DOES PEACEKEEPING WORK?

DOES PEACEKEEPING WORK?

SHAPING BELLIGERENTS' CHOICES
AFTER CIVIL WAR

Virginia Page Fortna

PRINCETON UNIVERSITY PRESS

PRINCETON AND OXFORD

Library of Congress Cataloging-in-Publication Data

Fortna, Virginia Page

Does peacekeeping work? : shaping belligerents' choices
after civil war / Virginia Page Fortna.

p. cm.

Includes bibliographical references and index.

ISBN 978-0-691-13281-5 (hardcover : alk. paper)

ISBN 978-0-691-13671-4 (pbk. : alk. paper)

1. Peace-building. 2. Peace-building—Case studies.
3. Civil war—Case studies. I. Title.

JZ5538.F67 2007

341.5'84—dc22   2007047168

British Library Cataloging-in-Publication Data is available

This book has been composed in Janson

Printed on acid-free paper. ∞

press.princeton.edu

Printed in the United States of America

1   3   5   7   9   10   8   6   4   2

For Pete

CONTENTS

FIGURES, MAPS, AND TABLES

Figures

Maps

Tables

ACKNOWLEDGMENTS

IT IS ALL TOO EASY, as a scholar sitting comfortably in an office in an American university, to treat civil war as a distant and abstract phenomenon; to forget that the conflicts we write about and treat as data points in our analysis have led to countless personal tragedies for the people caught up in them. This book grows out of a long-standing personal interest in conflict and the stability of peace that stems from having traveled and lived in war-torn places as a child. I have tried, as I researched and wrote this book, to remember the people I know whose lives were torn apart by the Intifada or by the wars in southern Africa. This book focuses on attempts by the international community to keep peace in such places, and on the decisions that leaders of governments and rebel groups make about waging war and peace. But it is the ordinary people whose lives and deaths are affected by these decisions that provide the motivation for this project.

My first research project was originally intended to cover the durability of peace after both interstate and civil wars. But there were neither the resources, nor the time, nor the data to cover both adequately. That project focused on the former, on attempts to maintain peace after conflicts between states. This project has allowed me to return to the subject of civil wars. It focuses, more narrowly than the first project, on one particular policy tool for maintaining peace—international peacekeeping. As such, it picks up on work I began before graduate school, as a research assistant at the Henry L. Stimson Center. While the literature on peacekeeping has exploded since then, at the time there was very little research on the topic. I had the good fortune to work there with Bill Durch, whose keen insights and policy-relevant research led the new wave of interest in the subject.

I am grateful to many people who have helped me write this book. Chuck Myers at Princeton University Press has supported the project from beginning to end. My colleagues in international relations at Columbia's Saltzman Institute of War and Peace Studies, Dick Betts, Nisha Fazal, Erik Gartzke, Pablo Pinto, and especially Bob Jervis and Jack Snyder, have created a truly wonderful intellectual community—friendly, supportive, and engaging. I have been the beneficiary of many insightful conversations there, about my research and about the larger questions we all study. Bob and Jack have each read several drafts of this book, and their thoughtful comments have helped me to improve it. Nisha deserves special mention, not only for commenting on several iterations of the manuscript, but also for being a sounding board on matters personal, professional, and academic. Over the last two years, we navigated together the exciting but often difficult territory of pregnancies, new parenthood, and juggling work with childcare. She has been a good friend through all of it. Ingrid Gerstmann, who makes the institute run, and run smoothly, helped with the logistics of research, from assisting with field trips and managing grants to the more mundane but still essential tasks that support research. Two at Columbia who are experts on peacekeeping, Kim Marten and Michael Doyle, gave me very constructive comments on the penultimate draft of the book. Andy Gelman and Shigeo Hirano generously advised me on statistical issues. A former student, Megan Gilroy, provided excellent research assistance, compiling information on each of the civil wars covered in the data set used here. Stephanie Pleschinger helped compile the index.

I have been the lucky recipient of a number of grants and fellowships that supported this research. The Carnegie Corporation of New York funded much of the early research as well as my field trips to Bangladesh, Sierra Leone, and Mozambique. I thank Steve del Rosso in particular for his support of this project. The American Academy of Arts and Sciences granted me one of its first Visiting Scholarships, allowing me to concentrate on research for this book rather than teaching. Finally, the Hoover Institution at Stanford provided another year of leave, during which I wrote the bulk of this manuscript. At Stanford, many of my thoughts on how peacekeeping operates were fleshed out over burritos with Barry Weingast, or in the "work in progress group" lunches where Jim Fearon, Jeremy Weinstein, Mike Tomz, and others contributed their considerable brainpower to the problems I was tackling.

The insights of several scholars of peacekeeping have been particularly helpful: Jean Krasno, Michael Gilligan, Steve Stedman, Nicholas Sambanis, who generously shared his detailed data notes on civil war cases, and Lise Howard, whose expertise I relied on heavily as I was coding peacekeeping missions.

I have also had the good fortune of many opportunities to present this work, while it was in progress, at conferences and seminars at many universities. I cannot name all of the people, formal discussants and members of the audience, whose insightful questions and constructive critiques helped me improve the book. Suffice it to say that this book is the product, not just of the intellectual community at Columbia, but of the wider international relations and political science community fostered by the American Political Science Association and the International Studies Association, and especially by speaker series at places like Berkeley, Emory, Georgetown, Harvard's Olin Institute, MIT, Princeton, Rice, Rutgers, the University of Southern California, Stanford's Center for International Security and Cooperation, the University of Washington, Wesleyan, the University of Wisconsin–Madison, and Yale.

Early versions of the theory and data presented in this book appeared, respectively, in two previous articles: "Interstate Peacekeeping: Causal Mechanisms and Empirical Effects," *World Politics* 56 (4) (2004): 481–519; and "Does Peacekeeping Keep Peace? International Intervention and the Duration of Peace after Civil War," *International Studies Quarterly* 48 (2) (2004): 269–92.

Anyone who has done field research knows that one owes a huge debt to the people, both at home and especially in the countries visited, who help make it happen. My trip to Bangladesh would not have been possible without the assistance and suggestions of Malgosia Madajewicz, Rounaq Jahan, Phil Oldenberg, and Mohammed Rashiduzzaman. I was overwhelmed by the hospitality of the Bangladeshis—many people invited me into their homes, or gave generously of their time to discuss the Chittagong Hill Tracts. I was the recipient not only of the insights, but also the gracious hospitality, of Amena Mohsin, Mizanur Rahman Shelley, Devashish Roy, and Shantu Larma. My trip to the Chittagong Hill Tracts would not have been possible without Mrinal Kanti Tripura, who gave me days of his time, driving hours to pick me up in Chittagong for the trip into the hills, helping me navigate military checkpoints, setting up interviews for me in Rangamati, and volunteering as chauffeur, tour guide, and occasionally interpreter.

Lotta Hagman, John Hirsch, and my good friend Ade Adebajo gave me good advice and contacts in Sierra Leone, while Raisedon Zenenga at the UN put in me touch with UNAMSIL (United Nations Mission in Sierra Leone) officials in Freetown. Margaret Vogt gave me contacts in both Sierra Leone and Mozambique. In Freetown, Ismail Diallo and Gilbert Ngesu of UNAMSIL helped me understand the Sierra Leone case and introduced me to several interviewees. In Sierra Leone, I owe the greatest debt of gratitude to Lory Dolar, who helped me set up interviews, including accompanying me on a wild goose-chase through Freetown looking for a politician who, we ultimately learned, had fled the city and been killed; getting me a seat on UN helicopter flights so I could see the diamond-mining areas and meet ex-combatants "up-country"; and even taking me and my husband to a spectacular beach outside Freetown on our day off.

Carrie Manning, Jeremy Weinstein, Andrea Bartoli, and Agostinho Zacarias gave me background information, practical advice, and contacts for my trip to Mozambique. Once I was there, João Honwana, Antonio Matonse, and Anícia Lalá helped me to set up interviews and to understand Mozambique's transition to peace. Abdul Manafi ably translated for me in interviews with officials who did not speak English. On all three trips, I was struck by how willingly and charitably people gave me their time to teach me about their countries and the conflicts from which they were emerging. Even interviews with the highest-ranking officials ended only when I ran out of questions.

Last, but most definitely not least, I am grateful to my family for their love and support through this and all my endeavors. I thank my parents, Robert and Evelyn, and my brothers, Ben and Ned, for so many things, including instilling in me a love of travel off the beaten track that made it easy to imagine field research in the places I went for this project. The newest member of my family, Rosina, has impeccable timing—she waited until just after I had sent this manuscript out for review to be born. Rosie also deserves thanks for being such a great sleeper and a generally easy-going baby. She has allowed me to wrap up final revisions without being too sleep deprived. And most important, she has filled the final year of this project with great joy. Finally, I thank my husband and true love, Pete, who has supported me and this project in countless ways. He endured long flights and hotel rooms with beds a foot shorter than he is to accompany me on my field trips. He cooked dinner every night he was in New York during my pregnancy so I could finish this manuscript. He drew the maps for the book. And he has kept me laughing through all of it. I am deeply grateful for his moral support, his love, and his friendship. This book is dedicated to him, with all my love.

Big House, Portland, Oregon
June 2007

DOES PEACEKEEPING WORK?

One

PEACEKEEPING AND THE PEACEKEPT

QUESTIONS, DEFINITIONS, AND RESEARCH DESIGN

The Questions

IN COUNTRIES WRACKED BY CIVIL WAR, the international community is frequently called upon to deploy monitors and troops to try to keep the peace. The United Nations, regional organizations, and sometimes ad hoc groups of states have sent peacekeepers to high-profile trouble-spots such as Rwanda and Bosnia and to lesser-known conflicts in places like the Central African Republic, Namibia, and Papua New Guinea. How effective are these international interventions? Does peacekeeping work? Does it actually keep the peace in the aftermath of civil war? And if so, how? How do peacekeepers change things on the ground, from the perspective of the "peacekept," such that war is less likely to resume? These are the questions that motivate this book.

As a tool for maintaining peace, international peacekeeping was only rarely used in internal conflicts during the Cold War, but the number, size, and scope of missions deployed in the aftermath of civil wars has exploded since 1989. Early optimism about the potential of the UN and regional organizations to help settle internal conflicts after the fall of the Berlin Wall was soon tempered by the initial failure of the mission in Bosnia and the scapegoating of the UN mission in Somalia.[1] The United States in particular became disillusioned with peacekeeping, objecting to anything more than a minimal international response in war-torn countries (most notoriously in Rwanda). Even in Afghanistan and Iraq, where vital interests are now at stake, the United States has been reluctant to countenance widespread multilateral peacekeeping missions. But the demand for peacekeeping continues apace. In recent years, the UN has taken up an unprecedented number of large, complex peacekeeping missions, in places such as the Congo, Liberia, Haiti, and Sudan.

---

[1] Note that the US-led and UN missions in Somalia (UNITAF and UNOSOM, respectively) were not peacekeeping missions as defined here, but rather humanitarian assistance missions (see definitions below). This distinction was lost, however, in the debates over the merits of peacekeeping after the fiasco in Mogadishu.

Through these ups and downs, scholars and practitioners of peacekeeping have debated the merits of the new wave of more "robust" and complex forms of peacekeeping and peace enforcement developed after the Cold War, and even the effectiveness of more traditional forms of peacekeeping.[2] However, this debate is hampered by shortcomings in our knowledge about peacekeeping. Despite a now vast literature on the topic, very little rigorous testing of the effectiveness of peacekeeping has taken place. We do not have a very good idea of whether it really works. Nor do we have an adequate sense of how exactly peacekeeping helps to keep the peace.

Casual observers and many policymakers opposed to a greater peacekeeping role for the international community can point to the dramatic failures that dominate news coverage of peacekeeping, but rarely acknowledge the success stories that make less exciting news. Meanwhile, most analysts of peacekeeping draw lessons from a literature that compares cases and missions, but with few exceptions, examines only cases in which peacekeepers are deployed, not cases in which belligerents are left to their own devices. This literature therefore cannot tell us whether peace is more likely to last when peacekeepers are present than when they are absent. Surprisingly little empirical work has addressed this question. Moreover, the few studies that do address it, at least in passing, come to contradictory findings. Some find that peacekeeping makes peace last longer, some find that it does not, and some find that only some kinds of peacekeeping are effective.[3] A closer look is clearly needed.

The literature on peacekeeping is also surprisingly underdeveloped theoretically. Causal arguments about peacekeeping are therefore often misinformed. Opponents of intervention dismiss peacekeeping as irrelevant, or worse, counterproductive.[4] Proponents, on the other hand, simply list the functions of peacekeeping (monitoring, interposition, electoral oversight, etc.), describing its practices with little discussion of how exactly the presence of peacekeepers might influence the prospects for peace. Little theoretical work has been done to specify what peacekeepers do to help belligerents maintain a cease-fire, or how peacekeepers might shape the choices made by the peacekept about war and peace.

Further, most existing studies of peacekeeping focus almost exclusively on the perspective of the peacekeepers or the international community. In discussions of mandates, equipment and personnel, relations among na-

---

[2] On this debate see, for example, Tharoor 1995–96 and Luttwak 1999.

[3] See Hartzell, Hoddie, and Rothchild 2001; Dubey 2002; and Doyle and Sambanis 2000, respectively. See also Doyle and Sambanis 2006; Gilligan and Sergenti 2007. For studies of the effects of international involvement on peace after interstate (as opposed to civil) wars, see Diehl, Reifschneider, and Hensel 1996; and Fortna 2004c.

[4] Luttwak 1999; Weinstein 2005.

tional contingents or between the field and headquarters, and so on, it is easy to lose track of the fundamental fact that it is the belligerents themselves who ultimately make decisions about maintaining peace or resuming the fight. Only by considering the perspective of the peacekept—their incentives, the information available to them, and their decision making—can we understand whether and how peacekeeping makes a difference.

In short, our current understanding of peacekeeping suffers from three gaps: we know too little about whether or how much peacekeepers contribute empirically to lasting peace, we lack a solid understanding of the causal mechanisms through which peacekeepers affect the stability of peace, and we know too little about the perspective of the peacekept on these matters. This project aims to rectify these shortcomings. The book draws on theories of cooperation and bargaining in international relations to develop the causal mechanisms through which peacekeepers might affect the decisions belligerents make about maintaining peace or returning to war. It assesses the empirical effects of peacekeeping by comparing (both quantitatively and qualitatively) civil conflicts in which peacekeeping was used to conflicts in which peacekeepers were not deployed. And it evaluates the causal mechanisms of peacekeeping by drawing on the perspective of the belligerents themselves.

Two simple questions drive this study: does peacekeeping work? And if so, how? Answering these questions is not so simple, however. To know whether peace lasts longer when international personnel are present than when belligerents are left to their own devices, we need to compare both types of cases. But we also need to know something about where peacekeepers tend to be deployed. Unlike treatments in a controlled laboratory experiment, peacekeeping is not "applied" to war-torn states at random. If the international community follows the common policy prescriptions to send peacekeepers when there is strong "political will" for peace and where the chances for success are high (that is, to the easy cases), then a simple comparison of how long peace lasts with and without peacekeeping would misleadingly suggest a very strong effect for peacekeeping. If, on the other hand, peacekeepers are sent where they are most needed—where peace is otherwise hardest to keep, then a simple comparison would lead us to conclude, again incorrectly, that peacekeeping is useless or even counterproductive.[5] To address whether and how peacekeeping works, I must first answer the question of why peacekeepers deploy to some cases and not others. The first empirical step in this project must therefore be to examine where peacekeepers go. The book therefore addresses three

---

[5] Peacekeeping is thus endogenous to processes that affect the duration of peace. The selection of peacekeeping must be accounted for before we can assess its effects.

questions: Where do peacekeepers go? Do they make peace more likely to last? Through what causal mechanisms do they operate?

This project aims to have a direct impact on the policy debates over peacekeeping. It furthers our understanding of why some conflicts draw in international peacekeepers while others do not. It goes on to provide clear evidence that this policy tool is indeed extremely effective at maintaining peace, substantially reducing the risk of another war. And it spells out how peacekeeping works, so that more effective strategies for maintaining peace can be developed by the international community.

Scope and Definitions

This study encompasses civil wars, those with peacekeeping and those without, in the post–Cold War period. Peacekeeping during the Cold War was used primarily in interstate conflicts. In the few exceptional cases of peacekeeping in civil wars prior to 1989 (for example, Cyprus and the Congo), the primary purpose was less to prevent the resumption of war than to contain the conflict to prevent direct superpower intervention. Examining civil wars that ended before 1989 thus sheds little additional light on analysis of peacekeeping as a tool for maintaining peace, while restricting the time period covered in the study allows me to focus more attention on the cases covered.[6]

Much of the theory proposed and tested here would apply to interstate conflicts as well as to conflicts within states.[7] But maintaining peace after civil conflicts presents particular challenges, as recent enemies generally have to disarm, agree to a single legitimate government and a unified army, and live alongside one another.[8] Some of the causal mechanisms discussed here, for example, managing electoral processes in an impartial manner, maintaining law and order, and helping former belligerents transform into political parties, apply only to civil conflicts. Wars within states have become the most common type of war, and create almost all of the current need for peacekeeping in the international system.[9]

The burgeoning literature on peacekeeping has brought with it a proliferation of definitions, distinctions, and taxonomies of the concept. Some clarification of what I mean by the term is thus in order. I use the term

---

[6] Cases from 1945 to 1989 do provide a baseline of what happens when peacekeeping is not a commonly used practice, however. See chapter 2.

[7] For a similar analysis of peacekeeping in interstate settings, see Fortna 2004b.

[8] Walter 2001. This is not the case when a rebel group successfully manages to secede, as in Eritrea or East Timor. Secession can raise additional problems, however, as formerly majority groups become ethnic minorities overnight, as in the Balkans.

[9] The recent peacekeeping mission between Ethiopia and Eritrea is a rare exception.

peacekeeping to refer to the deployment of international personnel to help maintain peace and security in the aftermath of war. All peacekeeping missions involve military personnel, though they may or may not be armed, and many missions include substantial civilian components as well.[10] This study encompasses peacekeeping performed by the UN and by regional organizations or ad hoc groups of states. While it is possible that a unilateral intervention could perform a peacekeeping role, peacekeeping has in practice been a multilateral activity. The multilateral nature of peacekeeping arguably helps to ensure its impartiality and to bolster its legitimacy, both in the eyes of the peacekept and in the eyes of the rest of the international community.[11]

This definition includes both operations based on the traditional principles of peacekeeping, specifically the consent of the belligerents themselves and the defensive use of force, as well as peace enforcement missions that relax these conditions considerably. Some studies use the term *peace operations* to encompass both consent-based and enforcement missions, reserving the term *peacekeeping* solely for the former.[12] I use the term *peacekeeping* to encompass both types of mission, in part because it allows me to refer to those keeping the peace as subjects—peacekeepers, rather than the awkward "peace operators," but also because much of what I have to say about the effect of peacekeeping on the duration of peace is applicable to both types of mission. When I need to distinguish between them, I refer to *consent-based peacekeeping*, and to *peace enforcement missions*. As shorthand, I also sometimes follow the UN lingo, using the terms *Chapter VI* and *Chapter VII missions*, respectively, though these are technically misnomers.[13] Until recently, it was rare for the mandates of peacekeeping missions to make explicit reference to the UN Charter,[14] and even Chapter VII–mandated missions rely to some extent on the consent of the belligerents.[15]

---

[10] With the advent of multidimensional peacekeeping with large civilian components (see below), former UN secretary-general Dag Hammarskjöld's quip that peacekeeping is not a job for soldiers, but only soldiers can do it (quoted in Smith 2003, p. 121) is less absolute than it once was.

[11] Finnemore 2003 notes that multilateralism marks an important normative shift in international humanitarian intervention and the ways in which it is legitimated.

[12] See, for example, Findlay 2002, pp. 3–7.

[13] Nowhere does the UN Charter refer to the concept of peacekeeping; it is an improvisation that falls somewhere between the actions envisioned by the charter in Chapter VI (pacific settlement of disputes) and those in Chapter VII (use of force against threats to the peace). Thus Hammarskjöld famously described peacekeeping as "Chapter six and a half."

[14] Findlay 2002, pp. 8–9, notes that resolutions never mention use of force explicitly. However, recent enforcement missions often note authorization under Chapter VII, indicating that the missions are mandated to use force.

[15] These semantics were debated over the course of the 1990s, as the role of the use of force in peacekeeping was explored explicitly. During the Cold War, the UN maintained the fiction that all peacekeeping was consent-based, even when missions that began with consent

While I use the term peacekeeping quite broadly, this study does not examine all types of peace operations. I do not assess the effects of humanitarian intervention during warfare, for example. And because I am interested in the effect of peacekeeping on the duration of peace, I study cases in which a cease-fire has been reached, however tenuous and temporary it might prove to be. This means that the peacemaking, or more accurately, the cease-fire-making,[16] efforts of the international community are not examined in this study. I do not assess the effects of preventive deployment to keep war from breaking out in the first place, nor the effects of mediation missions sent when the fighting is still raging, nor military interventions that attempt to bring about a cessation of hostilities. Many of these latter missions stay on once a cease-fire is in place, and these peacekeeping missions are included in this study. But I am examining their effects on whether peace lasts, not on whether peace is achieved in the first place. The latter is an important topic in its own right, but it is beyond the scope of this work.[17] In other words, this is not a study of all of the effects of peace operations; it is a study of the effects of peace operations on only one of their possible goals—that is, maintaining peace. Similarly, I do not include in this study international efforts to wage war in the name of collective security, as in Korea or the 1991 Gulf War.[18]

Of the range of operations covered by the term *peacekeeping*, not all missions are alike, of course. This study distinguishes among four types of peacekeeping operation (the first three of which are consent-based, Chapter VI missions, while the fourth is Chapter VII missions):

- *Observation missions* are small deployments of military and sometimes civilian observers to monitor a cease-fire, the withdrawal or canton-

---

slid into patently more robust operations, as in the Congo. Findlay 2002; Hillen 2000, p. 29. Malone and Wermester 2000, p. 50, note that the distinction between Chapter VI and Chapter VII missions had "become fairly moot" by the end of the 1990s, as the new operations of 1999 (Kosovo, Sierra Leone, East Timor, and the Democratic Republic of Congo) were all Chapter VII operations.

[16] The term *peace-making* is sometimes used to refer to efforts to solve the root causes of conflict, as opposed to simply reaching a cease-fire. See, for example, Furley and May 1998, pp. 3–4.

[17] On the effect of intervention on the termination of fighting (that is, on war duration) see Regan 2000, 2002; and Elbadawi and Sambanis 2000. See also Fortna 2005 for an argument that the availability of peacekeeping as a practice makes it easier for belligerents to settle.

[18] See Findlay 2002, pp. 6–7. Again, if a war-fighting operation is followed by a peacekeeping mission after a cease-fire is in place, as in Afghanistan or Kosovo, the latter incarnation is included in this study.

ment of troops, or other terms of an agreement, such as elections. They are unarmed, and their main tasks are simply to watch and report on what they see. The peacekeepers deployed in Angola in 1991 (UNAVEM II) or in the Western Sahara (MINURSO) are examples, as are the missions led by New Zealand and then Australia in Papua New Guinea in 1997–98 (the Truce Monitoring Group and Peace Monitoring Group, respectively).

- *Interpositional missions* (also sometimes referred to as *traditional peacekeeping missions*) are somewhat larger deployments of lightly armed troops. Like observer missions, they are meant to monitor and report on compliance with an agreement, but they also often serve to separate forces by positioning themselves in a buffer zone or to help demobilize and disarm military factions. Examples include the UN missions in Angola in 1994 (UNAVEM III) and in Guatemala in 1996 (MINUGUA).
- *Multidimensional missions* consist of both military and civilian components helping to implement a comprehensive peace settlement. In addition to the roles played by observer or interpositional missions, they perform tasks such as the organizing of elections,[19] human rights training and monitoring, police reform, institution building, economic development, and so on. The missions in Namibia (UNTAG), El Salvador (ONUSAL), and Mozambique (ONUMOZ) fall in this category.
- *Peace enforcement missions* involve substantial military forces to provide security and ensure compliance with a cease-fire. They have a mandate to use force for purposes in addition to self-defense. Examples include the West African and UN missions in Sierra Leone in 1999 (ECOMOG and UNAMSIL) and NATO missions in Bosnia (IFOR and SFOR). Some peace enforcement missions are also multidimensional in nature, including substantial military force as well as many of the civilian components of multidimensional missions. Most Chapter VII missions do enjoy the consent of the belligerents, at least at the beginning of the mission. But unlike Chapter VI missions, they are not obligated to depart should they lose that consent. Other peace enforcement missions enjoy the consent of one side (most often the government), but not necessarily the other. In other words, Chapter VII missions may have the consent of the belligerents, but it is not a necessary condition for their operation.

---

[19] Note that a number of observational or interpositional missions include in their mandates election observation, as opposed to the organizing or running of elections.

In the empirical analyses that follow, I pay particular attention to the difference between consent-based Chapter VI missions and Chapter VII enforcement missions because both the selection process by which they deploy to some cases and not others, and the causal mechanisms through which they operate may be very different.

Most peacekeeping is undertaken by the United Nations, but sometimes regional organizations or ad hoc coalitions have deployed missions to keep the peace. NATO did much of the heavy lifting of peacekeeping in the Balkans, Russia has deployed peacekeeping missions to its near-abroad, the Organization of African Unity sent a small mission to Rwanda,[20] and the Economic Community of West African States (ECOWAS) has deployed peacekeeping missions in West Africa.

I use the term *international community* as a catchall shorthand phrase to refer to interested states and international or regional organizations potentially involved in maintaining peace. It includes, most notably, the United Nations, but also organizations such as NATO, the European Union, the Organization of American States, and the Organization of African Unity (now the African Union). It also includes the great powers, especially the United States, although in some cases a former colonial power or a regional hegemon may be as important.

I use the term *peacekept* to refer to decision makers within the government and rebel organizations.[21] These are the people who decide whether to maintain peace or return to war. The wordplay in the term should not be taken to connote that they are "owned" or passively "kept" by outsiders. Quite the contrary; the focus on these actors is meant to emphasize the importance of these critical players as active decision-makers.

What do I mean by "work" when I ask, "Does peacekeeping work?" I mean simply, does peacekeeping increase the chances that peace will last? If peacekeeping works, conflicts in which peacekeepers deploy to help maintain a cease-fire will be less likely, all else equal, to slide back to civil war than cases in which no peacekeepers are present. If peacekeeping does not work or is ineffectual, the recidivism rate should be no different for peacekeeping and nonpeacekeeping cases. The conclusion I reach, that peacekeeping does indeed work, is a probabilistic one, not a deterministic one. The claim is not that peacekeepers will absolutely ensure lasting peace in every case, only that it will significantly improve the chances that peace will hold.[22]

---

[20] This mission was succeeded by the better-known UN mission, UNAMIR. On the Rwanda case, see Jones 2001.

[21] To my knowledge, the term was coined by Clapham 1998.

[22] Thanks to anonymous reviewers for suggesting this clarification, as well as the clarification about the connotation of the term *peacekept*.

Overview of the Book

The remainder of this chapter discusses the research design of the project, describing the statistical models and data used for the quantitative portion of the study, as well as the selection criteria for the case studies chosen for fieldwork and interviews.

Chapters 2 and 3 treat peacekeeping as the dependent variable, asking where peacekeepers tend to be deployed. Chapter 2 develops hypotheses about where peacekeepers are most likely to be sent, from both the supply side (where the international community is most likely to intervene) and the demand side (where belligerents are most likely to request or accept peacekeeping). It then uses statistical evidence to test these hypotheses empirically, examining the selection process that determines whether international personnel are deployed to keep peace, or whether belligerents are left to their own devices. Chapter 3 first introduces the case studies, providing background information on the Chittagong Hill Tracts conflict in Bangladesh, the Mozambique case, and the Sierra Leone case(s) (the Sierra Leone conflict encompasses three attempts to maintain peace). It then examines qualitatively why peacekeepers were deployed to some of these conflicts and not others. Together, chapters 2 and 3 demonstrate clearly that peacekeepers tend to deploy to the most difficult rather than the easiest cases. They also show that where peacekeepers go is determined not just by the international community, but also by the incentives of the peacekept.

Chapter 4 lays out a causal argument of peacekeeping. It draws on the existing literature on peacekeeping, moving beyond descriptions of peacekeepers' functions to hypothesize specific causal mechanisms through which their presence may make peace more stable. It suggests that peacekeepers can disrupt potential pathways back to war (1) by changing the incentives for war and peace of the peacekept; (2) by reducing their uncertainty about each other's intentions; (3) by preventing and controlling accidents or skirmishes that might otherwise escalate to war; and (4) by preventing either side from permanently excluding others from the political process. Through these causal mechanisms, peacekeepers can shape belligerents' decisions about whether to maintain peace or return to war.

Chapter 5 assesses the overall effects of peacekeeping, asking whether peace lasts longer when peacekeepers deploy than when they are absent. It employs primarily quantitative evidence to demonstrate that, all else equal, peacekeeping has a significant positive impact on the stability of peace. Conservative estimates indicate that peacekeeping reduces the risk of another war by more than half. Less conservative, but probably more accurate, estimates show that peacekeeping cuts the risk of renewed war by

75%–85%. A brief qualitative comparison of the cases supports this conclusion. In short, peacekeeping works.

Chapter 6 addresses the question of *how* peacekeeping works. It draws on the case studies, and especially evidence from interviews, to assess the causal mechanisms of peacekeeping. It pays particular attention to the perspective of the peacekept in evaluating the causal impact of the presence or absence of peacekeepers. Chapter 7 summarizes conclusions and implications of this study, emphasizing lessons for policymakers.

Research Design

This project employs both quantitative analysis of a data set encompassing cease-fires in all civil wars from 1989 to 2000 and in-depth case studies of three carefully selected conflicts. These methods complement each other and compensate for each other's weaknesses. The statistical analysis provides breadth, while the case studies provide depth. The quantitative analysis allows me to control for many variables to handle the fact that peacekeeping is not applied randomly, while the case studies allow me to investigate nuances lost when political processes are reduced to numbers. Most important, the statistical survey is best suited to establishing that peacekeeping has an effect, while the fieldwork and interviews conducted for the cases studies allow me to examine the causal processes of peacekeeping from the perspective of the peacekept.[23]

Quantitative Analysis

Statistical analysis is used to answer two questions: where peacekeepers go (chapter 2) and whether they make peace more durable (chapter 5). The quantitative analysis in chapter 2 employs logit and multinomial logit regression. These models are appropriate for dichotomous (no peacekeeping or peacekeeping) and discrete (no peacekeeping, consent-based peacekeeping, or peace enforcement) variables, respectively.[24]

The statistical analyses in chapter 5 employ duration models (sometimes also known as hazard, or survival models) designed for exploring the effects, in this case of peacekeeping, on the length of time something, such as peace, will last. And they can do this even for cases in which we know

[23] Lin 1998.

[24] One could argue that these discrete categories are ordered from less to more peacekeeping, making ordered logit models more appropriate. However, because I think the process by which Chapter VI and Chapter VII missions deploy may be quite different, I do not assume such an ordering.

that peace has lasted to date (the end of the data set), but do not know how long it will last in the future. This is known as "censored" data in the statistical jargon. For example, peace was holding in Kosovo when data collection for this project ended, and continues to do so as of this writing, but it may falter after the book goes to press. Duration models do not assume that peace that has lasted to date will continue to do so. Another advantage is that we can treat the duration of peace as continuous rather than specifying an arbitrary cutoff point (five years, say) as constituting "successful" peace. Peace that falls apart within a few months is thus treated as less stable than peace that lasts four years. And peace that falters after six years is treated as less successful than peace that has held to date.

Of the duration models available, I employ both Cox proportional hazard models and Weibull models. The Cox makes no assumptions about the underlying "hazard function" of war resumption. This means that it makes no assumptions about whether peace becomes more or less likely to last, given that it has held thus far, or whether this likelihood fluctuates over time. The Weibull can be preferable for use with relatively small data sets, but is more restrictive, assuming that the hazard is monotonically rising or falling; that is, that peace does not first become harder to keep over time and then easier, or vice versa.[25] In all cases, the results are robust to this model choice.

The data set created for this project consists of 94 cease-fires, or breaks in the fighting, from 1989 through 1999 in almost 60 civil wars.[26] The data build on those compiled by Doyle and Sambanis,[27] but I have added a number of short-lived cease-fires not included in their data or in other data on civil wars. For example, research on the war in Guinea-Bissau in 1998–99 identified several unsuccessful attempts to maintain peace, including a cease-fire negotiated in Cape Verde in August 1998 that faltered two months later, and a peace agreement reached in Abuja in November 1998 that lasted until the end of January 1999.[28] Inclusion of these ultimately unsuccessful attempts to maintain peace is particularly important for a study of postwar stability, as their omission would truncate variation in the dependent variable and introduce selection bias.[29] Adding these cases also

[25] However, it does not assume a particular shape, as some other possibilities do. Box-Steffensmeier and Jones 1997.

[26] Because some conflicts include more than one break in the fighting, not all cases in the data are independent of one another. In the statistical analyses, I take this into account by calculating robust standard errors with cases clustered by country. For example, the four cease-fires in the Sudan conflict are not treated as independent of each other, but they are considered independent of the cease-fires in Sri Lanka.

[27] Doyle and Sambanis 2000, 2006.

[28] On this conflict, see Adebajo 2002, chap. 5.

[29] See Geddes 1990.

provides more leverage in understanding why peace sometimes lasts and sometimes falls apart quite quickly.[30]

I include cases only through the end of 1999 for two reasons. Data for some key control variables are unavailable after that time. More important, this cutoff allows me to observe whether peace lasts for at least five years after the point of a cease-fire for all of my cases. So while to be included in this study, a break in the fighting must occur before the beginning of 2000, observation of the main dependent variable—whether peace lasts— continues to the beginning of 2005.

The data set compiled for this project includes information on the date of each break in the fighting, and the date, if any, war resumed. If war had not resumed by December 31, 2004, the observation is treated as censored at that point. The data also include information on the type of peacekeeping mission, if any, and on any changes in peacekeeping over time. In other words, the data record when peacekeeping missions arrive and depart, or significant changes in mission type over time.[31] The data set also incorporates information on a number of variables that may affect whether peacekeepers are likely to be deployed and the probability that peace will last. These include the outcome of the war at the time the fighting stops (victory for one side, a truce, or a settlement), the number of deaths caused by the war, the size of the government's army, economic indicators, measures of democracy, whether the parties have reached an agreement in the past, and so forth. Many of these control variables are taken from existing data sets, but the central variables in this study, the duration of peace and peacekeeping missions, I coded myself.

Data on civil wars are notoriously messy. It is not always clear how many factions are involved in the fighting, and data on war-related deaths are often very sketchy. It is not always obvious exactly when fighting starts or stops or even whether a particular case qualifies as a civil war. Wherever coding decisions had to be made, particularly those about how long peace

---

[30] I added cases when my own research (with the able assistance of Megan Gilroy) identified cease-fires that held for at least one month because I could be fairly confident of catching these systematically. In an ideal world, these data would include every break in the fighting, even if it lasted only days or hours. While a significant improvement on existing data, the list of cases here continues to omit some of the shortest-lived cease-fires. Adding these cases would almost certainly strengthen the argument that peacekeeping helps maintain peace. We are much more likely to have information about failed cease-fires when peacekeepers are present than when they are absent, since tracking and reporting on cease-fires is a central part of what peacekeepers do. Even given this bias in available information, of the approximately 50 cease-fires lasting less than a month identified in research on individual cases, fewer than a dozen occurred while peacekeepers were present. In other words, better data that include these even shorter-lived cease-fires would strengthen the main empirical findings of this study.

[31] This is known as a "time-varying" covariate.

lasted or the inclusion or exclusion of cases, I coded so as to work against my own argument that peacekeeping is effective. For example, some data sets on civil wars include a case for the secessionist rebellion in Cabinda in Angola, while others do not. This questionable case encompasses a number of short-lived attempts to make peace, none of them with peacekeepers present. Because their inclusion would support the argument that peacekeepers help maintain peace, I exclude them. Similarly, the first break in the fighting in the war in Congo-Brazzaville is variously dated in January 1994, December 1994, and January 1995. Because this is a case with no peacekeepers present, I use the earliest date so that peace is coded as lasting, if anything, longer than it actually lasted, thus favoring the counterargument that peacekeeping does not work. Therefore, the quantitative results reported here, if anything, underestimate the effect of peacekeeping on peace. The list of cases and information on data sources can be found in appendix A.[32]

Case Studies

While statistical analysis can give us a fairly good idea of *whether* peacekeeping works, it cannot tell us *how* works. For this we must look at individual cases in more detail. This study examines three conflicts in depth: the Chittagong Hill Tracts (CHT) conflict in Bangladesh, the civil war in Mozambique, and the conflict in Sierra Leone.

The first of these is a case of peace with no peacekeepers. Its inclusion is important to avoid the problem, mentioned above, of studies that examine only instances in which peacekeepers were actually deployed. The CHT conflict affords examination of the null case—what happens when belligerents try to maintain peace on their own, without the help of international peacekeepers? There are many cases of civil wars ending with no deployment of peacekeepers in the post–Cold War era; peacekeepers deploy in under 40% of the cases examined here. But to set up an especially difficult test of the argument that peacekeeping matters, I chose a no-peacekeeping case in which neither side clearly defeated the other, and in which peace has lasted to date. Of the conflicts that fit this description, I chose one with little international involvement and a relatively large total death toll.[33] An added benefit was that English is widely spoken in Bangladesh, making fieldwork and interviews much more feasible.

---

[32] The data and full coding notes are available on the web at http://press.princeton.edu/8705.html.

[33] The former criterion militated against using South Africa as a case, while the latter eliminated Djibouti 1994, Egypt, Mali 1995, Northern Ireland 1998, and Pakistan. I avoided the Algerian case because only one of several factions ceased fire in 1997. The other possibilities in this category are Azerbaijan-Nagorno Karabakh 1994, and Myanmar-Kachin 1993.

The Mozambique case provides a look at a consent-based peacekeeping mission widely touted as a success. Of the Chapter VI peacekeeping cases in which war has not resumed, I again chose a relatively large conflict in terms of numbers killed.[34] Mozambique makes for a potentially difficult test case for the argument that peacekeeping makes a difference. Most case studies of the Mozambican peace process emphasize the belligerents' "political will" for peace. If the parties were strongly committed to peace, the question arises whether the peacekeepers mattered or whether peace would have lasted regardless. I thus focus the analysis on determining whether and how the peacekept thought that peacekeeping was instrumental (as opposed to epiphenomenal) to maintaining peace. In-depth research on this case thus allows me to investigate whether the causal mechanisms hypothesized in chapter 4 were in fact at work.[35]

The war in Sierra Leone involved numerous attempts to make peace. Several of them were unsuccessful, including the Abidjan cease-fire of 1996 with no peacekeepers present, and the Lomé agreement of 1999, when peacekeepers were deployed. A final peace deal reached in Abuja in late 2000 and early 2001 has so far held, overseen by a large peace enforcement mission.[36] These three distinct attempts to maintain peace allow for comparison in a single setting of both failed and (so far) successful peacekeeping attempts. The variation within this case, while tragic for the Sierra Leoneans who lived through the conflict, makes it a good one for analysis. As in Bangladesh, Sierra Leone had the additional attraction of being an English-speaking country, facilitating fieldwork there.[37]

Together, the three case studies allow me to explore both successful (Bangladesh, Mozambique, and Sierra Leone–Abuja) and failed (Sierra Leone–Abidjan and Lomé) efforts to create lasting peace; as well as instances with no peacekeeping (Bangladesh and Abidjan), consent-based peacekeeping (Mozambique), and enforcement missions (Lomé and Abuja). The cases cover the range of variation in both the primary independent variable (peacekeeping), and the dependent variable (whether peace lasts), as indicated in table 1.1. Most important, they provide the insights

[34] Others in this category include Cambodia, El Salvador, Guatemala 1996, Namibia, and Nicaragua.

[35] Two practical reasons also directed the choice of Mozambique as a case for this study. I had done previous research on conflicts and peacekeeping in southern Africa, giving me some background knowledge of this case. I also had several contacts who had studied Mozambique or participated in resolution of the conflict who helped put me touch with interviewees.

[36] Only the first two of these are included in the data used for the quantitative part of this study, as the third takes place after the end of 1999.

[37] An unexpected benefit of choosing three relatively obscure cases, which have not been inundated by Westerners conducting research, was that I found participants in the conflict surprisingly willing, even eager, to give me ample time for interviews.

TABLE 1.1

Case Selection

	War Resumes	Peace Lasts
Peacekeeping	Sierra Leone 1999	Mozambique, Sierra Leone 2000–2001
No Peacekeeping	Sierra Leone 1996	Bangladesh

of the belligerents themselves into how the presence or absence of peacekeepers affected the prospects for peace.

In several trips over the course of 2002, I conducted field research in all three countries.[38] I interviewed over 75 political and military leaders from the government and from rebel groups (particularly those who were involved in negotiating and implementing the peace accords), diplomats, and members of NGOs and academics, both foreign and domestic. My intent was to learn from those on the ground, especially from the recent belligerents themselves, that is, the "peacekept," whether and how the presence of peacekeepers made a difference. In Bangladesh, I interviewed members of the government and the Shanti Bahini rebel group (including its leader, Shantu Larma), as well as members of a breakaway faction, the United People's Democratic Front (UPDF) that has not accepted the peace deal. In Mozambique, I interviewed political and military leaders from both the government and the former rebel group, Renamo (now an opposition party).[39] In Sierra Leone, I interviewed government officials, high-ranking members of the main rebel group, the RUF, as well as the head of the progovernment militia, the Civil Defense Forces (CDF).[40] In Sierra Leone, where I could observe peacekeeping "in action," I also interviewed military and political leaders in the UN mission. Interviews with the peacekept (or not peacekept in the Bangladesh case) in these three countries allow me to

[38] I traveled to Bangladesh in January, to Sierra Leone in November, and to Mozambique in December, spending about two weeks in each country.

[39] Government interviewees included Armando Guebuza, the chief negotiator at the time of the peace accords, who has since become president of Mozambique. I was unable to interview Renamo leader Dhlakama, but was able to interview high-ranking members of the former rebel organization, including several delegates to the peace negotiations.

[40] I was unable to locate Johnny Paul Koroma, the head of the AFRC, a faction that fought on both sides at various points and that temporarily held power after a coup. Not long after my trip, he was indicted by the war crimes tribunal in Sierra Leone, and shortly thereafter was found dead under mysterious circumstances. The CDF head, Chief Sam Hinga Norman, whom I did interview, was also since indicted and arrested by the tribunal. UN Document S/2005/777, p. 2.

examine the causal mechanisms of peacekeeping.[41] While chapter 5 briefly compares the outcome across the cases, I use them more for process tracing than for controlled case comparison.[42] Background information on these three cases is provided in chapter 3.

The research methods used in this project dovetail to allow me to address both whether and how peacekeeping works. By studying the full universe of cases, including those to which peacekeepers did not deploy, I can assess whether peacekeeping makes a substantive difference in the prospects for lasting peace. By conducting fieldwork and interviews with the government and rebel leaders in three carefully chosen conflicts, I can investigate the causal mechanisms through which peacekeepers make a difference in the decision making of the peacekept.

Conclusion

The "invention" of peacekeeping after World War II and its extension to civil conflicts after the Cold War represent crucial innovations in the international community's ability to make and maintain peace in war-torn areas around the globe. But despite a burgeoning literature on the subject, this policy tool remains poorly understood. We do not yet have many systematic studies of the effects of peacekeeping on the duration of peace, nor do we yet have a thorough understanding of how peacekeeping works on the ground from the perspective of the peacekept. This book aims to fill these gaps. It tests rigorously whether peace lasts longer when peacekeepers are present than when belligerents are left to their own devices, taking into account the fact that peacekeepers are not deployed to war-torn spots at random. It also examines how the presence of international personnel affects the decision making of the belligerents themselves, exploring the ways in which peacekeepers make peace more likely to last.

I show that peacekeeping is a very effective tool. Peacekeepers tend to go to the most difficult cases. And peace lasts significantly longer, all else equal, when international personnel deploy to maintain peace than when they do not. Moreover, I argue that peacekeepers make peace more likely by changing the incentives of the parties, providing them with credible information about each other's intentions, preventing and managing acci-

---

[41] Because one goal of this project is to focus on the perspective of the peacekept, I try to convey their views about peacekeeping in their own words. However, because I took notes and did not tape-record interviews, their statements are not necessarily exact quotes. I tried to record people's statements as faithfully as possible.

[42] On these distinctions and various uses of case studies, see Eckstein 1975; George and Bennett 2004; and Gerring 2004.

dental violations of the peace, and preventing either side from hijacking the political process during the transition to peace.

Peacekeeping does not guarantee stable peace in every case, but it greatly improves the chances that peace will last. This is true, not only of large, militarily robust enforcement missions, but also of smaller consent-based missions. This is because many of the ways peacekeeping works are not primarily military in nature, but rather economic and political.

The findings of this study have important implications for the conflicts that fill today's newspapers. They suggest, for example, that the fractured peace efforts in Palestine, both between Palestinians and Israelis, and among Palestinian factions, would be much more likely to succeed if international peacekeepers were actively involved. They suggest that the United Nations mission in the Sudan will improve the chances for stable peace between that government and the Sudan People's Liberation Movement, and that efforts to create and fund a peacekeeping mission in Darfur will be well worth it. They suggest that efforts to keep peace in Afghanistan should focus at least as much on maximizing political and economic leverage as on military efforts (but also that peacekeeping is particularly difficult where contraband financing, such as opium, fuels conflicts). This study does not tell us how to stop the fighting in Iraq. But now that civil war has begun, it does suggest that once a cease-fire is reached, whether through the defeat of one side, a political settlement, or even just a truce, peace will be much more likely to hold if an international peacekeeping mission deploys.[43] Such a mission will need to use economic and political leverage as well as military force to create incentives for peace, and will need to focus on alleviating the security and political concerns of the Iraqis. Peacekeeping may be the only hope for something resembling stability after a US military withdrawal.

The conclusions of this study are ultimately optimistic. Civil wars face a serious recidivism problem. It is not easy to maintain peace after civil war, but it is not impossible. Where the belligerents and the international community are willing to countenance peacekeeping, the risk of renewed war is substantially lowered. By showing not only that peacekeeping works, but how it works, I hope that this book will inform ongoing policy debates and improve the international community's efforts to maintain peace in states torn apart by civil war.

---

[43] The current US operation does not meet the definition of peacekeeping used in this study, among other reasons, because it was an interstate intervention to effect regime change, rather than a mission to keep peace in a civil war. US forces are probably far too implicated in the current crisis to provide effective peacekeeping. However, drumming up the personnel for an international peacekeeping mission for Iraq will be no easy task.

Two

WHERE PEACEKEEPERS GO I

HYPOTHESES AND STATISTICAL EVIDENCE

THIS CHAPTER AND THE NEXT INVESTIGATE the question of where peacekeepers go: What distinguishes conflicts that induce international peacekeeping missions from conflicts that do not? Why were peacekeepers sent to El Salvador and Namibia but not to the Philippines or Palestine, for example? Why peacekeeping in Mozambique and, eventually, in Sierra Leone, but not in Bangladesh? What explains this variation across cases of civil war? This chapter draws on existing research as well as a theory of the demand for peacekeeping to develop a number of hypotheses. It then uses the data on peacekeeping in civil wars to test them empirically over the full universe of cases. The next chapter looks at three conflicts in depth to examine the processes by which peacekeepers are sent to some cases but not others.

Conventional wisdom, journalistic accounts, and the small number of academic articles on the topic focus almost exclusively on where the international community chooses to deploy its personnel; that is, on the supply side of the peacekeeping equation. I contend that the demand for peacekeeping is equally important. Where do belligerents ask for peacekeepers to help them maintain peace? Enforcement missions may be driven primarily by where the international community chooses to intervene. But consent-based missions, by definition, also require that the belligerents themselves choose to have peacekeepers deploy.[1] Factors that affect either (or both) the supply of and the demand for peacekeeping are thus examined here. To address the selection issue discussed in chapter 1, I pay particular attention to whether peacekeepers are generally sent to easier or to harder cases. If the former, then any positive relationship between peacekeeping and durable peace may simply be spurious. If the latter, then successful peacekeeping attempts are all the more noteworthy.

The International Community's Supply of Peacekeeping

Because most peacekeeping operations are undertaken, or at least authorized by, the United Nations Security Council, and because the five permanent members (Perm-5) of the Security Council (United States, Britain,

[1] Durch 1993, pp. 22–23.

France, China, and Russia) can veto any operation they dislike, there has been understandable attention paid to the interests of the Perm-5 in determining where peacekeepers go. A number of scholars suggest that peacekeeping is more likely where these veto-wielding states have an interest in the conflict,[2] but less likely if a great power has intervened in the conflict directly, or where the target state is itself a great power.[3] In other words, the relationship is curvilinear: great power interests need to be engaged, but not *too* engaged. Gibbs suggests that the supply of peacekeeping is driven by outsiders' imperialist desire to exploit natural resources.[4] Other studies, however, cast doubt on these arguments,[5] while still others contend that peacekeeping is not driven solely by the realpolitik interests of the Perm-5 so much as their desire to remake war-torn nations in the liberal democratic image.[6]

Another line of argument suggests that because the Security Council responds to threats to international peace and security, peacekeeping is more likely in conflicts that threaten to spread beyond their borders.[7] Others maintain that the international community responds to a humanitarian impulse, with longer and more deadly conflicts more likely to receive intervention.[8]

Of particular interest to this book is whether the international community tends to send peacekeepers to the easy cases or to the hard ones. Studies of peacekeeping often suggest that peacekeepers should be deployed only where the chances for success are high. To what extent has the international community heeded this advice to intervene only where peace is relatively likely to last anyway (and the value added of peacekeeping is therefore low)?

Jakobsen finds that policymakers in the intervening countries consider the chances for success when deciding to launch a peace enforcement mission.[9] Carter argues that the UN strategically chooses peacekeeping cases

[2] de Jonge Oudraat 1996; Durch 1993, pp. 22–23. See also, Beardsley 2004; Bennis 1996; Gibbs 1997; Diehl 1993, p. 86.

[3] de Jonge Oudraat 1996; Mullenbach 2005.

[4] Gibbs 1997.

[5] Jakobsen 1996. Gilligan and Stedman 2003 find, for example, that peacekeeping is affected neither by former colonial relationships nor by natural resources. They find some geographic bias to the incidence of intervention, but the region most neglected is Asia, not Africa, as we might expect if Perm-5 interests drove the selection of peacekeeping. See also Beardsley 2004; Andersson 2000.

[6] Andersson 2000; Marten 2004; Paris 2004.

[7] de Jonge Oudraat 1996, pp. 517–18.

[8] Gilligan and Stedman 2003. See also Regan 2000, pp. 50–61; Beardsley 2004. Jakobsen 1996 argues that there must also be media attention to put humanitarian issues on the international agenda.

[9] Jakobsen 1996.

where the probability of success is high.[10] Gilligan and Stedman find that the UN avoids "the cost and risk" of intervening in militarily powerful countries.[11] They find no relationship between intervention and whether the belligerents have signed a peace treaty, something others have argued is a good indicator of their political will for peace.[12] Gilligan and Stedman chalk this finding up to multicollinearity, however, noting a strong positive bivariate relationship. Overall, their findings suggest that while the international community responds to the loss of life, it is more likely to react, and to react quickly, in easier cases.

de Jonge Oudraat argues just the opposite, however. By intervening where there is a larger threat to peace, the UN chooses conflicts where the probability of success is low:

> The UN Security Council is more likely to take action when problems are difficult, risks are high, and failure is entirely possible; and predisposed to do nothing when the chances of success are greater.[13]

In earlier work, I found evidence that peacekeepers, especially consent-based missions, tend to select into harder cases rather than easier ones.[14]

These studies begin to shed some light on the question of why peacekeepers are deployed to some civil wars and not others, but they are incomplete. With only a few exceptions, existing work has examined only the cases to which peacekeepers were deployed, not the comparison cases,[15] so we should take many of the findings noted above with a grain of salt. Of the exceptions, Gilligan and Stedman's analysis, is the most sophisticated.[16] It employs duration analysis to examine how quickly the international community responds to civil wars.[17] While important, that question is somewhat different from the one addressed here: Among civil wars that reach some sort of break in the fighting, what distinguishes those that see peacekeeping from those that do not?[18]

---

[10] Carter 2007.

[11] Gilligan and Stedman 2003, p. 48. They note that these risks and costs come from intervening without the country's permission, but by their measure, intervention consists mostly of consent-based peacekeeping that should not carry these risks.

[12] Doyle and Sambanis 2006, p. 103.

[13] de Jonge Oudraat 1996, pp. 525–26.

[14] Fortna 2004a, pp. 278–81.

[15] That is, they select on the dependent variable.

[16] Others are Andersson 2000, which focuses on who contributes to peacekeeping, providing only very preliminary bivariate analysis of the "targets" of peacekeeping; and Mullenbach 2005, which faces several methodological problems, including multicollinearity, and an unclear comparison category for variables such as ethnic, religious, and ideological wars.

[17] Gilligan and Stedman 2003.

[18] The latter question is particularly important for investigating the endogeneity of peacekeeping. What matters is whether peacekeepers were deployed as peace began, not how quickly the international community responded to an ongoing war. The difference in perspective also reflects a focus on a different effect of peacekeeping. For Gilligan and Stedman,

The analysis in the remainder of this chapter goes beyond existing studies in two ways. First, I examine both peace enforcement missions and consent-based peacekeeping missions, while distinguishing between them. These two types of mission are likely driven by very different processes. Examining one and not the other, or worse, lumping them together, may lead to very misleading results.

Second, and most important, I consider the motives of the potentially peacekept as well as the motives of peacekeepers. All of the existing literature focuses on the supply side of the peacekeeping equation. Where peacekeepers go is thus portrayed as the result only of the international community's choices. Scholars of peacekeeping acknowledge the need for the combatants' consent, at least for Chapter VI missions; however, these studies pay almost no attention to the choices made by the belligerents themselves in determining whether peacekeeping missions happen or not.[19] While a peacekeeping mission requires an active decision by the UN or a regional organization (or sometimes an ad hoc group of states) to deploy, it is quite rare for the international community to refuse peacekeepers if the belligerents themselves request them. Despite US admonitions during the 1990s that it learn to do so, the international community rarely "just says no."[20] Whether or not peacekeepers are deployed in civil wars is thus a decision made, at least in part, by the combatants themselves.[21]

The Belligerents' Demand for Peacekeeping

We might expect governments and rebel groups to be more likely to ask for international help maintaining peace when they are least able to manage the job on their own. When peace is likely to last anyway, there is no need for the intrusion of international personnel, but when peace is more fragile, there will be higher demand for peacekeeping. Following this logic, anything that, a priori, makes peace less stable should make peacekeepers more

---

the concern is with the international community's ability to stop the fighting. My concern is with the ability of peacekeepers to maintain peace in the aftermath of war, to prevent the resumption of fighting. Note that the data used in both our studies are more appropriate for investigating the latter question, as most peacekeeping missions deployed at or even just after the end of the war to keep peace in its aftermath, not to bring a halt to the fighting.

[19] Gilligan and Stedman 2003, p. 40, is a partial exception. They suggest two hypotheses that they describe as demand-side but that are either indirectly or partially supply-side arguments: that stronger states are better able to resist pressure to consent to peacekeeping, and that the war aims of rebels affect both the willingness of the government to agree to peacekeepers and the willingness of the UN to send them.

[20] President Clinton urged the UN to be more selective in sending peacekeepers, telling the General Assembly in September 1993 that "the United Nations must know when to say no." Quoted in Cohen 1995, p. 77.

[21] For a start in this direction, see analysis by Fortna and Martin, forthcoming.

likely. The deeper the animosity and the higher the level of mistrust between the belligerents, the greater the need for outsiders to help cement the peace. By the same token, wars that end with a clear victory by one side should be very unlikely to see peacekeepers. Not only is a clear military outcome most likely to lead to stable peace,[22] but the military winner is also unlikely to allow peacekeepers in to interfere with its own dealings with the losing side.

Whether or not peacekeepers deploy is likely to be an issue of serious contention between the belligerents; their interests are not the same in this regard. Belligerents will be strategic in their acceptance or refusal of peacekeeping as they bargain with each other. I propose two generalizations about how each side will view peacekeeping. First, unless they have won the war outright, rebels will be more likely than governments to want an international presence. If an agreement has been reached to share power or to open the political system to elections, rebels will have reason to fear the government will renege on political aspects of the agreement, or will use the trappings of state power to the rebels' disadvantage. As discussed further in chapter 4, peacekeepers can help hold the government to its promises to open its political system. Peacekeepers' dealings with both sides also tend to legitimize rebels as political actors with standing equal to governments.[23] Second, the more powerful belligerent is likely to desire peacekeeping less than its weaker antagonist, for peacekeepers tend to level the playing field by preventing military power from being translated into political gains. Even short of outright victory, the stronger side may prefer to manage the transition to peace without the interference of outsiders.[24] Exceptions to these generalizations include cases in which peacekeepers have a mandate to bolster an agreement that formalizes the stronger side's power, and wars that end with an agreement to restore the political status quo ante, in which case the government may be more desirous of an international presence.

The government and rebel groups do not have equal say in whether peacekeepers deploy. If neither side wants outside interference, a consent-based mission (by definition) will not occur. If both (or all, in the case of multifactional wars) sides desire peacekeepers, the international community is unlikely to say no and peacekeepers will deploy. If the government does not want peacekeepers, its wishes usually trump those of rebel

[22] Licklider 1995; Toft 2003.

[23] The rebels may believe that the sovereignty norm biases the international community toward the government side, but this concern is often outweighed by the benefits of international recognition.

[24] Such agreements are relatively rare. Normally, if the status quo ante is restored, this is the result of the government's military victory.

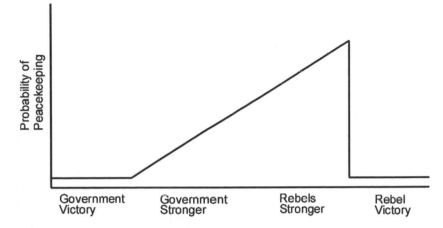

Figure 2.1. Relative Strength and Consent-Based Peacekeeping

groups,[25] unless rebels can wrest this concession from the government on the battlefield, coercing it to agree to peacekeeping. If the government wants peacekeepers and the rebels do not, the government may be able to convince the international community to intervene on its behalf, but the international community may be reluctant. If intervention takes place in this situation, it is likely to be an enforcement mission rather than a consent-based mission.

Taken together, these propositions suggest that consent-based peacekeeping is unlikely if either side wins outright, but that, short of clear victory for one side, it is more likely when rebels are relatively stronger and governments correspondingly weaker. Weak rebel groups may want peacekeeping the most, but are least likely to get it, as strong governments want outside interference the least and are best able to block it. Relatively weak governments, on the other hand, have fewer objections to peacekeeping (as it may help protect them), while relatively strong rebels are better able to push for a peacekeeping mission that may grant them legitimacy and protect them from abuse at the hands of the state. The relationship between government and rebel strength and the likelihood of consent-based peacekeeping should thus look something like figure 2.1.

Because these dynamics affect when belligerents will request or consent to peacekeeping, they should affect Chapter VI missions, but not necessarily Chapter VII operations. In general, the strategic interests of the belligerents

[25] Sovereignty norms, while substantially weaker than before the end of the Cold War, when they discouraged peacekeeping in civil conflicts altogether, nonetheless still dictate that much greater weight be given to government requests than to those by rebels.

will be similar to those discussed above, and perhaps even stronger, with enforcement missions. However, precisely because these missions do not require the consent of all belligerents, where they go will be less directly affected by these interests. Moreover, some enforcement missions deploy with the express intent of supporting one side in the conflict, protecting a government from a rebel group (as in Sierra Leone, for example), or, less often, protecting a group represented by rebels from abuse at the hands of the government (as in East Timor or Kosovo).[26] The strategic interaction between the belligerents therefore has much less effect on the deployment patterns of enforcement missions than consent-based peacekeeping. Chapter VI missions require the support of both the international community and all of the belligerents. Chapter VII missions require the support only of the international community (though in practice they usually have support from at least one side in the conflict). The difference between these two types of missions thus lets us investigate differences between supply-side and demand-side arguments for where peacekeepers go.

Hypotheses and Empirical Results

The remainder of this chapter lays out and tests empirically a number of hypotheses about where peacekeepers go. In this chapter (and the next), peacekeeping is the dependent variable rather than the independent variable, as it is in the rest of the book. Because I am interested not only in whether peacekeepers are deployed, but also in the distinction between consent-based and enforcement missions, I use multinomial logistic regression. Of the 94 cease-fires in civil wars in the post–Cold War period, consent-based peacekeeping missions were deployed to 23 (7 of these were monitoring missions, 10 traditional peacekeeping operations, and 6 multidimensional peacekeeping), enforcement missions were sent to 13 cases, and belligerents were left to their own devices in the other 58 cases. What accounts for this variation? I test, first, the overall relationship between the ease or difficulty of the case and the likelihood of peacekeeping. I then explore more specific hypotheses about where peacekeepers go.

Peacekeeping and the Degree of Difficulty

For the purposes of the rest of this book, the main hypotheses to investigate are whether peacekeepers tend to go to relatively easy or relatively difficult

---

[26] Peacekeepers in Kosovo initially served to protect Kosovar Albanians from Serbia, but as Kosovo has moved toward de facto independence, peacekeepers there have increasingly served to protect ethnic Serbs from majority Albanians.

cases. Critics of peacekeepers' independent effect, as well as those who argue peacekeepers should only deploy where the chances for success are good, expect (or hope) that

HYPOTHESIS: Peacekeeping is most likely where peace is relatively easy to keep.

I argue, however, that peacekeepers are most likely where they are most needed, in the more difficult cases.

HYPOTHESIS: Peacekeeping is most likely where peace is relatively difficult to keep.

In order to test these opposing hypotheses directly, I need to know the probability that peace would last if belligerents were left to their own devices in each case. That is, I need an assessment of the degree of difficulty at the time of a cease-fire. Unfortunately, making this determination is not straightforward.

From existing research on the stability of peace after civil war, we are beginning to understand the factors that tend to make peace harder or easier to keep.[27] The way the war ends, whether in victory for one side, a peace treaty, or only a truce, shapes the chances for peace.[28] The more death and displacement caused by the civil war, the harder it is to maintain peace.[29] The number of factions, whether or not rebels have access to lootable resources to fund their fight, and whether they have support from neighboring countries also appear to affect the prospects for peace.[30] Both a country's level of economic development and its level of democracy shape its vulnerability to repeated warfare.[31] Whether a war is fought along identity lines (e.g., ethnicity or religion), and whether or not it is a secessionist conflict, are also thought by some to affect the prospects for peace.[32]

I could use these variables to estimate a statistical model of the duration of peace and then use that model to predict the probability that peace will last at the time of a particular cease-fire. There is a problem, however.

[27] For a review of the quantitative literature on this topic, see Walter 2004b. For a qualitative assessment, see Downs and Stedman 2002.

[28] Licklider 1995; Toft 2003; Fortna 2004a; Doyle and Sambanis 2000; Downs and Stedman 2002.

[29] Doyle and Sambanis 2000; on refugees and internally displaced people and the resumption of war, see DeRouen and Barutciski 2005.

[30] Doyle and Sambanis 2000; Fearon 2004.

[31] Walter 2004a argues that the former is a matter of the opportunity costs for those deciding whether or not to pick up a gun and return to war. Others have argued it is a matter of economic grievances fueling repeated conflict. Collier et al. 2003. On democracy and recurrent war, see Dubey 2002; and Walter 2004a.

[32] The effect of these attributes remains a matter of debate. See Walter's 2004b summary.

If peacekeepers do in fact tend to deploy to more difficult cases, and if peacekeeping improves the chances that peace will last (as we will see in chapter 5 that it does), then the estimates of the degree of difficulty at the time of the cease-fire, before peacekeepers arrive, will be biased by the fact that peacekeepers affect the eventual outcome. The most difficult cases, because they are most likely to get peacekeepers, will appear less difficult than they really are (peace will last longer than it would have if no peacekeepers deployed). This will mute the estimated effects of variables that shape the prospects for peace. So our predictions about the overall degree of difficulty based on these estimates will be wrong. If peacekeepers instead go to the easiest cases, our estimates will also be biased, but in the opposite direction—the easiest cases will appear even easier than they really are and effects will be exaggerated. Either way, if peacekeeping is effective and if there is a systematic relationship between the difficulty of the case and whether or not peacekeepers deploy (the very thing we are trying to determine), our estimates will be incorrect.

Fortunately, there exists a set of cases that are not affected by this problem. As discussed in chapter 1, peacekeeping was only very rarely used in civil wars before the end of the Cold War. And when it was used (as in the Congo) its purpose was to contain ongoing conflict, not necessarily to prevent its recurrence. These cases thus provide information about the counterfactual—what would happen if no peacekeepers deployed to help maintain peace in the aftermath of civil war? How would characteristics of the conflict shape the prospects for peace? I therefore use these earlier cases to generate unbiased estimates of the effect of the variables discussed above on the ease or difficulty of keeping peace. I then plug the values for these variables from the post–Cold War cases into the model to generate the predicted probability of renewed war in each case since 1989.[33]

In appendix B, I describe a model of peace duration based on 10 characteristics that affect the degree of difficulty: infant mortality (as a proxy for economic development), democracy, war aims, identity conflict, numbers killed or displaced, military outcome, whether a treaty was signed, the number of factions, contraband financing for rebels, and a neighboring country's support for rebels. Using this model, I generated the predicted duration of peace[34] at the time of the cease-fire for each of the post–Cold

---

[33] Of course, we cannot assess the counterfactual perfectly. The duration of peace may be different now than it was during the Cold War. But unless the end of the superpower rivalry changed the effect of the variables investigated here on that duration (for example, unless something about the Cold War made contraband financing for rebels more, or less, detrimental to peace than it is now) this will not bias our results. Moreover, using these Cold War cases is better than using the post–Cold War cases in which we know our estimates will be biased by the presence of peacekeepers.

[34] Technically, the natural log of the predicted time to another war.

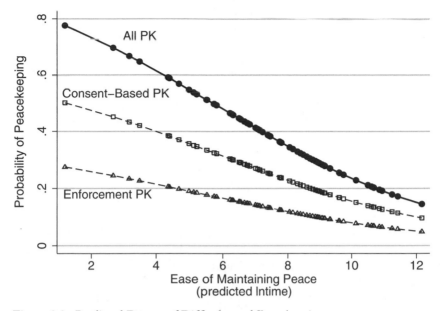

Figure 2.2. Predicted Degree of Difficulty and Peacekeeping

War cases.[35] Examples of cases with a long predicted duration of peace, representing relatively easy cases, include Northern Ireland (democracy, high standard of living, relatively few killed or displaced, a peace treaty signed, etc.) and Yemen (war ended in decisive victory, nonidentity war, only two factions, no contraband financing or neighbor support for rebels). Cases predicted to be much more difficult, likely to revert to war quickly, include Liberia and Cambodia, both with high infant mortality rates and low democracy scores, where the war had taken a huge toll in terms of those killed or displaced, and involved many factions, and where rebels enjoyed significant contraband financing and support from neighboring countries.[36]

These predicted indicators of the degree of difficulty provide strong evidence that peacekeepers tend to go to the most difficult cases. Figure 2.2 shows the relationship between the degree of difficulty of the case and the probability that peacekeepers deploy. The longer peace is expected to last at the time of the cease-fire, based on the model described above, the less likely the case is to receive peacekeepers. The top line shows the relation-

[35] Results are substantially the same if I use instead the predicted hazard, or risk, of renewed warfare.

[36] Peace is predicted to last hundreds of years in the former cases, but only a few weeks in the latter.

ship for all peacekeeping types combined. As the ease of maintaining peace increases, the probability of a peacekeeping mission declines. The lower lines show the relationship separated by consent-based and enforcement missions.[37] In short, there is no support for the notion that peacekeepers select easy cases. Rather, the evidence clearly indicates that peacekeepers tend to go where peace would otherwise be most fragile.

While indicative of the overall relationship between peacekeeping and the degree of difficulty, these are crude measures that explain only a very small amount of the variation across cases.[38] However, the existing literature's focus on where the international community chooses to intervene, and the idea, outlined above, that some sets of belligerents want peacekeeping more than others, lead to more specific hypotheses about how peacekeeping varies over civil war cases (some of which also bear on the issue of ease or difficulty of maintaining peace). By testing these hypotheses, we can paint a richer picture of where peacekeepers go. The following sections lay out these hypotheses and discuss the results of the multinomial logistic regressions used to test them.

With a relatively modest number of cases, and a large number of independent variables, many of which are dichotomous, and some of which are related to each other, it is important to test the robustness of findings to variations in model specification. Table 2.1 provides a representative sample of the many regressions run to evaluate the effects of these variables and their interaction with each other. A scan across the six models in table 2.1 gives a good sense of the direction and statistical significance of each finding. Negative coefficients indicate variables that make peacekeeping less likely; positive coefficients, variables that make peacekeeping more likely. The effects on both consent-based and enforcement missions are shown. How skeptical we should be of each result is indicated in the column marked "$P < |Z|$." Values lower than .05 meet the conventional standard for statistical significance: that there is less than 5% chance of seeing this result if no relationship existed.[39] See appendix A for more information on the variables used in this analysis.

[37] These results are obtained with logistic and multinomial logistic regressions of peacekeeping or peacekeeping chapter (respectively) on the predicted duration of peace from the model described in appendix B. Results are statistically significant at the .05 level for all peacekeeping and for consent-based peacekeeping. Because of the relatively small number of cases in this category, results for enforcement missions fall shy of this level of confidence, but are significant at the .10 level. We can therefore be fairly confident (90%–95% sure) that these effects are not the result of chance alone.

[38] The "pseudo-R^2" value indicating the percentage of variation accounted for by the model is less than 1.

[39] Note that because this data represents the full universe of cases, we are not attempting to infer from a sample to a larger population, as is often the case in statistical research.

TABLE 2.1
Where Peacekeepers Go

	Model 1				Model 2				Model 3			
	Consent		Enforce		Consent		Enforce		Consent		Enforce	
	Coef. (RSE)	P<|Z|	Coef. (RSE)	P<|Z|	Coef. (RSE)	P<|Z|	Coef. (RSE)	P<|Z|	Coef. (RSE)	P<|Z|	Coef. (RSE)	P<|Z|
P5 Affinity	-0.06 (2.18)	.98	0.83 (2.56)	.75								
P5 Alliance					-1.43 (1.36)	.29	-1.21 (2.46)	.62				
Former P5 Colony					-3.80 (1.63)	.02	-5.77 (2.13)	.01	-3.72 (1.67)	.03	-6.02 (2.08)	.00
Oil Exporter	-0.73 (1.21)	.55	-0.08 (0.83)	.92	-0.87 (1.31)	.51	-1.33 (1.31)	.31	-0.80 (1.30)	.54	-1.39 (1.30)	.29
P5 Contiguity	-3.03 (1.09)	.01	-1.78 (1.93)	.36	-5.59 (1.92)	.00	-2.52 (1.77)	.16	-5.36 (1.70)	.00	-2.68 (1.42)	.06
P5 Involvement					0.85 (1.33)	.52	0.18 (1.60)	.91	0.53 (1.26)	.67	-0.18 (1.30)	.89
Deaths	0.10 (0.15)	.51	0.10 (0.24)	.68	-0.01 (0.27)	.96	-0.17 (0.36)	.64	0.00 (0.28)	.99	-0.21 (0.26)	.43
Democracy	-0.03 (0.06)	.65	-0.27 (0.07)	.00	-0.04 (0.06)	.49	-0.36 (0.14)	.01	-0.05 (0.06)	.35	-0.34 (0.11)	.00
Government Army Size	-0.012 (0.005)	.03	0.001 (0.002)	.52	-0.011 (0.005)	.02	0.002 (0.001)	.28	-0.012 (0.004)	.01	0.001 (0.002)	.57
Contraband	-0.03 (0.81)	.97	0.36 (1.13)	.75	0.80 (1.40)	.57	1.37 (1.18)	.24	0.87 (1.12)	.44	0.15 (1.02)	.26

TABLE 2.1 (continued)
Where Peacekeepers Go

| | Model 1 | | | | Model 2 | | | | Model 3 | | | |
| | Consent | | Enforce | | Consent | | Enforce | | Consent | | Enforce | |
	Coef. (RSE)	P<|Z|	Coef. (RSE)	P<|Z|	Coef. (RSE)	P<|Z|	Coef. (RSE)	P<|Z|	Coef. (RSE)	P<|Z|	Coef. (RSE)	P<|Z|
Mountains	0.75 (0.27)	.01	−0.09 (0.35)	.80	1.32 (0.54)	.01	0.16 (0.59)	.79	1.35 (0.46)	.00	0.24 (0.41)	.56
Victory	−1.43 (1.12)	.20	0.90 (1.81)	.62	−4.22 (1.94)	.03	−0.80 (3.56)	.82	−4.05 (2.00)	.04	−0.84 (2.10)	.69
Treaty	0.14 (0.82)	.87	3.89 (1.73)	.02	−0.16 (1.65)	.92	4.43 (3.09)	.15	0.05 (1.64)	.98	4.36 (2.03)	.03
Secession	−0.41 (0.75)	.58	−1.18 (1.33)	.37	1.02 (1.86)	.58	0.79 (1.20)	.51	1.52 (1.85)	.41	1.10 (1.24)	.37
Past Agreement	0.02 (0.43)	.97	1.45 (1.04)	.17	0.17 (0.84)	.84	2.82 (1.60)	.08	0.21 (0.75)	.78	2.73 (1.24)	.03
Infant Mortality	0.00 (0.01)	.91	−0.03 (0.01)	.02	0.02 (0.01)	.09	−0.01 (0.02)	.78	0.02 (0.01)	.11	−0.00 (0.01)	.95
Constant	−1.52 (2.68)	.57	−3.17 (2.74)	.25	−2.45 (3.70)	.51	−1.92 (4.59)	.68	−3.19 (3.83)	.41	−1.91 (3.31)	.56
N	91				83				88			
Pseudo-R^2	0.33				0.51				0.52			
Log Pseudo-Likelihood	−55.52				−37.86				−38.90			

TABLE 2.1 (continued)
Where Peacekeepers Go

	Model 4				Model 5				Model 6			
	Consent		Enforce		Consent		Enforce		Consent		Enforce	
	Coef. (RSE)	P<|Z|	Coef. (RSE)	P<|Z|	Coef. (RSE)	P<|Z|	Coef. (RSE)	P<|Z|	Coef. (RSE)	P<|Z|	Coef. (RSE)	P<|Z|
Former P5 Colony	−6.24 (1.97)	.00	−6.05 (3.16)	.06	−2.60 (1.55)	.09	−5.00 (1.82)	.01	−4.47 (2.27)	.05	−8.31 (2.75)	.00
Oil Exporter					−0.71 (1.13)	.53	−1.44 (1.22)	.24	−2.88 (2.40)	.23	−0.04 (1.93)	.98
P5 Contiguity	−7.58 (2.66)	.00	1.19 (1.78)	.50	−4.95 (1.85)	.01	−2.88 (1.35)	.03	−5.26 (1.75)	.00	−3.78 (2.02)	.06
P5 Involvement					1.37 (1.03)	.18	0.33 (1.04)	.75	−0.39 (1.55)	.80	−1.33 (1.72)	.44
Neighbor Aids Rebels	−0.48 (0.95)	.61	1.29 (1.16)	.27								
Deaths					0.02 (0.21)	.92	−0.15 (0.30)	.61	0.03 (0.31)	.92	−0.72 (0.38)	.06
Democracy	−0.09 (0.06)	.12	−0.56 (0.20)	.01	−0.05 (0.06)	.45	−0.35 (0.12)	.00	−0.06 (0.09)	.47	−0.47 (0.18)	.01
Government Army Size	−0.022 (0.008)	.00	−0.006 (0.003)	.07	−0.009 (0.005)	.04	0.002 (0.002)	.33	−0.014 (0.006)	.01	0.001 (0.002)	.71
Contraband	1.82 (1.21)	.13	3.11 (1.04)	.00	0.35 (0.82)	.67	0.72 (0.83)	.39	1.00 (1.26)	.43	2.17 (1.76)	.22

TABLE 2.1 (continued)
Where Peacekeepers Go

	Model 4				Model 5				Model 6			
	Consent		Enforce		Consent		Enforce		Consent		Enforce	
	Coef. (RSE)	P<|Z|	Coef. (RSE)	P<|Z|	Coef. (RSE)	P<|Z|	Coef. (RSE)	P<|Z|	Coef. (RSE)	P<|Z|	Coef. (RSE)	P<|Z|
Mountains	1.83 (0.73)	.01	-0.73 (0.47)	.13	1.40 (0.51)	.01	0.21 (0.40)	.61	1.35 (0.45)	.00	0.45 (0.50)	.37
Victory	-2.89 (2.97)	.33	5.56 (2.39)	.02	-4.57 (2.42)	.06	-0.76 (1.98)	.70	-4.60 (2.63)	.08	-0.48 (2.67)	.86
Treaty	-0.49 (1.31)	.71	10.81 (3.79)	.00	-0.36 (1.66)	.83	4.28 (2.04)	.04	0.11 (1.93)	.96	5.65 (1.91)	.00
Secession	3.87 (1.50)	.01	3.25 (2.06)	.11					1.84 (2.65)	.49	1.84 (1.95)	.34
Identity War					-1.40 (1.29)	.28	-0.49 (1.18)	.68				
Past Agreement	-0.07 (0.85)	.94	5.90 (2.09)	.01	0.46 (0.71)	.52	2.59 (1.16)	.03	0.38 (0.63)	.55	3.21 (1.23)	.01
Infant Mortality	0.04 (0.01)	.01	-0.03 (0.01)	.01	0.01 (0.01)	.44	-0.01 (0.02)	.56	0.02 (0.02)	.14	-0.00 (0.02)	.92
Factions									-0.51 (2.46)	.84	5.03 (1.37)	.00
Constant	-4.70 (2.05)	.02	-9.68 (3.35)	.00	-1.58 (2.18)	.47	-1.18 (3.18)	.71	-2.27 (4.76)	.63	-2.04 (3.67)	.58
N	85				88				88			
Pseudo-R^2	0.61				0.52				0.58			
Log Pseudo-Likelihood	-30.44				-39.02				-33.80			

National Interests of the Great Powers

If the supply of peacekeeping is driven by the national interests of the great powers who wield a veto in the Security Council, then peacekeeping should generally be more likely in countries of strategic or historical interest to these powers. Unfortunately, great power interest is a difficult concept to measure. It consists of a number of factors, including geographic proximity, political, historical, or alliance ties, and strategic resources, among others. Rather than attempt to construct a singe measure of "interest," my approach here is to test the relationship between these component factors of interest and the likelihood of peacekeeping.[40] Perm-5 members may be most aware of and most concerned by civil wars in countries with whom they have close relations, such as alliance partners, or historical ties, such as their former colonies. The conventional wisdom and much of the peacekeeping literature would predict that

HYPOTHESIS: Peacekeeping is more likely the closer the political or historical ties between the country and United States, Great Britain, France, China, or Russia (the Perm-5).

If the cynical hypothesis that peacekeeping is driven by desired access to resources, then

HYPOTHESIS: Peacekeeping is affected by whether a country is rich in strategic resources, such as oil.

Note that scholars argue this hypothesis in both directions. Some contend that peacekeeping will be more likely because intervening powers want to get their greedy hands on such resources.[41] Others suggest that individual powers will be less likely to countenance peacekeepers because they do not want others interfering with their access or because they do not want to offend the governments from whom they buy oil (as for example, in the Sudan or Iraq).[42] Natural resources have also been used as a measure of the difficulty of maintaining peace, so if they drive where peacekeepers go, this effect will help us understand whether peacekeeping selects into the easy or the hard cases.[43] Measures of political "affinity" (based on voting in the

[40] For a similar critique of lumping the various components of "national interest" together, see Gilligan and Stedman 2003.

[41] Gibbs 1997.

[42] Kim Marten, email to the author, August 1, 2006.

[43] See, for example, Collier and Hoeffler 2004. For a review of the literature on natural resources and civil war, see Ross 2004.

UN), formal alliance ties, former colonial relationships,[44] and fuel exports are used to test these propositions.[45]

As table 2.1 shows, neither hypothesis is supported. Political affinity between a country and a Perm-5 member has no statistically significant effect on peacekeeping. And the negative coefficients for both alliance ties and former colonial ties indicate that whatever effects exist are the opposite of those predicted by this hypothesis. The former is not statistically significant, but peacekeeping is much less likely in former colonies of the Perm-5 than in other states (more on this below). Nor is there truth to the accusation that peacekeepers are motivated by access to strategic resources. If anything, peacekeeping is less likely in oil-rich countries, but the relationship is not significant.[46] Peacekeeping is not significantly more likely when the most powerful members of the UN Security Council are more interested or engaged than in other cases.

Indeed, when Perm-5 interests are *most* highly engaged, when conflicts occur in their own backyard, or where they have intervened directly on behalf of one side of the conflict, we might expect the great powers to prefer to handle crises without the interference of the rest of the international community.

HYPOTHESIS: Peacekeeping is less likely in conflicts in or contiguous to the territory of the Perm-5, or where a Perm-5 member has intervened, either militarily or politically, on behalf of one side in the war.

There is mixed support for this notion. When the conflict is in the territory of a Perm-5 member, or in its own backyard (*P5 contiguity*), peacekeeping is quite unlikely. This relationship is both quite robust and significant for consent-based peacekeeping, less so for enforcement missions. No peacekeepers were deployed to Afghanistan in 1992, or to Burma/Myanmar, nor, of course, have peacekeepers deployed to Chechnya or to Northern Ireland.[47] Interestingly, however, and contrary to what others

---

[44] Generally, these are former colonies of Britain or France, though the Philippines cases are also included as a former colony of the United States.

[45] I also tested the effects of primary commodity exports as a percentage of GDP (from Doyle and Sambanis 2000), but this variable is largely driven by exports of commodities such as coffee or tea, which are unlikely to drive peacekeeping. Thanks to Jim Fearon for pointing this out.

[46] Conventionally, variables that do not pass the traditional .05 level of significance are assumed to have no effect, as we cannot with confidence reject the null hypothesis. However, because a rationale for this chapter is to determine control variables that ought to be included in models of peacekeeping's effects, it is important to discuss marginally significant results (with appropriate caveats). We cannot conclude with confidence that there is *no* effect.

[47] Many of the conflicts in the backyard of Perm-5 members ended in a victory for one side, but this effect holds up even controlling for victory.

have argued,[48] peacekeeping is no less likely when a great power has intervened in the war on one side (*P5 involvement*). Indeed, in most model specifications the relationship is positive, though generally insignificant.

In short, only one aspect of great power interest in a conflict has the expected effect on peacekeeping. When civil wars take place in or next to their own territory, the Perm-5 are unlikely to countenance peacekeeping.[49] Other aspects of "strategic interest" evidently do not much shape where peacekeepers go.

Threat to Peace, Cost of War, and Democracy

A less cynical view of peacekeepers' motives is that the international community uses peacekeeping not to protect the narrow interests of its most powerful members, but to safeguard international peace and stability, for humanitarian reasons, or to foster democratization.

HYPOTHESIS: The more a civil war threatens international peace by spilling across borders, the more likely a peacekeeping operation.

If peacekeeping is driven by a humanitarian impulse, then it should be more likely in more deadly wars. The death toll of the war should also affect belligerents' choices. The higher the human cost of war, the more valuable the peace, and the more belligerents should be willing to endure the intrusion of outsiders to help them secure it.

HYPOTHESIS: The more deadly the war, the more likely a peacekeeping operation.

If the international community hopes to use peacekeeping to democratize war-torn states, peacekeeping should be most likely in countries in which democracy is lacking. On the demand side, rebel groups may feel less need to push for international oversight of the postwar political process if democratic institutions exist at the time of a cease-fire.[50]

HYPOTHESIS: More democratic countries are less likely to receive peacekeeping operations.

[48] E.g., Mullenbach 2005, p. 537.

[49] Even this finding runs counter to some arguments about strategic interest: for example, that NATO peacekeeping occurred in Bosnia and Kosovo because of (not despite) geographic proximity.

[50] Democracies might also be more susceptible to public pressure not to allow infringement on their sovereignty, but this pressure may also be high from the "selectorate" in countries where the military is politically powerful. Bueno de Mesquita et al. 2003. For an example of military institutions' sensitivity in this regard, see Perlez 2005.

As a proxy for the threat to international peace, I denote wars in which a neighboring country intervened on behalf of a rebel organization.[51] This hypothesis is not supported. Such intervention has no positive effect on the likelihood of consent-based peacekeeping. Enforcement missions may be more likely; the coefficient is consistently positive across model specifications, and sometimes approaches statistical significance, but we cannot have much confidence in this result. See model 4 in table 2.1.[52]

The humanitarian hypothesis also fares poorly. Peacekeeping is no more or less likely in low-cost wars such as Djibouti, Mali, or Northern Ireland than in very deadly wars such as Angola, Cambodia, and Afghanistan. In the multivariate analysis, the effect of the death toll on the likelihood of peacekeeping is inconsistent; its sign flips across models and is never significant.[53] Humanitarian crises may make intervention more likely during war in order to stop it, but they do not have a strong effect on the likelihood of peacekeeping afterward.[54]

The democratization hypothesis fares better. Peacekeeping, specifically enforcement, is less likely in more democratic countries than in more authoritarian ones, as expected.[55] This effect is consistent across model specifications but not significant for Chapter VI missions, while it is both significant and robust for Chapter VII missions. That this effect is stronger for enforcement than for consent-based missions indicates that it is a supply-side dynamic more than a demand-side phenomenon and suggests that the international community is indeed using peacekeeping to try to democ-

[51] The number of refugees displaced by the war is another possible proxy. However, existing measures (e.g., Doyle and Sambanis 2000) combine true refugees—those who have fled across a border—and internally displaced people, making this another measure of the overall humanitarian crisis rather than a measure of the threat of spillover.

[52] Note that this measure may undercount interventions, but does not appear to do so in a way that is biased with respect to peacekeeping. Note also that missing data when this variable is included make some results unstable.

[53] The measure used here is the natural log of war deaths, including both battle and civilian deaths. Measures that include the number of people displaced by the war yield similar results but have more missing data problems. I also examined the effect of the war's duration but found it to have no consistent effect on the likelihood of peacekeeping. In some tests, enforcement missions appear more likely after shorter wars. But because some enforcement missions initially deploy during ongoing wars to stop them, and then stay on to maintain peace, it is more likely that these missions shorten wars than that the length of the war affects decisions about peacekeeping. In other words, the causal arrow is reversed.

[54] See Gilligan and Stedman 2003. The discrepancy in our conclusions is likely because they model how quickly peacekeepers deploy during an ongoing conflict, but as they acknowledge, the measure of deaths includes some that take place after peacekeepers arrive, as in Rwanda.

[55] I lag the democracy measure because data for the year the war ends may be picking up postwar democratization (for example, if the cease-fire occurs early in the year), which may be the result rather than the cause of peacekeeping.

ratize war-torn countries.[56] In this regard, as in others, peacekeepers go where the job of keeping peace is more difficult.

Relative Strength of the Government and Rebels

There are both supply and demand reasons to think that the military strength of the government should affect the likelihood of peacekeeping, but these reasons affect different types of peacekeeping. The international community will be less willing to intervene against the wishes of countries that are strong militarily. The supply argument thus suggests that

HYPOTHESIS: Enforcement missions are less likely the stronger the government's military.

On the demand side, militarily stronger governments will generally not want outside interference (both because they control the state apparatus and because they are relatively more powerful militarily). If stronger militaries also have lower costs of war, they will be less likely to concede to peacekeeping even if the rebels would like it. As depicted in the middle portion of figure 2.1:

HYPOTHESIS: Consent-based peacekeeping is less likely the stronger the government's military.

The distinction between consent-based and enforcement missions in table 2.1 shows that the supply-side hypothesis does not hold up, but the demand-side hypothesis is strongly supported. Government army size has no consistent or significant effect on the likelihood of Chapter VII peacekeeping, but larger government armies significantly reduce the probability of Chapter VI missions. Consent-based missions are more likely in places such as Angola, Cambodia, and Mozambique, for example, than in countries with large armies like India, the Philippines, or Ethiopia.

I also explore two other possible aspects of the relative strength of governments and rebels: mountainous terrain and rebels' access to contraband goods with which to fund their cause.[57] First, rough terrain is generally thought to provide an advantage to rebels and to disadvantage government forces.[58] By increasing the government's cost of war, and decreasing that of the insurgents, mountainous territory should allow rebels to extract con-

---

[56] The same is true if democracy is measured before the war begins, suggesting that the international community tries to democratize countries where this objective is least likely rather than most likely to succeed, where there is little history of viable democracy. For analysis of how well this democratizing mission succeeds, see Fortna 2008.

[57] Neighboring countries' support for rebels, discussed above, also obviously relates to rebel strength.

[58] See DeRouen and Sobek 2004; Fearon and Laitin 1999, 2003.

cessions. As rebels are more likely to want peacekeepers, mountains should increase the probability of peacekeeping. Rougher terrain may also make it harder for belligerents to monitor each other's activities, making verification by outsiders relatively more attractive.

HYPOTHESIS: Consent-based peacekeeping is more likely if the war has been fought in mountainous territory.

If peacekeepers tend to deploy to easy cases, they should avoid rough territory for two reasons. First, it should make operations more difficult and costly. Second, because rough terrain increases the chance of civil war in the first place,[59] it may also make the resumption of war more likely. On the other hand, if peacekeepers select into more difficult cases, there should be a positive association with mountainous territory.

As table 2.1 indicates, consent-based peacekeeping is significantly more likely the more mountainous the country in question, as expected. Peacekeeping is less likely in relatively flat Mali, Senegal, or in Israel-Palestine and more likely in more mountainous places such as Georgia, Western Sahara, and Guatemala. This along with the previous finding on government army strength provides evidence for the relationship depicted in figure 2.1. In the absence of a clear victory by either side (see below), consent-based peacekeeping is more likely the stronger the rebels relative to the government. And as we might expect, these demand-side dynamics do not affect enforcement missions; there is no significant effect of terrain on enforcement. These results also provide further evidence that peacekeepers go to tougher rather than easier cases—where rebels are relatively strong and the terrain is difficult.

Another proxy for relative strength of the belligerents is access to contraband financing. We might expect rebels who control independent and illegal sources of funding, such as drugs or gems, to be militarily stronger and therefore able to extract promises of peacekeeping during negotiations. However, because they are illegal, these sources of funding will make rebels much less willing to have the international community monitoring their behavior. I therefore do not expect a strong relationship between contraband financing for rebels and Chapter VI peacekeeping. I include this measure nonetheless, as it is a good indicator of the difficulty of maintaining peace (see appendix B).

HYPOTHESIS: Consent-based peacekeeping is unrelated to rebels' access to contraband financing.

As expected, there is no relationship between contraband financing for rebels and Chapter VI peacekeeping. The sign of this variable's coefficient

---

[59] Fearon and Laitin 2003.

flips across model specifications and is never significant. While contraband financing strengthens rebels, it presumably also makes them wary of outside monitoring. Enforcement missions, however, may be more likely when rebels enjoy contraband financing; this effect is consistent though rarely significant. In these cases, the rebels have less say about whether peacekeepers deploy.

War Outcomes

As figure 2.1 depicts, consent-based peacekeeping should be more likely the stronger the rebels relative to the government, and we have seen that it is. But as the figure shows, this relationship should not hold at the extremes, where one side has defeated the other. Here, the probability of consent-based peacekeeping should drop off. If the war ends with one side defeating the other outright, there will be little need for peacekeeping, and little desire for it on the part of the winner. The loser's wishes will be irrelevant.

HYPOTHESIS: Peacekeeping is unlikely if the war ends in a victory for one side.

Note that enforcement missions may be more common when one side has won outright, but that the causal relationship here is unclear. Some enforcement missions start as operations to end the fighting, often by taking sides, so are more likely causing the victory of one side than caused by it.

Of cases that end without a clear victory, there are two other possible outcomes. The fighting may stop with a truce or cease-fire, or the war may end with a political settlement.[60] If the international community heeds the advice to try to keep peace only where the belligerents signal their support for it, then

HYPOTHESIS: Peacekeeping is more likely if a peace treaty has been reached.

However, the belligerents themselves may be more likely to request international help when there is only a fragile cease-fire or truce in place. This suggests just the opposite hypothesis:

---

[60] Military victories and negotiated agreements are not necessarily mutually exclusive categories; there may be negotiations between an evident winner and loser to stop fighting before one side is eliminated. Kecskemeti 1964. However, this is less common in civil wars than in interstate wars. Moreover, the way the outcome data used here (based on categories from Doyle and Sambanis 2000) are coded, unfortunately precludes an analytical distinction between these two dimensions of war outcome, at least in the quantitative analysis.

HYPOTHESIS: Consent-based peacekeeping is less likely if a peace treaty has been reached than if the war ends with a truce.

Two dichotomous variables mark whether the war ended in a victory for one side and whether a treaty was signed—the comparison category here is wars that ended with a cease-fire or truce. As expected, consent-based peacekeeping is much less likely if one side has completely defeated the other. This relationship is consistent and generally statistically significant. All but two of 23 consent-based peacekeeping missions deployed where neither side had won the war outright (the exceptions are Rwanda in 1994[61] and Guinea-Bissau in 1999, both cases in which peacekeepers were present from an earlier failed cease-fire).[62]

Contrary to expectations, however, there is no clear or consistent relationship between the signing of a peace treaty (as opposed to a cease-fire or truce) and the probability of Chapter VI peacekeeping.[63] Interestingly, there is a strong positive correlation between Chapter VII missions and peace treaties. While one might expect that the international community would be more concerned that the parties indicate their "political will" for peace through a treaty when deciding whether to deploy a consent-based mission than an enforcement mission, this does not appear to be the case. This result may be due to reverse causality, as mentioned above. Where intervention occurs to end the fighting, interveners may insist on a peace treaty rather than a truce.

Sovereignty, Trust, Economic Conditions, and Factions

While peacekeeping can bring material benefits in the way of aid, it entails significant infringements on a country's sovereignty, and may also diminish its prestige. Allowing peacekeepers in means permitting foreign troops to be stationed on one's soil, and letting outsiders monitor one's actions and interfere with one's domestic political institutions. And just as providing troops to peacekeeping missions is a source of pride for many countries, being on the receiving end of intervention is a matter of state embarrassment. As noted above, peacekeepers can confer legitimacy on rebels as recognized political actors. While this is all to the good for rebels, govern-

---

[61] The RPF's military victory ended the genocide. UNAMIR II was present in Rwanda until 1996.

[62] There is no consistent relationship between victory for one side and Chapter VII missions. As noted above, it is not clear which way the causal arrows run in this relationship.

[63] Note that this contradicts earlier findings in my own work that peacekeeping is more likely when war ends in a truce rather than a treaty. Fortna 2004a. The addition of new cease-fires missed in the earlier data set (many of which are truces with no peacekeepers present, which is presumably why they were overlooked in the original Doyle and Sambanis list of cases) changes this result.

ments are understandably uncomfortable with this aspect of peacekeeping's infringement on sovereignty. The international community may also be worried about infringing on sovereignty when deciding whether or not to deploy peacekeepers. These sovereignty concerns obtain in all countries to some extent, but may be stronger in some cases than others. I explore two possible proxies to measure sovereignty concerns. First, states faced with secessionist challenges may be most sensitive about their sovereignty.[64] The demand for peacekeeping should thus be lower in secessionist conflicts than when rebels aim for other goals. A supply-side argument would suggest that third parties will be less willing to intervene in secessionist conflicts because doing so violates the territorial integrity norm.[65]

HYPOTHESIS: Peacekeeping is less likely, all else equal, in secessionist conflicts.

Second, former colonies of the Perm-5 states may be most wary of any peacekeeping presence that smacks of neocolonialism, while the international community may also want to avoid such charges.[66] Note that this last argument is exactly the opposite of the one suggested earlier by the notion that peacekeeping is driven by the interests of the Perm-5.

HYPOTHESIS: Peacekeeping is less likely, all else equal, in former colonies of the Perm-5.

The first hypothesis does not hold water. Neither the demand-driven argument that governments will be most prickly about sovereignty and therefore least willing to consent to peacekeeping when they face secessionist conflicts, nor the supply-side notion that the international community will be least willing to interfere in these conflicts, is right. There is no consistent or significant relationship between secessionist conflicts and peacekeeping. I also explored the effects of identity conflicts, which are correlated with but do not perfectly overlap with secessionist conflicts.[67] Peacekeeping, particularly of the consent-based variety, is, if anything, less likely in identity conflicts than in conflicts over ideology or other issues (see model 5), but this finding is not terribly robust over model specifications.

However, as noted above, peacekeeping is least likely in former colonies of the Perm-5. It is unclear whether this is because former colonies are most resistant to anything that might smack of neocolonialism, because

[64] Thanks to Stacie Goddard for this suggestion.

[65] Mullenbach 2005.

[66] There has been something of a norm within the UN against peacekeeping in former colonies of the permanent members of the Security Council, precisely to avoid charges of neocolonialism. Thanks to Carola Weil for pointing this out.

[67] Rwanda is an example of an identity war that is not secessionist. Yemen and Djibouti are secessionist wars that are not identity based, or think of the American Civil War.

the Perm-5 members are reluctant to appear to be recolonizing former territories, or because both of these dynamics are at work. In any event, former Perm-5 colonial status seems to be a better proxy for sovereignty concerns than are the war aims of rebels.

The demand for peacekeepers should be higher to the extent that the parties mistrust each other. The lower the level of trust, the more both sides will want an outsider to monitor the other's behavior and help prevent its defection. While mistrust will be high after any civil war, it may be more so in some than in others. For example, mistrust will be particularly high if the belligerents have reached a cease-fire or peace agreement in the past, only to see war flare up again when one or both sides renege. If the belligerents have previously tried and failed to make peace stick, they may also have less confidence in their ability to do so on their own. A failed agreement in the past may also influence the international community's decision about what type of peacekeeping force to send in. That a previous attempt to make peace has failed suggests the presence of strong spoilers, making an enforcement mission more appropriate than a less robust Chapter VI mission.

> **HYPOTHESIS:** Failed past agreements between the same belligerents make peacekeeping more likely.

Past rounds of warfare, particularly those that end in an agreement, are also a good indicator of the degree of difficulty of the case. If peacekeepers deploy to hard cases, this positive relationship between past agreements and intervention should hold. It should be reversed if peacekeepers choose easy cases.

As expected, cease-fires that follow previous (by definition) failed attempts to agree to peace are more likely to see peacekeeping, and especially Chapter VII missions.[68] The fact that this effect is stronger for enforcement missions suggests that the trend is driven at least as much by the international community's wariness about dealing with spoilers without a robust mission as it is by the belligerents' demand for peacekeeping. In cases where the belligerents reached an agreement in the past only to see one or both sides renege, such as Angola, Liberia, or Sierra Leone, the international community has intervened, often with enforcement missions authorized under Chapter VII. This finding is another indicator that peacekeepers go to more difficult cases, where peace has failed in the past and mistrust is likely to be especially high.

---

[68] This effect is fairly consistent across model specifications for Chapter VI missions (the exception in model 4 is likely due to missing data), but only significant for Chapter VII missions.

There are both demand- and supply-side reasons to think that where peacekeepers go is driven by a country's economic development. A demand perspective would suggest that wealthier countries, less dependent on international aid, may be less concerned about the possible adverse effects to their reputations should they renege while peacekeepers are present. Governments of richer countries may thus be more willing to accept peacekeepers. On the supply side, the international community has been accused of caring more about keeping peace in more developed countries than in poorer ones. Infant mortality rates provide a proxy for economic and living standards.[69]

HYPOTHESIS: Consent-based peacekeeping is less likely the higher the infant mortality rate.

Again, whether peacekeepers are more likely to go to richer or to poorer countries will help us assess whether they deploy in easy or in hard cases, as previous research has shown peace to be harder to keep when poor economic conditions reduce the opportunity costs of fighting.[70]

Neither the supply nor the demand argument gets it right on economic development. Enforcement missions may be less likely in disadvantaged states, but this effect is not robust, nor generally significant. Meanwhile, consent-based peacekeeping is, if anything, more likely the lower the living standards in a country; quite the opposite of the relationship hypothesized. Again, however, this suggests that Chapter VI missions, at least, tend to deploy to more difficult cases, where dim economic prospects lower the opportunity costs of returning to war.

A final indication of the ease or difficulty of maintaining peace is worth exploring. If peacekeepers go to the hardest cases, as I argue, a deployment will be more likely in complicated cases involving many factions (that is, more than just the government and one rebel group).

HYPOTHESIS: Peacekeeping is more likely when the war involves many factions.

The opposite will be true if peacekeepers go to the easiest cases.

There is no significant relationship between the number of factions and Chapter VI peacekeeping. However, Chapter VII peacekeeping is, as expected, significantly more likely when the war involved not just the government and one rebel group, but many factions (see model 6). Indeed, all but one of the enforcement missions studied here took place in conflicts with several factions (the sole is exception is Kosovo 1999). Chapter VII

---

[69] Other proxies, such as GDP per capita or literacy rates, yield similar results. Of these, the infant mortality measure is most robust and least plagued by missing data.

[70] Walter 2004a; Collier et al. 2003.

peacekeeping is more likely in complicated wars with many groups fighting, such as Bosnia, Liberia, and Sierra Leone, than in simpler wars pitting just two sides against each other, as in Congo-Brazaville, Mali, or Yemen.

Conclusion

To summarize, the strategic interests of the great powers are not generally a good predictor of where peacekeepers go, with one notable exception. Peacekeeping is very unlikely in conflicts in or near these states' territory. But feelings of historical responsibility for former colonies, political or alliance ties, and strategic resources have not generally made peacekeeping more likely. Nor do the less cynical hypotheses about the international community's motives hold up well. Peacekeeping is driven neither by threats to international peace and security, nor by a humanitarian imperative to intervene after the most deadly conflicts. However, there does appear to be a desire by the international community to send peacekeepers to less democratic countries, perhaps with the hope of fostering democracy.

The relative strength of governments and rebel groups provides a better explanation for peacekeeping, particularly consent-based missions. As depicted in figure 2.1, short of complete victory for one side, peacekeeping is more likely the stronger the rebels. And, again as depicted, peacekeeping is quite unlikely at the extremes where one side has defeated the other outright. For Chapter VI peacekeeping, there is no clear difference between a peace treaty and merely a cease-fire as the end to war, while for Chapter VII missions, the correlations may be the result of reverse causation.

There is mixed evidence that variable sovereignty concerns are a factor in determining where peacekeepers go—former colonies of the Perm-5 are unlikely to receive peacekeeping, though whether or not the conflict is a secessionist one does not appear to matter. Economic conditions are not a strong predictor of peacekeeping. But the levels of mistrust (whether high or very high) and the number of factions involved in the fight are both strong determinants of where enforcement missions deploy.

Overall, the models in table 2.1 do a fairly good job of explaining where peacekeepers go. They account for between one-third and two-thirds of the variation in outcomes. Two key points emerge from this statistical investigation. First, peacekeeping is the result of both supply-side and demand-side considerations. Second, and most important for the rest of this study, peacekeepers tend to deploy to more difficult cases rather than to easier ones.

The unwillingness of the great powers to countenance peacekeeping in their own backyards is clearly a supply-side phenomenon. That enforcement missions in particular are more likely in less democratic countries and where past agreements have failed to keep peace suggests that the international community uses peacekeeping to further a democratizing agenda, and that it responds to the possible presence of spoilers by sending more robust missions, both supply-side phenomena. That peacekeeping is unlikely in former colonies of the Perm-5 could reflect either a norm on the part of the international community against neocolonialism, or the belligerents' desire not to invite old colonial masters to keep the peace; or both of these causes may be at work.

Other findings clearly reflect the interests of the peacekept (or not peacekept, as the case may be). That consent-based peacekeeping, but not enforcement, is affected by the strength of the government's army is consistent with an argument about stronger governments being less likely to consent to peacekeeping, but not with the supply-side argument that outsiders will be less willing to intervene against the wishes of a strong government. That consent-based peacekeeping is more likely in more mountainous countries supports demand-side explanations: that the advantage rough terrain gives to rebels makes governments more willing to concede to peacekeeping, and that outside help with monitoring is more valuable in rougher terrain. Similarly, that Chapter VI missions are unlikely when one side has defeated the other suggests that the belligerents themselves often determine whether there is peacekeeping or not in a given case.

In short, both the decisions of the international community, especially the great powers, and the decisions of the potentially peacekept explain why peacekeepers deploy to some places and not to others.

Most important for the purposes of the rest of this study, these findings also provide strong evidence that peacekeeping is more likely in the most difficult cases, rather than the easy ones. Only one finding gives any support to the opposite conclusion: that Chapter VII peacekeeping is more likely when a treaty has been signed. But the preponderance of the evidence goes the other way, with peacekeepers clearly selecting the more difficult cases on most other counts. Peacekeeping is more likely when neither side has won outright (an outcome that may not be the most desirable on other grounds but is empirically the most likely to lead to stable peace). Chapter VI missions are, if anything, more likely in countries with lower living standards. And these consent-based operations are more likely where rebels are relatively strong—where government armies are smaller, and where terrain is rougher. Chapter VII missions, meanwhile, are more likely in less democratic states, where levels of mistrust are higher, and where there are multiple factions.

These results on specific hypotheses confirm the conclusions from figure 2.2 that peacekeeping is most likely in cases where peace is predicted to be particularly difficult to maintain, not in the easy cases. This finding, that peacekeepers go to the more intractable conflicts, is crucial to our under-standing of the causal effect of peacekeeping. If it were not true, if peacekeepers were "cherry-picking" the easy cases in which peace is likely to last no matter what, then one could argue that peacekeepers' effect on peace is merely spurious. One cannot make that argument given the statis-tical evidence provided here. As we shall see in the next chapter, both of the broad conclusions that emerge from this survey of the full universe of cases are supported by the more detailed and nuanced evidence from the case studies.

Three

WHERE PEACEKEEPERS GO II

EVIDENCE FROM THE CASES

THE STATISTICAL RESULTS IN THE PREVIOUS chapter provide some broad answers to the question of where peacekeepers go. They allow us to see patterns across the full universe of cases. But many of the statistical measures are crude proxies, and quantification likely misses nuances in the politics of where peacekeepers go. The case studies can shed more focused light on decisions by the international community and by the belligerents themselves about whether to send or accept peacekeeping. This chapter examines three conflicts, involving five attempts to maintain peace, in more detail to see why peacekeepers deployed in some cases but not others. Before answering this question, however, some background information on the cases, particularly the somewhat obscure Chittagong Hill Tracts conflict in Bangladesh, and the convoluted conflict in Sierra Leone, is in order.

Case Study Background

Mozambique: A Peacekeeping Success Story

After ten years of struggle against Portuguese colonial rule, Mozambique gained independence in 1975. The anticolonial movement Frente de Libertação de Moçambique (Frelimo) took power. However, the abrupt departure of the Portuguese devastated the economy and left Mozambique virtually devoid of educated or trained personnel to manage the country. Threatened by majority rule and by Mozambique's support for the black liberation movement in Rhodesia/Zimbabwe, Ian Smith's minority regime in Rhodesia established a force to disrupt Mozambique. The Resistência Nacional Moçambicana (Renamo) consisted of disgruntled Portuguese and black Mozambicans. On the eve of majority rule in Zimbabwe in 1980, apartheid South Africa took over as the rebel group's patron.[1] Afonso Dhlakama has led Renamo since 1979. By the early 1980s it numbered 6,000–7,000 fighters, attacking railway lines, power lines, hospitals, and schools. While the extent to which Renamo was motivated by a coherent political

---

[1] On the origins of Renamo see Vines 1996, chap. 2. For a more sympathetic view, see Hoile 1994.

program has been debated, the movement benefited from disenchantment with Frelimo's frequently heavy-handed Marxist-Leninist policies.[2]

Over the next decade, the war would devastate the lives and livelihoods of Mozambicans, killing an estimated one million people and displacing several times that number. The war quickly reached a stalemate: Renamo could not overthrow the Frelimo government; Frelimo could not eliminate Renamo. Fueled by the Cold War, the war in Mozambique continued throughout the 1980s, despite the stalemate, until the end of the superpower rivalry and the beginning of the end of apartheid in South Africa meant dwindling support for both sides. A severe drought further sapped both sides' capacity to fight.

In this context, peace initiatives began to gain momentum, and in 1990 negotiations between Renamo and the Mozambican government began in Rome. The talks took place in twelve rounds over two years, eventually resulting in the General Peace Agreement (GPA, or AGP in Portuguese), signed on October 4, 1992. The agreement called for the cessation of armed conflict, the cantonment and demobilization of both the Mozambican military and Renamo forces, and the creation of a new integrated army, as well as multiparty elections.

A Supervisory and Monitoring Commission, representing both sides and chaired by the UN, was established to oversee the entire peace process, with subsidiary commissions to oversee its various components. The UN was also asked to send a large peacekeeping mission. Security Council Resolution 797 (1992) established the United Nations Operation in Mozambique (ONUMOZ), with an authorized strength of 7,000 military personnel.[3] The mission was led by Special Representative to the Secretary-General Aldo Ajello. There were significant delays in getting the peace process started, and ONUMOZ was not fully deployed until May 1993. Elections, originally scheduled for October 1993, were eventually held in October 1994. Frelimo won the vote, and despite Renamo's initial threats to contest the election outcome by force, peace held. ONUMOZ withdrew by the end of the year.[4]

The UN's mission in Mozambique is hailed as a great peacekeeping success. Peace has held for over a decade and the chance of another war between Renamo and Frelimo is considered virtually nil. A second round of elections in 1999 and a third in 2004 have begun to cement democracy.[5]

---

[2] In addition to Hoile 1994 and Vines 1996, see Venâncio and Chan 1998.

[3] Reed 1996.

[4] For detailed descriptions of the mission see, Alden 2001, chap. 3; Synge 1997; Reed 1996; and Salomans 2003. For an overview and compendium of UN documents on the mission, see United Nations 1995.

[5] On demoralization in Mozambique, see Mannning 2002. For a more pessimistic assessment, see Weinstein 2002.

Mozambique

Mozambique is still extremely poor, but its economy has recovered significantly from its war and drought-stricken state in the early 1990s. The extent to which peacekeepers were responsible for maintaining the peace in Mozambique is explored in chapters 5 and 6.

Bangladesh: Peace without Peacekeepers
in the Chittagong Hill Tracts

The Chittagong Hill Tracts (CHT) is an area of over five thousand square miles in the southeast corner of Bangladesh, bordering Myanmar and the Indian states of Tripura and Mizoram. It constitutes 10% of Bangladeshi territory, and contains significant natural resources.[6] It is an area of steep hills and jungle very unlike the plains in the rest of Bangladesh. As a former Bangladeshi army commander put it, "The CHT is as ideal an area as one could find for waging guerilla war."[7]

The CHT is home to about a dozen "indigenous" ethnic groups, the largest being the Chakma, Tripura, and Marma.[8] The languages, culture, and religions of the hill people are quite distinct from the otherwise very homogenous population of Bangladesh.[9] The CHT now also contains a sizable Bengali settler population.[10]

The odd shape of Bangladesh and the even odder shape of India, with the northeastern states barely attached to the rest of India, give some idea of the politics of border drawing at partition. When India and Pakistan split along religious lines in 1947, the CHT as a non-Muslim area might logically have gone with India.[11] But for several reasons, including economic connections between the hill areas and the port in Chittagong, the importance of

[6] These include natural gas, the country's largest hydroelectric dam, and 60% of Bangladesh's reserve forests. Ibrahim 1991, p. 31; Minorities at Risk 2004a.

[7] Ibrahim 1991, p. 3.

[8] The hill people often refer to themselves collectively as Jumma, after their *jhum* (slash and burn) cultivation practices. They are also known, especially by others, as "tribals."

[9] Physically and linguistically, the indigenous hill people have more in common with the Burmese and inhabitants of India's northeastern states than with the Bengalis of the plains of Bangladesh. The Chakma and Marma are predominantly Buddhist, the Tripura predominantly Hindu. Other hill groups are Buddhist, Christian, or animist. Mohsin 2003, p. 18.

[10] According to the 1991 census, there were about 530,000 hill people in the CHT, and 430,000 Bengalis. Shelley, Khan, and Kabir n.d., p. 1. This figure for hill people does not include an estimated 50,000–70,000 refugees in India at the time (see below). The figure for Bengalis includes both those who have been settled in the CHT recently by the government, and those who migrated "naturally" much earlier. The latter are known as Adivashis, or "indigenous" or "original" Bengalis, and are not necessarily aligned politically with the settlers. Resentment of economic perks given to the settlers by the government often seems to trump ethnic identity. Mohsin 2003, p. 30; Alam interview, Rangamati; see also Ibrahim 1991, p. 3.

[11] Local chiefs favored recognition as native states, or, when it became clear that would not happen, union with either India or Burma. Mohsin 2003, p. 18.

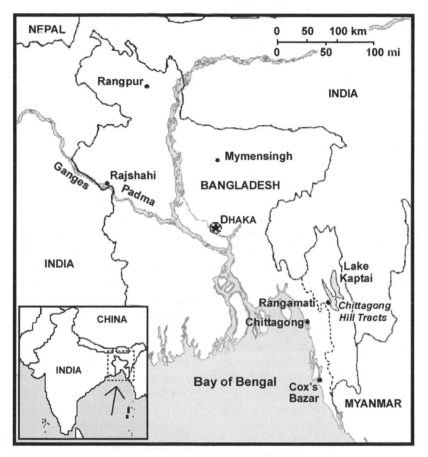

Bangladesh

energy resources in the CHT, and to compensate for other territory being granted to India, the CHT was granted to Pakistan by Cyril Radcliffe.[12]

The CHT had maintained a fair degree of local autonomy both in the Mughal period and under the British. This autonomy was codified under the British in the Hill Tracts Regulation of 1900, which set up special administrative rules, prohibited the settlement of outsiders in the CHT, and restricted the transfer of land to nonindigenous people. Pakistan revoked the special status of the CHT and began to encourage outsiders to settle there.[13] The economic grievances of the hill people began in earnest with

[12] Behera 1996, p. 987; Mohsin 2003, pp. 18–19. See also Chester 2002.

[13] The central government lacked the ability completely to implement this revocation, however, so in practice, some measure of autonomy remained until Bangladesh's secession in 1971. Larma interview, Rangamati.

the building of the Kaptai dam in 1962. The dam submerged 400 square miles, including 54,000 acres of much of the best arable land in the CHT (and the palace of the Chakma king). The resulting lake displaced some 100,000 people, mostly Chakma, about a quarter of the population of the CHT at the time.[14] The displaced were never fully compensated. Lake Kaptai is known among the hill people as the "lake of tears."

In 1971, when eastern Pakistan broke away to become Bangladesh, many in the Bengali resistance (Mukti Bahini) perceived the hill people to support Pakistan, and after independence the forces of the nascent Bangladeshi army took reprisals against them.[15] Relations between the hill people and the new government of Bangladesh thus got off to an unfortunate start.

As Bangladesh formed its constitution in 1972, the only member of Parliament from the CHT, Manobendra Narayan Larma, called on Prime Minister Sheikh Mujibur (Mujib) Rahman, demanding autonomy for the CHT, the retention of the 1900 regulations in the constitution, the continuation of the offices of the tribal chiefs, and a ban on the influx of nonindigenous people into the area.[16] These demands were interpreted as secessionist and a challenge to Bengali nationalism and were rejected outright.[17] Mujib advised the hill people "to do away with their ethnic identities."[18]

Soon thereafter, Larma founded the Parbattya Chattagram Jana Samhati Samiti (PCJSS, the Chittagong Hill Tracts People's Solidarity Association). Its armed wing, the Shanti Bahini ("Peace Force"), was headed by his brother, Jyotirindra Bodhipriya (Shantu) Larma. M.N. Larma was assassinated in 1983 by a hard-line faction of the PCJSS, led by Priti Kumar, that advocated outright secession. From the mid-1970s until the 1990s, the PCJSS and the Shanti Bahini waged a low-level guerilla war in the hills against the Bangladeshi military to press for autonomy, and to protest the ongoing policy of settling the CHT with Bengalis from the plains. Meanwhile, Bangladesh stepped up its settlement policy as a counterinsurgency tactic.[19]

[14] Minorities at Risk 2004a; Mohsin 2003, p. 24.

[15] Behera 1996, p. 989.

[16] Mohsin 1997, p. 22; Behera 1996, p. 990.

[17] M. N. Larma's attempt to distinguish between Bengali and Bangladeshi nationalism fell on deaf ears. As he said before parliament, "I am a Chakma not a Bengali. I am a citizen of Bangladesh, Bangladeshi. You are also Bangladeshi but your national identity is Bengali. . . . They [Hill people] can never become Bengali." Quoted in Mohsin 2003, p. 23.

[18] Quoted in Ghosh 1989, p. 73.

[19] Mohsin 2003, p. 30; Shelley, Khan, and Kabir n.d., p. 10. On the political and military rationale for the settlement policy, see Ibrahim 1991, pp. 31, 37–38. The demographic shift in the CHT has been dramatic. The nonindigenous population has risen from less than 10% in 1951 to over 25% by 1974 and is now estimated at 49%. Shelley, Khan, and Kabir n.d., p. 5.

The Bangladeshi army numbered about 100,000, a third to a half of whom were deployed in the CHT. Shanti Bahini's numbers varied between 2,000 and 15,000.[20] For much of the insurgency, the PCJSS and Shanti Bahini enjoyed the backing of India, establishing headquarters in Tripura and receiving military training and assistance from the Indian military. The fighting, which also involved massacres of indigenous villagers by the military, and of Bengali settlers by the Shanti Bahini, killed between 3,500 and 25,000, and caused 50,000 to 70,000 refugees to flee into India.[21]

Negotiations began in the late 1980s under H. M. Ershad's regime.[22] In 1989, Hill District Councils were set up in an attempt to assuage demands for autonomy and undermine the PCJSS by co-opting local leaders.[23] The peace talks picked up momentum after the return to democracy in 1991. In response to an overture from the Bangladesh Nationalist Party (BNP) government of Khaleda Zia, the Shanti Bahini declared a temporary cease-fire on August 1, 1992. Despite a number of violations of the truce, it was routinely extended, so that violence sputtered along at a relatively low level in the 1990s, as several rounds of negotiations failed to resolve the basic issues of autonomy and land ownership.[24]

The negotiations began to move quickly, however, after the 1996 election of Sheikh Hasina Wajed. Hasina's Awami League government was less nationalist and traditionally more pro-India than was the BNP. The PCJSS certainly believed it could get a better deal from the more secular Awami League than from the BNP. But more important, India put significant pressure on the PCJSS to concede on the outstanding issues and reach an agreement. India was increasingly concerned by the cost of destabilization from the CHT conflict and its refugees among its own "indigenous" minorities (e.g., the Mizos) waging ethnic insurgencies in India's northeastern states. Moreover, with a friendly Awami League government in power, India no longer needed the CHT insurgency as leverage against Bangladesh. In January 1997, India and Bangladesh agreed to cooperate against insurgencies in their border region. India cut rations to refugees from the CHT on its soil and asked the PCJSS to leave.[25]

---

[20] SIPRI 1992–97; Ghosh 1989, p. 75; Shelley, Khan, and Kabir n.d., p. 7; anonymous interview with an international embassy official, Dhaka.

[21] Estimates vary widely, from under 3,000 to 25,000 or even 50,000 killed, with 50,000–70,000 refugees. SIPRI 1998; Bercovitch and Jackson 1997; Doyle and Sambanis 2000, 2006; Maxwell 1998.

[22] Shafriqul Islam and Ibrahim interviews, Dhaka; Larma interview, Rangamati.

[23] Ibrahim interview, Dhaka; Ibrahim 1991, pp. 35–36.

[24] See Minorities at Risk 2004b for reports of clashes and extensions of the truce. The cease-fire was extended 35 times, in three-month intervals. Mohsin 2003, pp. 40–41.

[25] India's termination of support for the PCJSS was apparently a quid pro quo for Bangladesh signing an agreement on water use from the Ganges in December 1996. Mohsin interview, Dhaka; Mohsin 2003, p. 42; Shelley, Khan, and Kabir n.d., pp. 11–12.

On December 2, 1997, the government of Bangladesh and Shantu Larma formally signed a peace agreement restoring some measure of autonomy to the CHT. The agreement set up a Regional Council (RC) of which the chairmanship and 14 of the 22 seats are reserved for "tribals." The RC is a slightly more powerful version of the Hill District Councils set up in 1989, responsible for public administration, provision of basic services (primary education, health, social welfare, etc.), law and order, and development. But the exact nature of the RC's authority was left quite ambiguous, with some of its powers only "advisory" and not mandatory.[26] The treaty is similarly vague or silent on the timetable for withdrawal of the military, definitions of "permanent residence" in the CHT, criteria for settling land disputes between those (usually settlers) with documents and those (hill people) whose claims are based on custom and ancestral use, and other crucial matters. These provisions were deliberately left ambiguous so as to make an agreement possible.[27]

While the agreement stipulates that land cannot be sold or transferred to nonindigenous people without permission from the RC, it is silent on the issue of the existing settlers in the CHT. Shantu Larma claims that, while Hasina was unable politically to include it in the formal written treaty, she promised Larma personally that the settlers would be removed. The government subsequently denied this, although one participant of the government's negotiating team, since retired, confirmed that an informal and unwritten promise to reduce the number of settlers was indeed made.[28] In any case, no settlers have been repatriated.

At a ceremony in February 1998, Shantu Larma formally disbanded the Shanti Bahini, and some 740 rebels handed in their weapons. More followed suit later in the month. Altogether almost 1,500 fighters surrendered their weapons.[29] While many observers believe that the Shanti Bahini maintained some of its arms caches, and surrendered mostly its older weapons, the government certified that the Shanti Bahini had disarmed. The disarmament of the Shanti Bahini is notable because the Bangladeshi military had not yet (and still has not) withdrawn from the CHT as called for under the agreement, nor were most of the provisions of the agreement yet implemented.

Since then, the politics of the CHT have been marked by disagreement about how to interpret the vague peace treaty, and about how much of it has been implemented.[30] Meanwhile, the United People's Democratic Front

[26] Maxwell 1998, p. 68. The text of the agreement is reprinted in Mohsin 2003, pp. 129–40.

[27] Anonymous interview, Bangladesh.

[28] Anonymous interview, Bangladesh.

[29] Minorities at Risk 2004b.

[30] For a detailed account of the differences, see Shelley, Khan, and Kabir n.d., pp. 6–7; see also Chowdhury 2002.

(UPDF) was formed, representing those disaffected with the peace process and members of the Shanti Bahini who did not disarm. The UPDF has refused to accept the peace accord, claiming that the PCJSS has sold out.[31] Branded as "terrorists" by both the government and the PCJSS, it continues to wage low-level violence and disruption in the CHT.[32] The BNP, which had railed against the agreement while an opposition party, did not renounce the treaty after coming to power in 2001, but neither did it move to implement it further.[33]

Sierra Leone: A Complicated War

When Sierra Leone gained independence from Britain in 1961, the transition from colonial rule was peaceful. Sierra Leone was in fairly good shape relative to its West African neighbors, enjoying its status as "a hub of education and commerce on the Atlantic."[34] But decades of extremely poor governance led to Sierra Leone's collapse.

A brief period of democracy in the 1960s soon degenerated to one-party rule under the "staggeringly corrupt" rule of President Siaka Stevens.[35] Stevens dismantled or corrupted state institutions for personal, political, and financial profit.[36] His All People's Congress (APC) regime used privately recruited armed thugs to intimidate the opposition and to control diamond revenues. Setting a precedent for conduct during the coming war, these groups were remunerated largely through the opportunity to prey on and loot from civilians.

The diversion of diamond and other mineral revenues from official state coffers to private ones left Sierra Leone with virtually no resources for the provision of social services such as health, education, policing, or transportation. The processes of economic decline and state collapse continued after Stevens stepped down in 1985, appointing the inept and politically weak Maj. Gen. Joseph Momoh as his successor. Under Momoh, the state went bankrupt and stopped paying civil servants or teachers. Much of the professional class left the country.[37] When the civil war began, Sierra Leone was virtually stateless.

[31] The PCJSS and other Jumma rights groups allege that local military and local government administrators are aiding the UPDF as a means of divide and rule. Larma interview, Rangamati; Peace Campaign Group 2002, p. 10.

[32] From the signing of the accord through 2001, this violence claimed some 134 lives, over 1,000 wounded, and 740 kidnapped. Shelley, Khan, and Kabir n.d., p. 2.

[33] As Larma put it, the BNP sees the agreement as "Hasina's baby." Interview, Rangamati.

[34] Lord 2000, chronology, p. 2.

[35] Adebajo 2002, p. 81.

[36] Hirsch 2001a; Lord 2000; Reno 2003.

[37] Adebajo 2002; Hirsch 2001a.

Sierra Leone

In March 1991, a small group of rebels invaded Sierra Leone from Liberia. They numbered only about one hundred fighters initially, consisting of Sierra Leoneans, Liberians, and mercenaries, and calling themselves the Revolutionary United Front (RUF). They were led by Foday Sankoh, a former corporal in the Sierra Leone army and an itinerant photographer. The RUF was backed by then rebel leader, later president of Liberia, Charles Taylor.[38]

---

[38] The government was largely Mende, while most fighters with the RUF were Temne, but the war was not primarily about ethnic grievances as much as intergenerational, economic, and political ones. Malan, Rakate, and McIntyre 2002, p. 13; Keen 2005.

The Sierra Leone army (SLA) was notoriously ill-trained and ill-equipped. In April 1992, after three months without pay, a group of frustrated soldiers left the front lines for Freetown and toppled Momoh. Later that year, the war escalated when the RUF took Kono, the most important diamond-mining region. The Sierra Leone army was beset with discipline and morale problems, with many soldiers defecting or engaging in banditry and looting, and often colluding with rebels. The term *sobel* came to describe the "soldiers by day, rebels by night" phenomenon. With the government unable to protect the populace from the RUF or even from its own soldiers, militia and vigilante groups sprung up, some based on the traditional hunting groups known as Kamajors. Later these would be organized as the Civil Defense Forces (CDF), fighting alongside the government against the RUF. The government also relied on the mercenary outfits Executive Outcomes and later Sandline to back and train its forces.

The Abidjan Agreement, 1996

By the end of 1995, the war had reached a military and political stalemate.[39] After another coup, and the beginnings of peace talks between the government and the RUF, elections were held in March 1996, giving Ahmed Tejan Kabbah the presidency. Though Sankoh refused to recognize the elections, he eventually met with Kabbah and his government over the course of 1996. On November 30, the RUF and the government reached a cease-fire agreement in Abidjan. Under the accord, the RUF was to demobilize and would be granted amnesty. A Neutral Monitoring Group was to observe implementation of the agreement, but it was never established because Sankoh refused to accept the 750-person UN peacekeeping mission.[40] Within weeks fighting had resumed, both between progovernment forces and the RUF, and between SLA soldiers and Kamajors vying for control of diamonds and other resources.[41] Sankoh was arrested in Nigeria in March, and the Abidjan accords collapsed completely.

On May 25, 1997, a military junta calling itself the Armed Forces Revolutionary Council (AFRC) staged a coup and installed Major Johnny Paul Koroma as head of state. The AFRC immediately allied itself with the RUF, confirming suspicions of "sobel" collusion.[42] AFRC/RUF forces overwhelmed the few hundred West African troops stationed in Sierra Leone to provide staging bases for the ECOWAS peacekeeping force's operations in Liberia (ECOMOG), and to help protect Freetown from the

---

[39] Gberie 2000.
[40] Hirsch 2001b, p. 157.
[41] Lord 2000, chronology, p. 5.
[42] Keen 2005.

RUF. The ECOWAS countries, led by Nigeria, imposed a blockade, and deployed a large force to Sierra Leone.[43] In October, the UN Security Council imposed sanctions against Sierra Leone.[44] In February 1998, after another brief round of negotiations in which the AFRC/RUF agreed to disarm but quickly reneged,[45] the Nigerian troops, along with CDF militia units, forced the AFRC/RUF from Freetown and restored Kabbah to nominal power in the capital. Kabbah was almost entirely dependent on outside military support. Most former SLA troops were fighting for the AFRC, and even the CDF forces aligned with Kabbah were controlled not by him but by his deputy defense minister, Chief Hinga Norman.[46]

A very small contingent of about 50 UN observers (the UN Observer Mission in Sierra Leone, or UNOMSIL) deployed to Sierra Leone in June 1998 to monitor the security situation and the disarmament and demobilization of Sierra Leonean forces by ECOMOG.[47] This mandate proved premature, however, as no cease-fire was in place. ECOMOG and pro-Kabbah forces were unable to contain the AFRC/RUF forces, and in January 1999, the rebels overran the capital.[48] UNOMSIL evacuated its personnel.

THE LOMÉ AGREEMENT, 1999

In heavy fighting throughout January, ECOMOG managed to retake the capital, reinstalling Kabbah once again. Meanwhile, the restoration of democracy in Nigeria after Sani Abacha's death in June 1998 had a profound effect on Sierra Leone. A democratic Nigeria was much less willing to pay in blood and treasure for peacekeeping in the Sierra Leone morass. Of ECOMOG's 13,000 troops at this point, 12,000 were Nigerian.[49] The mounting Nigerian casualties were unsurprisingly unpopular at home, and Nigeria announced it would soon withdraw its forces. This led to a peacemaking scramble by West African leaders, the British, and the

[43] By October 1997, ECOMOG II forces numbered about 4,000, by June 1998, 13,000, all but 1,000 from Nigeria. Conciliation Resources 1997, p. 1; Adebajo 2002, pp. 90–91.

[44] Hirsch 2001a, p. 64; Adebajo 2002, p. 8.

[45] See discussion of the Conakry agreement of October 23, 1997, in Hirsch 2001a, pp. 64–65; Adebajo 2002, p. 88.

[46] Bangura 2002.

[47] UN Document S/1998/486, p. 13.

[48] Hirsch 2001a, pp. 72–74, attributes ECOMOG's inability to defeat the RUF to poor leadership, and to limited resources and logistics capability. Its military effectiveness was not helped by a deep split within ECOMOG. For a detailed discussion of the internal politics of ECOMOG, see Adebajo 2002, pp. 88–91.

[49] Adebajo 2002, p. 91. Hundreds of Nigerian soldiers lost their lives in Sierra Leone, and the operation reportedly cost Nigeria a million dollars a day. Rashid 2000, p. 1; Adebajo 2002, pp. 95, 97.

United States, and to significant pressure on Kabbah to reach a deal with rebel forces.[50]

Negotiations with the RUF led to a cease-fire in May 1999 and then to the Lomé Peace Agreement on July 7. The agreement not only exonerated Foday Sankoh (who was still in prison and facing a death sentence), but gave him the status of vice president and cabinet positions including control of "strategic" resources (read diamonds). Most controversially, it provided a blanket amnesty for RUF, AFRC, CDF, and SLA combatants. The RUF was to become a political party, combatants were to be disarmed, demobilized, and reintegrated into society, and a new national army was to be created including ex-RUF, CDF, and SLA soldiers.[51] Few of the terms of Lomé were ever implemented, however.

As ECOMOG began to pull out, UNOMSIL was transformed from a small monitoring mission to a much larger peacekeeping mission, with an accompanying name change to the United Nations Mission in Sierra Leone (UNAMSIL). The new UN mission, initially authorized at a troop strength of 6,000, began to deploy in December 1999. To avoid a complete power vacuum during the transition, four ECOMOG battalions simply changed their hats and became UN peacekeepers.[52]

UNAMSIL got off to a rocky start, to put it mildly. Cease-fire violations were frequent, the RUF refused the UN access to many areas under its control, and disarmament, demobilization, and reintegration (DDR) fell well behind schedule. From its inception, UNAMSIL was technically a peace enforcement mission, authorized under Chapter VII of the UN Charter, but it did not deploy with a robust force posture and therefore did not present a credible deterrent on the ground. In April and May 2000, as UNAMSIL attempted to deploy to diamond-mining areas, the RUF attacked its positions in Magburaka and Makeni, killing a number of peacekeepers and taking over 500 of them hostage. The RUF then used captured UN equipment, including armored personnel carriers, to advance on Freetown.[53]

This triggered a British intervention. Meanwhile, the Security Council raised UNAMSIL's authorized troop level to 13,000.[54] In August, there was relatively heavy fighting between British forces and a breakaway faction of the RUF known as the West Side Boys in the Occra Hills outside of Freetown.[55]

[50] Rashid 2000, pp. 2, 4.

[51] Hirsch 2001a, pp. 82–83. See also Rashid 2000.

[52] Malan, Rakate, and McIntyre 2002, p. 21.

[53] Ibid.

[54] UN Document S/Res/1299, 2000.

[55] The West Side Boys' name refers to the American rapper Tupac Shakur, whose deadly dispute with Biggie Smalls (aka Notorious B.I.G.) was construed as a West Coast–East Coast rivalry. Reno 2003. Tupac Shakur was named after Tupac Amaru, the leader of an indigenous

THE ABUJA AGREEMENTS, 2000–2001

After the RUF attacks on the UN and on British forces, the emphasis of the international community shifted from implementing Lomé, which was now considered dead in the water, to defeating the RUF. After being marginalized and reportedly held prisoner by RUF commander Sam "Maskita" (Mosquito) Bockarie, Johnny Paul Koroma switched sides, calling on AFRC forces now to fight alongside government forces against the RUF. Sankoh was arrested again in May 2000. In September, after an attack across the Guninean border by RUF-supported dissidents, Guinea joined the fray. Taylor, under strong international pressure, cut his support for the RUF, and with Sankoh back in prison, the rebel group began to fracture. The combined forces of the SLA, now backed and trained by Britain, the CDF militia, the AFRC, and the Guinean army, finally broke the back of the RUF as a viable military force.

In November 2000, a substantially weakened RUF signed an agreement in Abuja, and after continued clashes with the CDF and Guinean forces, another agreement the following May. The first of these agreements called for resumption of the DDR process and unimpeded movement of UNAMSIL. The RUF, not surprisingly, dragged its feet on aspects that threatened its military strength or its access to diamonds.[56] But the combination of military setbacks, the threat of a new offensive by progovernment forces, increasingly robust patrols by UNAMSIL[57] (and the perception that these were backed by British forces) elicited greater RUF compliance. UN officials also credit Force Commander Opande with convincing RUF leader Issa Sesay that noncompliance would not be tolerated, but that UNAMSIL would protect Sesay if he cooperated.[58]

The peace process reached a turning point with the second Abuja agreement in May 2001. The RUF and the CDF disarmed in areas where they had been fighting, the DDR process got going again, and UNAMSIL

---

uprising in Peru against the Spanish, and the namesake of the more recent rebel group in Peru. So in an odd series of connections between pop culture and civil war, a rebel group in Sierra Leone was named for an American musician, whose namesake in turn was a rebel group in Peru.

[56] UN Document S/2001/228, p. 15.

[57] Command-and-control problems within UNAMSIL between the Nigerians and the Indians were settled with the latter's departure. The new force commander, Lt. Gen. Daniel Opande of Kenya, interpreted UNAMSIL's mandate much more aggressively than his predecessor. In March 2001, UNAMSIL's troop level was raised again to 17,500. UN Document S/Res/1346, 2001.

[58] Opande, an imposing figure and many years Sesay's elder, reportedly gave the RUF leader a stern dressing down that left an impression. Ellery interview, Freetown. When I met Sesay briefly in November 2002, he seemed cowed by and dependent on the UN for protection and even for food, notwithstanding allegations that he profited from illegal diamond mining.

began preparing Sierra Leone for elections. By January 2002, disarmament of CDF and RUF forces was considered complete. Elections were held without major incident in May and June 2002. Kabbah was reelected president, and his Sierra Leone People's Party (SLPP) won two-thirds of the seats in Parliament. A fifth of the seats went to the APC. Koroma received 3% of the presidential vote and his party won two seats in Parliament. The RUF mustered less than 2% of the vote. Fewer people voted for the RUF than had fought under its banner.[59]

In September 2002, UNAMSIL began a slow and cautious process of drawing down its presence in Sierra Leone, gradually turning security functions over to the government of Sierra Leone. UNAMSIL's mission terminated in December 2005. It has been replaced by a small political mission, the UN Integrated Office for Sierra Leone. Ten years of a war notorious for brutality to civilians by one estimate killed 70,000, left 20,000 surviving amputees (many more died of their wounds), displaced 2.5 million people—half the population of Sierra Leone—and involved 27,000 child soldiers, many of them abducted to fight.[60]

Where Peacekeepers Go

Case Study Evidence

What do these conflicts tell us about where peacekeepers tend to be deployed? Why were peacekeepers sent to Mozambique but not Bangladesh? Why to Sierra Leone by the agreements in 1999 and 2000–2001 but not in 1996? Why an enforcement mission in Sierra Leone, but not Mozambique? Were the answers to these questions driven primarily by the international community, or also by the belligerents? In other words, whose decisions affected peacekeeping deployment? Was the presence of peacekeepers (or lack thereof) a response to factors that made peace generally harder or easier to keep?

Bangladesh

Why were there no peacekeepers sent to the Chittagong Hill Tracts? The PCJSS issued a demand in April 1987 for UN mediation of the conflict, and Shantu Larma requested a UN peacekeeping force to protect the hill people.[61] The government of Bangladesh was decidedly unreceptive to this

---

[59] Ellery interview, Freetown. A significant number of the RUF soldiers were child combatants not eligible to vote. Many others had been kidnapped and forced to fight and felt no strong political allegiance to the RUF.

[60] Malan, Rakate, and McIntyre 2002, p. 13.

[61] Ghosh 1989, p. 76; Maxwell 1998, p. 67.

idea, having nothing to gain from increased attention to the plight of the hill people. This was the last time the issue of peacekeeping was raised, at least in public.

Despite the efforts of a few human rights organizations and the small diaspora of hill people, the CHT conflict was simply not on the international agenda. It was a low-level conflict, generating no massive humanitarian impulse to intervene. Compared to other wars and crises in the mid-1990s, the CHT was extremely low priority to the rest of the world. Nor was it strategically important to any state other than Bangladesh and India. The PCJSS got very little response from the international community. As Larma put it:

> We appealed to the international community, but the response was not enough to get a third-party role. We didn't get very positive responses—[we received] some encouragement from human rights organizations, such as Amnesty International and the Anti-Slavery Society. We appealed to governments, in both the Western and Eastern blocs, but no one came forward.[62]

The refugee situation was perhaps the most likely to generate international interest and assistance, but India resisted a large role for the UN High Commissioner for Refugees (UNHCR). PCJSS secretary of international relations Rupayan Dewan expressed his disappointment in the organization: "they could have come unofficially."[63]

So there was no pressure from the side of the international community or the UN to get involved. Moreover, the most powerful external party to the conflict, India, was extremely reluctant to allow outside peacekeepers to deploy. Since the late 1960s, India has consistently pushed to minimize the role of peacekeepers in the Kashmir conflict, preferring to keep the issue on a bilateral footing with Pakistan.[64] India was thus ill-disposed to call for a strong peacekeeping presence in another conflict along its borders.

The United Nations may well have responded positively to a direct request for peacekeeping from the parties themselves, particularly to a call from the government of Bangladesh. But the government was quite resistant to such an idea, for several reasons. First and most important, as the more powerful side in the conflict, the government had little to gain and much to lose from outside involvement. This was especially true as the peace agreement called for the disarmament of the Shanti Bahini before

---

[62] Larma interview, Rangamati.

[63] R. Dewan interview, Rangamati.

[64] This is partly the result of disappointment with the UN's failure to acknowledge Pakistan's role in starting the 1965 war, partly the result of general concerns about infringement on its sovereignty, and partly because it perceives UN involvement would favor Pakistan. Blinkenberg 1972, p. 153; Fortna 2004c, p. 138.

the government was required to implement its side of the agreement. There was thus no pressing need, from the government's perspective, to bring in monitors or troops to ensure that the Shanti Bahini laid down its arms. Nor did it seem terribly concerned that the PCJSS would renege on its side of the deal.[65] Meanwhile, a strong international presence would have made it more difficult for the government to delay implementation of autonomy provisions, removal of army camps, and so forth. A peacekeeping mission would have pressured the government to fulfill its promises, but would not have significantly improved the chances of PCJSS compliance, at least in the short term.

Second, allowing an international peacekeeping mission to deploy would have been politically costly. For both domestic political reasons and international diplomatic reasons, peacekeepers' infringement on Bangladesh's sovereignty would have been hard to swallow. The BNP (in opposition at the time of the agreement), already antagonistic toward the agreement, would have capitalized on nationalist sentiment against allowing foreign soldiers on Bangladeshi soil. Internationally, Bangladesh would have felt the arrival of peacekeepers as a huge blow to its prestige. As a poor country, generally on the receiving end of international aid, Bangladesh is extremely proud of its role as one of the largest contributors of troops to UN peacekeeping in other war-torn places.[66] When it comes to peacekeeping, Bangladesh sees its role as helping other "basket case" countries to stabilize. Accepting peacekeepers itself would be tantamount to admitting to being a "basket case" country itself.

In short, the government had no desire to see peacekeepers deploy. The rebel side would very much have liked a peacekeeping presence, but was not strong enough to insist on one during the negotiations. The PCJSS was pressed militarily, given India's decision to turn off the spigot of support. And it would have been especially difficult to hold out for a peacekeeping presence since India itself was opposed.[67] Nor was the leadership of the PCJSS politically strong enough to demand peacekeepers.[68] To some extent, this may have been the result of naïveté. The PCJSS leadership seemed willing to trust the government's promises without any apparent enforcement mechanism other than the threat of a return to war.[69]

[65] Anonymous interview with European diplomat, Dhaka.

[66] This pride was palpable when I toured a Bangladeshi battalion's encampment in Sierra Leone.

[67] It might have been possible to request an Indian rather than UN peacekeeping presence, but this was presumably a nonstarter for Bangladesh.

[68] This was the accusation of the UPDF leaders. Anonymous interviews, Dhaka.

[69] Some, including a number of hill people, argued that PCJSS was too inexperienced, and that hill people in general were too willing to trust others. Mohsin and K. Chakma interviews, Dhaka.

Shantu Larma's own explanation for why he did not insist upon peacekeepers was, in part, that the CHT was a domestic issue ("Ours was not an independence movement"), so that international peacekeeping was not appropriate.[70] This may have reflected lack of knowledge about the use of peacekeeping in civil wars after the Cold War, but it also suggests that Larma was concerned not to make his own movement appear too threatening to Bangladeshi sovereignty. The PCJSS strategy was to reassure Bangladesh that its demands for autonomy were not a precursor to secession. So perhaps Larma was unwilling to push too hard for a peacekeeping force that would itself undermine the country's sovereignty. Alternatively, he may have been trying to save face, since in the event he was not successful in his demands for peacekeeping.

In sum, with no international impulse for a peacekeeping mission, and with both the government of Bangladesh and India opposed, the PCJSS had little hope of gaining a peacekeeping mission to oversee the agreement, much as it would have liked one.

Mozambique

In Mozambique, the dynamic was quite similar, except that the rebel group was relatively stronger and was able to get the government to concede to peacekeepers. Though outsiders had been involved in Mozambique's war from the beginning, no powerful state took the lead in mediating or keeping peace. With the end of Cold War and the end of apartheid, both regional states and great powers were in favor of a peaceful solution in Mozambique, but the issue was not high priority. The role of mediator fell to Sant'Egidio, a lay Catholic organization in Italy. As former US assistant secretary for African affairs Chester Crocker put it, "U.S., British, and Portuguese attention was directed elsewhere."[71]

The initiative for peacekeeping came from the belligerents themselves, specifically from the rebels. From the very beginning of the negotiations, Renamo pushed for an international presence, while the Frelimo government resisted. The first mention of UN peacekeeping during the peace talks came in a proposal from the Renamo negotiator, Raul Domingos, in August 1990. Frelimo negotiator Armando Guebuza (now Mozambique's president) insisted that the government would accept no such infringement on Mozambican sovereignty.[72] Renamo initially pushed for a UN transitional authority, modeled on the peacekeeping mission in Cambodia,

---

[70] Larma interview, Rangamati.

[71] Foreword to Hume 1994, p. xi.

[72] Hume 1994, pp. 37, 42. For a time, Frelimo proposed an Organisation of African Unity rather than UN mission. Synge 1997, p. 18.

UNTAC. That the UN would take over the administration of the country was a nonstarter for the government. But Cameron Hume, the US observer during the peace talks, notes that this proposal

> reflected the depth of RENAMO's skepticism that the FRELIMO government . . . could be trusted to conduct fair, multiparty elections.[73]

By early 1991, the government softened its refusal to allow any infringement on its sovereignty and accepted in principle that there would be some sort of peacekeeping operation. Frelimo realized that Renamo's deep mistrust of the government would make it very difficult to reach peace without a peacekeeping mission.[74] Renamo gradually dropped its demand for a Cambodia-style international transitional administration. Slowly, over the course of the negotiations, the gap between the two sides' positions on peacekeeping narrowed, but throughout, Renamo demanded as large and intrusive a mission as possible, while the government pushed for a small and limited peacekeeping presence.[75] For Renamo, the presence of peacekeepers was crucial to hold the government to its promises.[76] At a press conference in November 1991, Dhlakama justified his demand for an international guarantor by saying "When we have laid down our weapons, who will guarantee that Frelimo will not step back from its commitments?"[77] An international presence would also confer on Renamo some recognition as a legitimate political player in Mozambique. The government, meanwhile, was extremely prickly about any possible infringement on its sovereignty.[78] Because Frelimo insisted that Renamo recognize it as the legitimate government, anything that trampled on its sovereignty or suggested that Frelimo and Renamo were parties of equal status was anathema.[79]

That the initiative for peacekeeping came from the parties themselves is clear from the fact that the United Nations, which would have to provide peacekeepers, was not involved in the negotiations until June 1992, two years into the formal negotiation process and only a few months before it ended.[80] Until the last moment, the desire of the international community

---

[73] Hume 1994, p. 59; see also p. 66.

[74] Guebuza and Hunguana interviews, Maputo. See chapter 6, below.

[75] Hume 1994 provides a very detailed account of the negotiations.

[76] Interviews with Renamo leaders de Castro and Almirante, Maputo.

[77] Quoted in Hume 1994, p. 79.

[78] This was very apparent, even 10 years later, in my interviews with Frelimo officials.

[79] The government's resistance to peacekeeping appears to have been a matter of principle, not motivated by a desire to maintain the ability to renege on the peace deal. Granted, however, even if it were at least partly the latter, direct evidence to that effect (other than the government's eventual behavior) would be almost impossible to come by.

[80] Synge 1997, p. 19.

was to keep the peacekeeping role limited. US diplomat Jeffrey Davidow advised the mediators to resist Renamo's demand for an extensive UN peacekeeping role.[81] The United States wanted as small, and as cheap, a mission as possible. The UN, facing an unprecedented number of peacekeeping operations and fearful of overcommitting itself, concurred.[82] It was only in the last few months of the negotiations, as it became clear that a small and cheap peacekeeping mission in Angola had been penny-wise but pound-foolish, that the members of the Security Council became convinced of the need for a substantial mission.[83]

Renamo, at least in principle, was all too happy to have a more substantial mission, while the government objected to a larger peacekeeping mission and to any expansion of its mandate.[84] This continued to be a bone of contention even after the peace agreement was signed. Renamo refused to demobilize until there was a large UN presence, while the government stated its objections to a larger force. A government official argued, "We are not a protectorate of the Security Council; we are a member of the United Nations. The UN is here as observers, not as a peacekeeping force." Another accused the UN of wanting to be "an occupation force."[85] While the government had been able to resist Renamo's call for a larger mission, once the UN was pushing for this too, the government relented. As Guebuza put it:

> Our understanding was of a small force, not a huge one. Renamo had also agreed to a small force, but battalions and battalions came. The UN was nervous without a big force. Later they saw it was not necessary to have so many troops, but it is better to prevent than to remedy.[86]

In short, whether there would be peacekeepers in Mozambique was determined by the negotiations between Renamo and Frelimo. The size and cost of the mission, however, was affected by decisions made by the suppliers.

Sierra Leone

In Bangladesh and Mozambique, the rebels pushed for peacekeepers and governments resisted. In Sierra Leone, the situation was reversed. The

---

[81] Hume 1994, p. 75.

[82] Synge 1997, pp. 20–21.

[83] Ibid., 30–32.

[84] Renamo, too, was concerned with its pseudo-sovereignty as the UN began to deploy into Renamo-controlled territory. The rebel group wanted to control delivery of humanitarian assistance.

[85] Unnamed officials, quoted in Synge 1997, pp. 36, 39.

[86] Guebuza interview, Maputo.

government depended on international forces to stay in power, and the peacekeeping mandates were designed to support it, while the rebels funded their war through contraband diamond mining and had no desire for international oversight. However, the rebel strategy was not to refuse to sign agreements calling for peacekeepers, but to resist the actual deployment of international personnel.

During the negotiations between Kabbah and the RUF that led to the Abidjan accord in 1996, the rebels demanded the withdrawal of foreign mercenary forces, particularly Executive Outcomes. The government initially refused, as such a withdrawal would leave its weak army vulnerable to an RUF attack.[87] In the end, the Abidjan agreement called for withdrawal of foreign forces and the establishment of a Neutral Monitoring Group. Who would provide these monitors or how many there would be was left unspecified in the agreement. Sankoh refused to discuss the details with the UN special envoy mediating the talks, whose impartiality he mistrusted.[88] Sankoh was deeply suspicious of the entire UN system.[89] Despite the evident reluctance of the RUF to consent to peacekeepers, the UN began to plan for a small monitoring mission of about 750 troops.[90] In the event, Executive Outcomes withdrew, Nigeria provided Kabbah with some bodyguards, and the RUF refused to allow UN monitors to deploy. The international community was not yet contemplating enforcement action in Sierra Leone, so the RUF's nonconsent meant there would be no peacekeeping during this short-lived peace spell. As then US ambassador to Sierra Leone, John Hirsch, put it, the international community

> did little to follow up on implementation [of the Abidjan accords]. . . . Sankoh's rejection of the 750-man peacekeeping force saved the United Nations Security Council from having to make such a commitment.[91]

Spending money and risking lives on peacekeeping in Sierra Leone was unpopular with the major powers, particularly the United States.[92]

---

[87] Hirsch 2001a, p. 52.

[88] UN Document S/1997/80, p. 3; Hirsch 2001a, p. 52; Adebajo 2002, p. 86.

[89] He believed, in what became a self-fulfilling prophecy, that the UN was biased against him. His suspicion of the UN was reportedly rooted in his mistrust of international agencies' ability to offer protection, for example to prevent the assassination of Patrice Lumumba in the Congo in the 1960s and later of Samuel Doe in Liberia. Bright 2000, p. 4.

[90] See UN Document S/1997/80. There had been some discussion earlier of US and EU funding for an OAU role in supervising disarmament. Gberie 2000, p. 5. But the idea of an OAU mission seems to have been dropped.

[91] Hirsch 2001a, p. 97.

[92] Keen 2005, p. 204.

After the Abidjan agreement collapsed, and the AFRC/RUF attacked Nigerian soldiers stationed in Sierra Leone, ECOWAS briefly attempted to negotiate with Koroma.[93] When this failed, ECOWAS imposed a blockade and greatly expanded its force in Sierra Leone, dubbing its new mission ECOMOG II.[94] However, the reaction of the rest of the international community to these developments is summed up by Ambassador Hirsch as "little and late."[95] Sierra Leone is a small, strategically unimportant country, and in the years after the Somali debacle and failure in Rwanda, the United States had no stomach for peacekeeping in Africa.[96] The United States and other powers saw Sierra Leone as Britain's problem. But the UK was unwilling to offer material support to the ECOWAS mission as long as Nigeria's military leader, Abacha, was at the helm of the West African organization. The great powers were happy, for the time being, to leave the problem of Sierra Leone to the West Africans. The UN sent a token mission, UNOMSIL, of 50 monitors in June 1998. But withdrew quickly when AFRC-RUF forces retook Freetown.

By this point, however, international attention to and concern with Sierra Leone was growing rapidly. A political scandal in Great Britain over violations of the sanctions on Sierra Leone by Sandline International had put the war in the British news.[97] Meanwhile, its humanitarian toll, and especially RUF atrocities, including its practice of amputating the hands and limbs of civilians, were beginning to generate a "CNN effect" (or more accurately, a "BBC effect") creating political pressure for Western governments to do something to halt the violence. The threatened withdrawal of newly democratic Nigeria from ECOMOG generated discussion of replacing the West African mission.

In the talks leading up to the Lomé agreement, the RUF had a much stronger hand than it had in Abidjan.[98] In the Abidjan negotiations, the RUF had been under significant military pressure, particularly from Execu-

[93] Nigeria had about 700 troops in the country at this point, some of them providing security in Freetown. Hirsch 2001a, p. 61; Adebajo 2002, p. 87, and personal correspondence with the author, April 16, 2003.

[94] Adebajo 2002, p. 87.

[95] Hirsch 2001a, pp. 63ff.

[96] This doctrine of reluctance is the basis of Presidential Decision Directive (PDD) 25 of 1994. See Hirsch 2001a, p. 63.

[97] Ellery interview, Freetown. Sandline was a private company run by a former British army colonel, hired by Kabbah to repel AFRC/RUF forces from diamond-mining areas in return for concessions managed by a businessman wanted for embezzlement in Thailand. The scandal turned on questions of whether the British Foreign Office knew ahead of time of Sandline's intention to run arms to Sierra Leone, and whether the sanctions applied only to the junta or also to Kabbah, whom the sanctions were meant to help restore to power. Hirsch 2001a, pp. 66–67.

[98] Hirsch 2001a, p. 81.

tive Outcomes. Now it had proven it could not easily be defeated even by the much larger ECOMOG force. Moreover, the political future of this force, on which Kabbah's government was utterly dependent, was in question. The RUF-AFRC negotiating position included, inter alia, demands for the immediate withdrawal of ECOMOG and the creation of an independent peacekeeping force.[99] That the RUF wanted the ECOMOG force that had been fighting against it to leave was not surprising. That it wanted any peacekeeping mission in Sierra Leone is surprising. The RUF-AFRC seems to have believed, reasonably enough, that Kabbah's government and his international backers would not accept ECOMOG's withdrawal without a substitute mission to protect it. The RUF was also, at this point, trying to portray itself as "reasonable and credible" by accepting an international mission.[100] ECOMOG's role in the transition to peace was a major sticking point in the negotiations. In the end, the parties agreed to Nigerian forces remaining in an ECOMOG mission that was to be given a new peacekeeping (as opposed to fighting) mandate until peace was consolidated and a new UN peacekeeping force could be put in place.[101]

UNOMSIL was transformed into UNAMSIL, initially intended as a force of about 6,000 (though it would eventually reach three times that size). Britain played the lead role on the Security Council in pushing for this mission. Despite Britain's strong support for the mission, its size and the resources provided to it were fairly limited. The international community was preoccupied with the missions in Kosovo and East Timor and was reluctant to spread itself even thinner with another large expensive mission in Sierra Leone.[102]

While the RUF agreed on paper to a larger role for the UN peacekeepers, it contested UNAMSIL's legitimacy from the start. As the political head of UNAMSIL, Special Representative Oluyemi Adeniji, later reported:

> From its induction in Sierra Leone, Sankoh had displayed an antagonism which proved implacable to the UN mission UNAMSIL. He denounced its deployment as illegal and inconsistent with the Lomé Agreement, done without his agreement and threatening to his party. Every effort made to explain the link between UNAMSIL and article XVI of the Lomé Agreement met with a pretence at understanding, only for UNAMSIL to be denounced again shortly thereafter. With

---

[99] Rashid 2000, p. 4.

[100] Ismail Rashid, email to the author, February 8, 2005.

[101] Rashid 2000, pp. 5, 8.

[102] Hirsch 2001a, p. 86; Adebajo 2002, p. 94. The Sierra Leone government had little leverage to gain a larger or better funded mission. Ismail Rashid, email to the author, February 8, 2005.

that posture, RUF obstructed UNAMSIL from deployment throughout the country.[103]

Sankoh's mistrust of the UN had not diminished, nor was his consent to
peacekeeping forthcoming. Unlike Abidjan, however, this time the international community was willing to provide peacekeepers despite the RUF's
resistance, but this lack of consent necessitated an enforcement mission.

After the RUF attack on UNAMSIL in April and May 2000, this enforcement capacity was put to use. The reaction of the international community was not, as it had been in Somalia and Rwanda, to withdraw when
the going got tough. Rather, the British intervened, and international
forces in Sierra Leone, along with Kabbah's forces, set about defeating the
RUF militarily. The peacekeeping crisis in Sierra Leone came just as the
UN was evaluating its peacekeeping stance and deciding to take a much
more robust military approach to spoilers when necessary.[104] Between the
Abidjan agreement in 1996 and the crisis in 2000, the attitude of the international community (particularly the United States and Britain) to
peacekeeping in Sierra Leone changed from "We cannot afford to get involved in another Somalia- or Rwanda-like situation" to "We cannot afford
to fail at peacekeeping again."[105]

By late 2000, the military tide had turned against the rebels, and the
largely defeated and fractured RUF signed the Abuja agreements in November 2000 and May 2001. The RUF continued to drag its feet on disarmament and on conceding diamond-rich territory, but could not resist the
arrival of a much more robust UNAMSIL, now 17,500 troops strong and
taking a much more forceful posture in the countryside. This mission,
helped by the perception that UNAMSIL was backed by British forces,
managed to deploy throughout the country to disarm the RUF and the
CDF and to prepare Sierra Leone for elections. In the end, a cowed RUF
acceded to peacekeepers who, while certainly not neutral in the conflict,
took a less aggressive stance toward the RUF than did the British and progovernment forces in Sierra Leone.[106]

Conclusion

In all three of the case studies, whether or not consent-based peacekeepers
deployed depended entirely on the belligerents themselves. It is possible
that had the Bangladeshi government and the Shanti Bahini agreed to

---

[103] Quoted in Bright 2000, p. 2.
[104] See the Brahimi Report (UN Document A/55/305-S/2000/809).
[105] Hirsch and Zenenga interviews, New York.
[106] Anonymous interviews with UNAMSIL officials, Freetown.

peacekeeping, India would have tried to block supply at the international level. But while India is influential at the UN, it does not have a veto, nor was it an elected (nonpermanent) member of the Security Council in the late 1990s.[107] Whether or not peacekeepers were sent to the CHT was determined by the relative bargaining strength of the rebels, who pushed for peacekeepers, and the government, which resisted. The same was true in Mozambique. The interests of the great powers did not play a large role in this case. No Perm-5 member objected to peacekeeping, but nor did any of them push hard for it. The former colonial power, Portugal, was not on the Security Council at the time. In Sierra Leone, when it appeared that there was a desire for peacekeepers on the part of the belligerents, as in the Abidjan agreement, the UN was willing to put together a mission. But when it was clear that the RUF objected, the mission did not deploy.

However, considerations of supply were not entirely absent from consent-based peacekeeping. Given that there would be a mission in Mozambique, its size and therefore its cost were driven by decisions made by the international community. Resource constraints at the UN, particularly as it faced mushrooming demand for peacekeeping elsewhere, limited the initial plans for ONUMOZ. The decision to enlarge the mission considerably was the result of lessons learned in Angola, so was essentially a fluke of timing. Had the Mozambicans reached an agreement before the attempt to keep peace in Angola faltered, ONUMOZ would have been much smaller and cheaper.

Whether or not an enforcement mission deploys is, of course, a matter of supply. Enforcement missions were never considered in Bangladesh or Mozambique. In Sierra Leone, there was no stomach for such a mission early on as visions of Mogadishu danced in Western policymakers' heads. It was Nigerian interests that yielded ECOMOG. Adebajo describes these as threefold: Abacha's desire to end his regime's international isolation by being a valuable player in peacekeeping; corruption opportunities afforded by the mission (ECOMOG earned the epithet "Every Conceivable Moving Object Gone"); and Nigeria's interest in containing the regional conflict in its own neighborhood lest it spill over into Nigeria itself—"to put out the fire in order to stop it from extending to our own houses," as the Nigerian chief of staff in Sierra Leone put it.[108] By Lomé, Western powers, particularly Britain but also the United States, were willing to send an enforcement mission, though its size and cost were constrained by missions elsewhere. It was only after the peacekeeping hostage crisis in Sierra Leone, and considerable soul-searching on the general issue of peacekeeping (epit-

[107] See http://www.globalpolicy.org/security/membship/mem2.htm. It is conceivable, but not likely, that China would have vetoed a UN mission.
[108] Quoted in Adebajo 2002, p. 92.

omized in the Brahimi Report)[109] that the international community was willing to send a large and robust mission to Sierra Leone rather than leaving the job to the underfunded West Africans.

These cases shed light on some of the specific hypotheses outlined in the previous chapter, and these in turn help answer the question of whether peacekeepers tend to deploy to easy or difficult cases. Variations in the strategic interests of the Perm-5 cannot explain variation across these cases because such interests were not at stake in any of these countries. Both Bangladesh and Sierra Leone are former British colonies. That historical relationship was clearly important in Britain's decision to send its own force to Sierra Leone in 2000, and it was Britain that took the lead in pushing for UNAMSIL. However, Perm-5 colonial ties cannot account for the peacekeepers in Mozambique but not in Bangladesh.

Sierra Leone is endowed with much richer natural resources, including diamonds, bauxite, and rutile, than is either Mozambique or Bangladesh. These assets may help account for Nigeria's willingness to deploy ECO-MOG,[110] and diamonds were at least indirectly responsible for the Sandline scandal, but they do not otherwise seem to have been a factor motivating peacekeeping. These resources, as with oil, tend to be available whether war is raging or not. They might inspire intervention, but it is not clear why they would inspire peacekeeping. Easy access to these resources, did, however, fuel the conflict, making Sierra Leone a much more difficult place to keep the peace.

A comparison of these three cases supports the notion that the international community responds to threats to regional peace.[111] There were 50,000–70,000 refugees from the CHT in India, and there was some reciprocal cross-border support for rebel groups between India and Bangladesh, but the CHT conflict posed little threat of engulfing the region. The war in Mozambique created almost two million refugees,[112] and was much more closely entwined with the prospects for stability in southern Africa. The much shorter war in Sierra Leone caused 500,000 to flee by 1999,[113] and

---

[109] The Brahimi report, named for Algerian diplomat Lakhdar Brahimi, who chaired a panel in 2000 to draft a "comprehensive review of the whole question of peacekeeping operations in all their aspects," articulated the need, inter alia, to provide peacekeeping operations with sufficient resources (personnel, equipment, and funding) and sufficiently robust mandates, including the ability to use force if necessary. UN Document A/55/305-S/2000/809. On the report, and reforms implemented in its wake, see also Durch et al. 2003.

[110] Adebajo 2002, p. 93. Adebajo notes, however, that commercial interests alone cannot explain Nigeria's intervention, as it could have cut a deal to protect them without intervening.

[111] This hypothesis was not, however, supported by the statistical evidence in chapter 2 that used neighbors' support for rebels in the war as a proxy.

[112] Synge 1997, p. 80.

[113] Adebajo 2002, p. 99.

was a poster child for conflicts both caused by and contributing to spirals of instability and state collapse in West Africa.

The desire to reinstall Kabbah as the democratically elected president of Sierra Leone motivated the international response in Sierra Leone (including, ironically, Abacha's ECOMOG). While ONUMOZ helped usher in a much more democratic Mozambique, regime type does not seem to have been an important consideration in decisions about whether peacekeepers would deploy to Mozambique or the CHT (though the restoration of democracy in Bangladesh in 1991 did help the negotiations to reach a peace deal).

The clear evidence that bargaining power between the government and the rebels shapes the prospects for peacekeeping suggests that the demand-side interpretations of the statistical findings in the previous chapter about government army strength and mountainous territory are correct. The Bangladesh and Mozambique cases indicate that peacekeeping is more likely when rebels are relatively stronger. In Sierra Leone, the government was so weak militarily that it actually depended on peacekeepers for its survival, and it was a progovernment enforcement mission that deployed.[114]

The cases suggest that peacekeeping's infringement on state sovereignty is an important concern for governments. The government of Sierra Leone was in a particularly weak position on this front, as its tenuous grip on power was entirely dependent on outside forces, but the resistance of both the Mozambican and Bangladeshi governments was based on concerns about their sovereignty. While there is at least indirect evidence (through Shantu Larma) that the Bangladeshi government dug in its heels even more for fear that the PCJSS's push for autonomy might shade into secessionist sentiment, the real difference between Mozambique and Bangladesh was that the latter was in a relatively stronger bargaining position, so could prevent peacekeepers' infringement on its sovereignty. In other words, sovereignty is an important concern for governments contemplating peacekeeping on their soil, but it is relatively constant across cases (except where the government is so weak that it needs peacekeepers to help prop it up, as in Sierra Leone).

It is also clear from the cases studied that levels of mistrust drive the demand for peacekeeping. The parties to the Bangladesh conflict were relatively trusting of each other (perhaps to a fault in the PCJSS's case), while Renamo's mistrust of Frelimo was a direct cause of its demand for peacekeepers. In Sierra Leone, this was mitigated by Sankoh's distrust not only of the government, but also of the UN, though in the end the RUF

---

[114] I chose these three cases in part because the wars ended without a clear victory for one side but with peace agreements, so they cannot shed much light on the relationship between war outcomes and peacekeeping.

preferred UN peacekeeping to ECOMOG. Finally, as the statistical evidence indicated, enforcement missions are more likely in conflicts, such as Sierra Leone, with several factions, but this is not necessarily true of consent-based peacekeeping.

In these cases, did peacekeepers tend to go to the easy cases or the hard ones? It is difficult to assess the degree of difficulty of each conflict at the time of the cease-fire without letting our knowledge of whether peace subsequently held affect our judgment (and this eventual outcome is affected by whether peacekeepers were deployed). But of the five cases evaluated here, the two most precarious cease-fires were probably Mozambique and Lomé in Sierra Leone. The first case in Sierra Leone, Abidjan, is hardest to assess because there is least information available on it. But Lomé was arguably a harder case than Abidjan because the RUF (the main spoiler group) was stronger militarily, and levels of mistrust were higher after the failure of the Abidjan agreement. By the Abuja agreements, the RUF was much weaker militarily, making this a relatively easier situation in which to keep peace. The CHT conflict in Bangladesh was likely the easiest case of the five cease-fires studied here. It was less intense and the rebels relatively weaker than in Mozambique or the first two cases in Sierra Leone, while the government was fairly satisfied with the postwar status quo. In the short term at least, neither side had much incentive to derail the peace agreement.[115] Levels of mistrust were also much lower in this conflict than in others examined here.

If this assessment is correct, that the Mozambique case and the Lomé agreement in Sierra Leone were more difficult than Abidjan and Abuja, which were in turn more difficult than the Bangladesh conflict, then these cases support the conclusion that peacekeeping, especially consent-based peacekeeping, is more likely to deploy to more difficult situations.[116] The Chapter VII mission in Sierra Leone after Abuja runs counter to this conclusion, but the peacekeeping mission there was part of an intervention that led to the RUF's defeat, so as with the statistical finding in the previous chapter about war outcomes and enforcement missions, the causal arrows run the other way in this instance.

Beyond this general comparison across the cases, the more detailed qualitative evidence on many of the specific hypotheses evaluated here also supports the conclusion that peacekeepers are more likely to deploy to more difficult cases. Peacekeeping missions are more likely in circumstances that pose a higher threat to regional peace in terms of refugee crises, and they are more likely where rebels are relatively stronger

[115] See chapter 6 for further discussion of these incentives.

[116] The peacekeeping mission in Lomé was technically a Chapter VII mission, but did not deploy as such on the ground until after this agreement faltered.

(Mozambique rather than Bangladesh, for example). There is also qualitative evidence from all of the cases that higher levels of mistrust make peacekeeping more rather than less likely. Furthermore, the international community did not shy away from peacekeeping in Sierra Leone after the failure of previous attempts to maintain peace; rather it beefed up its response.

In short, both the statistical findings in the previous chapter and the case studies in this one indicate that it is not only the decisions of the international community about whether to intervene, but also the demand for peacekeeping on the part of the belligerents themselves, that shape where peacekeepers go and where they do not. The evidence from these two chapters also makes clear that peacekeepers tend to go where peace will be most difficult to keep. Peacekeepers usually deploy where neither side has been able to win outright, where refugee flows cause conflicts to spill over borders, threatening regional peace, and where the level of mistrust between belligerents is particularly high. Consent-based missions are particularly likely where rebel groups are relatively strong and where decent living conditions provide no bulwark against renewed warfare. Enforcement missions are more likely in less democratic states and in complicated wars with many factions. None of these factors is conducive to stable peace. In short, peacekeepers are most likely to be asked for, and to go, when peace is otherwise least likely to last. Whether and how they improve the odds for peace are the questions to which I now turn.

Four

A CAUSAL THEORY OF PEACEKEEPING

THE PROBLEMS WITH PEACEKEEPING are legion. Peacekeeping missions are often thrown into conflicts when the great powers want to be seen as "doing something" but do not really want to act. Mission mandates are often ambiguous, reflecting the lowest common denominator of agreement among sending states and among the belligerents themselves. Peace operations are usually improvised and ad hoc; they are too often planned at the last minute and are perennially understaffed, underfunded, and underequipped. "Muddling through has been the order of the day" in peacekeeping missions.[1] Troop levels are based on what member states are willing to provide, not on any realistic assessment of need.[2] With demand for peacekeeping personnel often outstripping supply, missions are patched together with begged-for soldiers. If there are choices to be made about who supplies forces, troop-contributing countries are often chosen more for geographic representation than for military effectiveness. Interoperabilty of forces is generally poor; troops that have to work together often do not even speak a common language. Command and control is loose at best, with peacekeeping soldiers likely to "phone home" before complying with orders from the force commander.[3] The way in which most peacekeeping missions are managed is, frankly, no way to run an effective military operation.[4]

It would thus not be surprising if the presence of peacekeepers made no difference at all; if their contribution to stable peace was virtually nil.[5] And yet, as we will see in chapter 5, peacekeepers do make a positive difference; peace is much more likely to last, ceteris paribus, when they are present than when they are not.

It is possible to argue that this positive effect is simply coincidence, that the effect is spurious. Studies of peacekeeping frequently note that the

---

[1] Cousens 1998, p. 99.

[2] Rarely, for example, do missions have a force-to-space ratio adequate for their military tasks. Hillen 2000, p. 34.

[3] Doyle 2001, p. 529.

[4] For detailed analyses of the military and political dysfunction of peacekeeping operations see Hillen 2000; Wesley 1997; Cockayne and Malone 2005, p. 333. See also Jett 1999. For recommendations on reform, see the Brahimi Report (UN Document A/55/305-S/2000/809); and United Nations 1996b.

[5] As Howard 2008, p. 3, points out, "The interesting question is not why [UN peacekeeping] fails, but why it succeeds. Failure is to be expected."

success of a mission depends on the cooperation of the parties to the conflict. The conventional wisdom is that peacekeeping works only "when there is real peace to keep" and depends crucially on the "political will" on the part of the peacekept; that is, on their commitment to peace. These ideas have become almost clichés in the peacekeeping literature.[6] But this raises the distinct possibility that peacekeeping is irrelevant—that peacekeeping only "works" in circumstances where peace would last in any case. Where there is already a strong peace and the belligerents support it wholeheartedly, war is unlikely to resume whether peacekeepers are present or not.[7] The evidence presented in this book shows this argument to be wrong—peacekeeping does have an independent effect on the prospects for peace—but it is important to take this charge seriously. The "value added" of peacekeeping is by no means obvious.

Nor is it straightforwardly obvious *how* peacekeeping works. This is particularly true for consent-based peacekeeping. How well-armed enforcement missions, operating with mandates that allow the use of heavy force if necessary, might make a difference is not quite so puzzling. But, as we shall see, consent-based peacekeeping is as effective as more robust enforcement missions. How does the presence of unarmed or lightly armed international personnel, deployed with the consent of both sides, make a difference? Through what causal mechanisms do peacekeepers keep peace? This chapter attempts to answer these questions. It lays out a number of ways in which peacekeepers might make peace more likely to last. The remainder of this book, particularly chapter 6, tests whether these hypothetical causal mechanisms are in fact at work in peacekeeping missions.

Causal Mechanisms in the Peacekeeping Literature

The peacekeeping literature is surprisingly vague on the question of how peacekeepers effect peace. Many studies list the functions of peacekeeping (interposition, monitoring, disarmament, police training, election observation, etc.) without linking these functions explicitly to a causal theory of how it works.[8] Even studies that purport to present a theory of peacekeep-

---

[6] See, for example, Rotberg 2000, pp. 5, 9; Doyle and Sambanis 2006, p. 50; Zongwe 2002, p. 1. See also Chopra 1998, p. 9; Clapham 1998, p. 318; Durch 1996a, p. 22; Hillen 2000, pp. 18, 37, 50, 55; James 1990, pp. 368–69; Wesley 1997, pp. 23, 28; the Brahimi Report (UN Document A/55/305-S/2000/809).

[7] As Doyle 1995, p. 45, notes, "Without the cooperation of the parties, [the UN mission] could not effectively control [the political process in Cambodia]. Yet had the parties been prepared to cooperate, control would not have been needed." See also James 1990, pp. 1, 5.

[8] For examples, see Berdal 1999, p. 53; Diehl 1993, pp. 9–11; James 1990, pp. 4–5; Rikhye 1984; Wesley 1997, p. 66.

ing do not spell out a specifically *causal* explanation of how it keeps war from resuming.[9]

Much of the literature makes only a very limited claim for an independent effect, often falling back on the idea that peacekeeping is a "self-help" technique that merely facilitates peace. Alan James's discussion of the definition of peacekeeping is fairly typical. He notes that the "dictionary definition" of peacekeeping "suggests . . . an independent and influential impact on the situation" but that in practice peacekeeping refers to something less ambitious: "it offers help to disputants with the help dependent on the willingness of all sides to accept it."[10] But what this help entails or why those willing to accept peacekeepers need their help, why they cannot reach peace on their own, is not specified.[11]

Similarly, a number of authors note that peacekeepers are not able to create the conditions of their own success.[12] While few authors say as much, this suggests that peacekeepers have little or no independent effect on whether or not peace will last. Hillen goes further than most when he notes that "tangible evidence offering a direct relationship of causality between UN military observers and mission success (or failure) is hard to find."[13] But he shies away from concluding that peacekeeping has no effect.

Other studies, especially case studies of peacekeeping missions, state that an operation "helped" keep peace, or was "crucial to" or "instrumental in" ensuring peace, but have at most an implicit argument about how peacekeepers made a difference.[14] The often unstated counterfactual is that, had peacekeepers been absent, war would have been more likely to resume.[15] However, little is done to back this claim up or to explain how peacekeepers reduced the probability of another war.

---

[9] Fetherston 1994 laments the lack of theorizing about how peacekeepers might create positive peace rather than simply maintain a cease-fire (negative peace), but does not discuss how peacekeepers might cause even negative peace. Her most explicit causal argument suggests that peacekeeping works by setting a peaceful example (p. 14). Doyle and Sambanis 2006 place peacebuilding in a conceptual "triangle," along with local capacity and local hostilities, to explain peace outcomes. Their theory chapter lays out causal mechanisms much more clearly than most, but even they often do not specify exactly how peacekeepers make a difference. Rikhye 1984 notes the difference between peacekeeping in practice and the concepts of maintaining peace and security spelled out in the UN Charter.

[10] James 1994, pp. 4–5.

[11] James's other work on peacekeeping (1969, 1990) is somewhat more explicit. See below.

[12] See, for example, Mackinlay 1995, p. 54.

[13] Hillen 2000, p. 54.

[14] See for example, Fortna 1995, p. 282; Hampson 1996b, pp. 96–97.

[15] Rikhye 1984, p. 100, is more explicit about his counterfactual assessments than many. In reference to the mission in Cyprus, for example, he notes, "If UNFICYP were withdrawn or its capability reduced, daily occurrences of minor incidents could detonate a resumption of fighting."

The dearth of specifically causal arguments is the result, first, of the literature's almost exclusive focus on cases in which peacekeepers are deployed, as opposed to those wars in which combatants are left on their own. Much of the literature consists of individual or collections of case studies of peacekeeping missions, many of which draw out general "lessons learned" from peacekeepers' experience.[16] Case comparisons are used to examine why peacekeeping sometimes succeeds and sometimes fails,[17] or to address the doctrinal debate about the propriety of the use of force by peacekeepers.[18] With few exceptions, the more basic question—What difference does it make having peacekeepers present rather than absent?— has not been asked.[19]

Second, the lack of a causal theory reflects a focus in the literature on the perspective of the peacekeepers rather than the peacekept.[20] The interests and preferences of the belligerents—their "political will" for peace— is taken as exogenous. The success or failure of peacekeeping is often attributed to the level of cooperation from the parties, but there is little discussion of how the presence or actions of peacekeepers might shape belligerents' "will," that is, how peacekeepers might change the incentives of the parties to the conflict.[21]

Identifying explicit causal links between the presence or absence of peacekeepers and the stability of peace has not been the main goal of existing studies.[22] Nonetheless, the literature does suggest, at least in passing, a number of plausible ways in which the presence of peacekeepers might causally shape the prospects for peace. Some authors point to the effect of

---

[16] Among numerous examples are Charters 1994; Cousens and Cater 2001; Doyle 1995; Durch 1993, 1996b; Holiday and Stanley 1993; Smith 2003; Synge 1997; Zacarias 1996.

[17] For example: Hampson 1996a; Howard 2008; Jett 1999.

[18] Examples include Findlay 2002; Otunnu and Doyle 1998; Pugh 1997.

[19] The quantitative analyses in Doyle and Sambanis 2000, 2006; Dubey 2002; Hartzell, Hoddie, and Rothchild 2001; and Gilligan and Sergenti 2007 are exceptions. These studies do not test causal mechanisms, however.

[20] A notable exception is the work by Clapham 1998, 2000.

[21] Stedman 1997 discusses strategies for managing "spoilers" of a peace process, including inducement, socialization, and coercion. He argues that the strategy should match the type of spoiler present (limited, total, or greedy). This assumes, however, that peacekeepers can identify spoiler type a priori, before war has resumed. The need to deal with the possibility of spoilers has found its way into UN strategy, particularly in arguments for more robust enforcement capacity. See, for example, UN Document A/55/305-S/2000/809; UN Document S/2001/394. But other than the need for deterrence, and sometimes for economic development, there is little explicit discussion of how peacekeepers might make would-be spoilers less interested in spoiling.

[22] Notable exceptions are Last 1997, whose central research question is, "How can peacekeepers control and de-escalate violent situations?" (p. 7); and Krasno, Hayes, and Daniel 2003, who focus in part on leverage to deter parties from returning to conflict (see especially chap. 8).

the moral authority of peacekeepers or to their symbolic effect as representatives of the international community.[23] Others note that peacekeepers improve communication between belligerents, and note the "calming influence" of a peacekeeping presence.[24] Much of the literature suggests that simply having peacekeepers watching makes peace more likely to hold,[25] and some argue that peacekeepers can serve as a trip wire for more robust intervention should peace break down.[26] The facilitating role that peacekeepers play in disarming and demobilizing troops is emphasized,[27] as is the role the international community can play in institutional reform and development so as to deal with the economic and political causes of war.[28] Much of the doctrinal debate over the use of force in peacekeeping focuses on the need for (while acknowledging the absence of) a strong deterrent against violations of the cease-fire.[29] The literature thus suggests a broad array of potential causal mechanisms that might link peacekeepers to more durable peace. In most cases, however, these mechanisms are implicit in discussions of peacekeepers' functions, in case analyses, or in prescriptive arguments about the need for peacekeeping reform.[30]

The aim of this chapter is to build on these insights in the existing literature, moving beyond description of what peacekeepers do, to explain in a more comprehensive and explicit way how what they do might shape

[23] See, e.g., Diehl 1993, p. 10; Durch 1996a, p. 17; Doyle and Sambanis 2000, p. 785; Rotberg 2000, p. 5. For discussions of the need to move beyond merely symbolic deployments, see the Brahimi Report (UN Document A/55/305-S/2000/809), p. 9; and Chopra 1998, p. 3. For more skeptical views see Hillen 2000, pp. 51, 102; James 1969; Wesley 1997, p. 13; and Mackinlay 1995, pp. 52–53.

[24] Hillen 2000, pp. 52–54; Rikhye 1984, p. 16; Rotberg 2000, p. 1; Doyle and Sambanis 2006, p. 53. Durch 1996a, p. 23, notes that improving communication can help "break the prisoner's dilemma." However, communication by itself does not change the equilibrium outcome in a prisoner's dilemma game.

[25] Among many examples, see Rikhye 1984, p. 15; Diehl 1993, p. 9; Hillen 2000, p. 52.

[26] Durch 1996a, p. 17; UN Document S/2001/394, p. 3.

[27] UN Document A/55/305-S/2000/809, p. 7; Rotberg 2000, p. 7.

[28] Durch 1996a, p. 4; Ryan 2000, p. 39; Ramsbotham 2000; UN Document S/2001/394, pp. 2ff.; James 1994, p. 4; Doyle and Sambanis 2000, p. 782; Doyle and Sambanis 2006, pp. 5, 15; Last 1997, p. 19.

[29] Jakobsen 2000, p. 44; Last 2000, pp. 81–82.

[30] Doyle 2001, p. 532, is more specific than most, noting that "first generation" (i.e. observation or interpositional mission) peacekeepers "provided transparency—an impartial assurance that the other party was not violating the truce—and raised the costs of defecting from and the benefits of abiding by the agreement with the threat of exposure, the potential resistance of the peacekeeping force, and the legitimacy of UN mandates." But he does not explore in detail how unarmed or lightly armed peacekeepers might resist defection, or why exactly the peacekept would care about exposure or UN legitimacy. See also Doyle and Sambanis 2006, esp. pp. 45–66.

belligerents' choices, thereby making peace more likely to last. For example, how does the moral authority of peacekeepers affect the incentives of the peacekept? Under what conditions will warlords or militia leaders be concerned about their reputations in the international community? How exactly does improved communication make the resumption of war less likely? What actions by peacekeepers are able to calm belligerents down in ways that make them less likely to fight? What difference does it make to the peacekept if monitors are watching their actions? Under what conditions will the presence of peacekeepers serve as a trip wire? Why are peacekeepers necessary during the disarmament process; what prevents belligerents from conducting this process themselves?

Assumptions

The argument spelled out below rests on a number of conditions and assumptions. The first is that there has been a civil war, and there has been some sort of break in the fighting. This break may prove to be very short-lived, or it may last a long time (that is the dependent variable of interest); it might come about because one side has been defeated, or be the result of outside pressures or simply war weariness. But to be considered in this study, there must be at least some cease-fire in place.

Another assumption is that there are at least two combatant parties making decisions about whether to maintain peace or return to war. If one side has been not just defeated but completely eliminated in the fighting, there is no possibility of the war resuming, and there can therefore be no effect of peacekeeping. There may well be more than two groups in a civil war. For the sake of simplicity, the argument that follows describes a strategic situation between two main actors; however, the argument applies as well to conflicts with many factions.[31] I do not, however, assume that each group represents a unitary actor. The parties are often riven by conflict between hard-liners and moderates and may splinter into separate factions. Command and control within both rebel and government armies is often extremely loose. Unauthorized action by rogue factions or individuals can cause serious obstacles to peace.

A third assumption is that the belligerents are rational. That is simply to say that they take purposeful action to further their own goals and to protect their own interests. They do not act at random, or take actions that

---

[31] The number of factions is an important control variable in the empirical analysis.

they expect will do themselves harm.[32] But this assumption does not imply that belligerents are omniscient. They often lack information and may face considerable uncertainty about their opponents, about the likely actions of peacekeepers, or about the outcome of future political processes.

I also assume that belligerents have deeply conflicting goals. This is relatively safe assumption given that they have, until recently, been killing each other to further these goals. The parties may (or may not) have a shared interest in stable peace, but they are certain to have very different ideas about the ideal political outcome of their struggle. On the other hand, I assume that their contest is not perfectly zero sum—there is at least some room for cooperation. This rests on the assumption that war is costly.[33] It takes resources to finance fighting, and of course war is extremely costly in terms of human life. It is also, though this may be of less concern to leaders making decisions about war and peace, horribly destructive to the general economy and social fabric. In civil wars, perhaps more so than in interstate conflicts, there may well be economic gains from war. Instability provides opportunities for looting, and often for highly lucrative trade in drugs, diamonds, illegally mined timber, and so on.[34] There may well be actors whose interests are better served by war than by peace, and these groups are particularly likely to try to spoil the peace, but even these spoilers do not prefer war for its own sake, but because of the opportunities it provides. In any case, because I select cases in which some break in the fighting has taken place, we can assume that there is at least some shared benefit to peace, even if this shared interest is only temporary or tenuous.

Paths to Renewed Fighting

To develop a causal theory of peacekeeping, I begin by thinking about the ways in which peace might fail. In the immediate aftermath of civil war, peace is quite fragile. War resumes within a year in almost a third of the cases examined here, and within five years in over half of the cases. Civil wars face a severe recidivism problem. Once belligerents have reached

[32] Civil wars are often described in journalistic press accounts as senseless and irrational. While the violence in civil wars, particularly that aimed at civilians, is horrific, sometimes beyond imagination, it generally reflects rational, if terrible, calculations. Violence against civilians may be used to control or move populations, to pay soldiers (through opportunities to loot), or as in terrorism, to gain attention. See Kalyvas 2006; Weinstein 2007; Stanton, forthcoming. For articulations of the contrary view that civil war is driven by emotion, hatred, and revenge, see Enzensberger 1994; Kaplan 1996.

[33] Fearon 1995.

[34] See, for example, Collier and Hoeffler 2004; Ballentine and Sherman 2003; Pugh and Cooper 2004; Ross 2004; and the articles in Ron 2005.

some sort of cease-fire, war might resume: through deliberate aggression, through a security dilemma spiral of fear and uncertainty, by accident, because one side reneges on the political deal reached at the cease-fire, or some combination of these pathways.

Aggression

By definition, recent combatants are deadly enemies with deeply conflicting goals, willing to fight to further them. Just because there has been a break in the fighting does not mean that parties who until that point had been killing and maiming each other to advance their own interests have suddenly become peace-loving actors, committed to nonviolent resolution of their differences. The end of the fighting, even if accompanied by a comprehensive peace settlement, is extremely unlikely to have given all sides what they want. On the other hand, if one side has gotten what it wants through victory, the other, by definition, will be dissatisfied. While the cost of fighting, and possibly international pressure, may have led all sides to choose at least a temporary cease-fire over continued warfare, strong incentives for aggression remain.

Despite agreeing to peace, one or more sides may be biding time for a more advantageous moment to attack in pursuit of military victory or a better deal at the bargaining table. Even if a combatant agreed to peace in good faith at the time of the cease-fire, if it comes to believe its interests will be compromised by the settlement, that is, if it is "losing the peace," or if it sees an unanticipated opportunity for gain at its enemy's expense, it may decide that renewed hostilities are a better option. Such a change of heart might come about because of a shift in power after the fighting stops,[35] or because one side obtains new information about its relative position. For example, if an erstwhile external ally of one side makes clear that it will no longer support its proxy, the other side may seize the chance to defeat its rival. If the peace settlement calls for disarmament and demobilization, and there is any imbalance in this process, the side that is temporarily stronger militarily is likely to grab the chance for victory. Similarly, the disarmament process may reveal one side's weaknesses (in terms of troop strength, morale and commitment to fight, or equipment) to the other. This new information may change the calculation for war or peace. The demobilization and disarmament process leaves belligerents extremely vulnerable, for there is little to prevent either side from cheating at this stage and launching a surprise attack as the other disarms.[36]

[35] Werner 1999 makes this argument with respect to interstate wars.
[36] Walter 1997, 2001.

In short, all sides in the immediate aftermath of a civil war have strong incentives to take advantage of each other; they all have aggressive motives to some extent.

Fear and Mistrust

Even if neither side would choose to reinitiate the war of its own accord, mistrust and fear can upset the peace. Deeply ingrained suspicion of the enemy will make both sides extremely wary. Both sides know that the other has at least partially aggressive motives. Neither side can be certain whether the other intends to maintain peace or is plotting an attack. Combatants in civil wars often lack the manpower and technology to monitor their own agreements effectively, nor is it easy for them to offer each other access to sensitive sites or information that would be needed for assurances of peaceful intentions. In this atmosphere of deep mistrust, security dilemma spirals are extremely likely. Moves that one side makes to protect itself, either militarily or politically, are likely to be interpreted as evidence of hostile intentions by the other.[37]

Both sides, to take one very pertinent example, are likely to hedge their bets if possible by maintaining a fighting capability. If a peace agreement requires disarmament and demobilization, all sides are likely to hold some forces and some arms in reserve, lest they be attacked. There are perfectly good defensive motives for such cheating on the agreement, but the other side is likely to view this noncompliance as evidence of aggressive intentions. This side will then be more inclined to keep its own fighting force available to protect itself, which will feed, in turn, the mistrust of the first side. At best, these security dilemma spirals will stall implementation of the peace process; at worst they can escalate until war seems inevitable and one side preempts rather than waiting to be attacked. Even parties with peaceful intentions have trouble credibly committing to peace.[38]

Accident

Given the levels of mistrust and mutual hatred in the aftermath of civil war, accidents or incidents between soldiers or civilians can also escalate and drag the country back toward war. Accidents and unauthorized incidents can be a problem even for disciplined armies, but in many civil wars command and control is quite loose. Leaders' decision to cease fire may not translate immediately and effectively into peace in all reaches of the country. Hard-liners within either side may deliberately try to derail the

---

[37] Jervis 1978; Walter and Snyder 1999.
[38] Walter 2001; Walter 1999, p. 8.

peace. Ongoing fighting after a cease-fire is in place, or occasional flare-ups by poorly organized, undisciplined troops, or by rogue elements, may be interpreted as signals of bad faith, or they may simply get out of hand, escalating beyond the control of those nominally leading forces.

Abuses by soldiers against civilians may continue after a cease-fire, especially in conflicts in which targeting the civilian population has been either a military strategy or a means of financing an army. Particularly in identity-based conflicts, in which protection of ethnic kin is a primary motivation to fight, attacks by opposing soldiers against one's own civilian population are likely to lead to retaliation. Similarly, incidents that start among civilians (rather than soldiers), such as demonstrations, rock throwing, and vigilantism, may set off larger conflagrations among polarized populations. In countries wracked by recent war, awash in weapons and often ill-disciplined troops, even small incidents or unintended provocations can escalate into much more serious fighting.

Political Exclusion

Much more so than in interstate wars, maintaining peace in civil conflicts entails a political process. States can and often do agree to live with their differences in the aftermath of war,[39] but ending internal war requires setting up a governance structure that both sides can tolerate. (Secession or partition avoids this problem, but creates a host of new difficulties concerning political exclusion of those who find themselves minorities in the new states.)[40] Former combatants will return to war if they feel they are losing the peace politically. If a power-sharing agreement that induced them to end hostilities is not complied with, if police forces abuse their members, if elections are not free and fair (or if a side that expected to win the election fails to), war is likely to resume. The transition from a state of divided sovereignty, in which each side controls its own military forces and territory, to a unified country is particularly dangerous. Rebels will be particularly unwilling to disarm if they fear the government will use the instruments of state power to exclude them.[41] All sides have a strong incentive to make a power grab that shuts the other out politically. The excluded side is likely to return to war if it is able to do so.

[39] Fortna 2004c.

[40] As, for example, the Serbs in many of the successor states to Yugoslavia. The problem of securing the peace in Croatia was therefore quite similar to the problem in countries that remain unified after civil war. On partition and the stability of peace, see Kaufmann 1996; Kumar 1997; and Sambanis 2000.

[41] For examples of this dynamic in El Salvador and Cambodia, see Howard 2008, pp. 118, 152.

The distinctions between outright military aggression, fear and security dilemma spirals, accidental escalation, and political exclusion outlined above are more useful analytically than in practice. In reality, civil wars are likely to resume through some combination of these overlapping pathways.[42] Small incidents and clashes between civilians or individual soldiers are likely to escalate because neither side is sure of the other's intentions, and fears the worst. The belief that drives the security dilemma, that the other side is inherently hostile, is fostered by the fact that both sides probably would, if unconstrained by the prospect of retaliation and another war, like to do harm to each other. The same mix of aggression and fear that drives military calculations also drives incentives and worries about the political process. Combatants' fears of each other are not unreasonable.[43] But thinking about aggression, fear, accident, and exclusion as four potential causal pathways to war suggests ways in which peacekeepers might be able to interfere and block renewed hostilities, thereby reducing the recidivism rate.

The Causal Mechanisms of Peacekeeping

Peacekeepers can have a causal, rather than spurious, effect on the stability of peace if (1) they reduce the likelihood of aggression by raising the costs of war or the benefits of peace for the peacekept; (2) they disrupt spirals of fear and security dilemmas by reducing belligerents' uncertainty about each other's actions and intentions; (3) they prevent accidents from occurring or control them so that they do not escalate to war; or (4) they can deter or prevent one side from reneging on a political deal and excluding the other from power. As with the pathways outlined above, these mechanisms overlap in practice. Measures that raise the cost of war will also tend to reassure parties that the other will not attack, and will make less appealing political exclusion that might trigger renewed fighting. Actions that build confidence about intentions will make it less likely that accidents

[42] In this, I disagree with those, such as Doyle and Sambanis 2006, who argue that one can identify the problem in a particular case and should design a peacekeeping mission accordingly. Even if a conflict is plagued by only one of these obstacles to peace rather than a combination, it is difficult, if not impossible, to know a priori which problem pertains. This makes arguments that the most effective peacekeeping missions are those that "fit well" with the underlying problem difficult to falsify—if peace falters, one can always argue after the fact that the mission was a bad match.

[43] Snyder and Jervis 1999, pp. 19–21 argue that while it is important to distinguish security dilemmas (which are driven by fear and uncertainty) from predation (what I call aggression), "elements of each are present in almost every specific situation. . . . The security dilemma gives rise to predators, and predation intensifies the security dilemma."

spiral out of control. Again, these are distinctions more useful analytically than in practice, but they provide an organizing framework for considering the causal mechanisms of peacekeeping.

Changing Incentives

RAISING THE COST OF WAR: DETERRENCE

How might the presence of a peacekeeping mission make outright aggression less likely? The ability of peacekeepers physically to deter aggression depends on the type of mission, specifically on the distinction between Chapter VI consent-based missions, and Chapter VII enforcement missions.

Walter maintains that a third party capable and willing to use force against a party that tries to renege on a peace deal can overcome the commitment problem inherent in civil war peacemaking.[44] Similarly, Last argues that for negotiated peace to hold, a third party must act as a "retaliator" against any defection, and argues for "coercive tools necessary to stop violence."[45] Or as Jakobsen puts it,

> More often than not a force capable of defeating any armed attempts to derail a peace process will be required to keep a peace process on track. Such a force is obviously more likely to be successful in reassuring parties fearful of cheating and deterring spoilers than lightly-armed peacekeepers or unarmed monitors. Should deterrence fail, it will also take a combat capable force to stop spoilers who have taken up arms to derail the peace process.[46]

A large, well-equipped enforcement mission, mandated to fight if necessary, can make deliberate aggression much more costly. Rather than fighting only the enemy faction, an aggressor will have to take on both the enemy and the intervening force.[47] The presence of a Chapter VII mission can thus serve as a deterrent.

The credibility of such a force is obviously an issue. The ability and willingness of peacekeepers to fight if push comes to shove is by no means assured. A number of embarrassing cases in the mid-1990s in which peacekeepers were unable even to defend themselves from hostilities let alone to protect vulnerable populations, as in Bosnia and Rwanda, led to serious soul-searching by the international community, and by the UN in

---

[44] Walter 2001.

[45] Last 2000, pp. 81–82.

[46] Jakobsen 2000, p. 44. Note the overlap between deterring aggression and reassuring those fearful of it.

[47] In this capacity, peacekeepers might be thought of as analogous to the podesta in medieval Genoa, hired by warring clans to maintain a military balance and keep peace. Greif 1998.

particular. A large literature on peacekeeping doctrine and the proper use of force emerged from this process.[48] Intrinsic to this debate is discussion of deterrence as a causal mechanism of peacekeeping. As is well understood in the wider literature on military deterrence, credibility is central to successful deterrence in peacekeeping.[49] If peacekeepers are likely to withdraw rather than fight in the face of resistance or hostilities, the legal technicality of a Chapter VII mandate means nothing. However, if a large, well-armed enforcement mission signals by its force posture and its early actions that it will use violence against spoilers if necessary, it can provide an important deterrent. Peacekeeping missions that follow military interventions to impose a cease-fire, such as those in Kosovo or East Timor, will be more credible than others because they are proof that the international community is willing to use force.[50] Leaders of government and rebel groups considering aggression will include in their calculations the likelihood and cost of having to fight the outside forces as well as the original enemy.

Chapter VI peacekeeping missions, on the other hand, are at most lightly armed and are not authorized to use substantial force. Furthermore, they operate with the consent of the belligerents themselves, so are constrained from taking direct action against either side lest they undermine that consent. Their ability to stop deliberate aggression is thus severely limited. Studies of traditional, consent-based forms of peacekeeping tend to argue that the presence of peacekeepers has some sort of symbolic deterrent effect based on the moral authority of peacekeepers, but these studies also note that such missions cannot deter deliberate aggression (more on this below).

Nonetheless, the presence and actions of even consent-based peacekeepers may make aggression more costly, and maintaining peace more lucrative. Peacekeepers' monitoring of demobilization and troop movements may make a surprise attack much more difficult. The presence of a Chapter VI mission may also serve as a trip wire with the potential to trigger a larger enforcement mission if necessary. Peacekeepers are "potentially a vehicle through with the outside world might be drawn into the fight against whichever side breaks the peace."[51] Historically, the international community has not responded to the tripping of a peacekeeping wire with forceful intervention. In Rwanda, the Interahamwe's killing 10 Belgian peacekeepers led not to a forceful response but to withdrawal of the peacekeeping mission. British intervention in Sierra Leone in response to attacks on UN peacekeepers in 2000 serves as a counterexample, however.

---

[48] Examples include Findlay 2002; Jakobsen 2000; Berdal 1999.
[49] See, for example, George and Smoke 1974; Huth 1988; Morgan 1977; Schelling 1966.
[50] This hypothesis is tested in chapter 5.
[51] Durch 1996a, p. 17. See also Doyle and Sambanis 2006, p. 56.

In Croatia, the UN peacekeeping mission UNTAES was able to present a strong and credible deterrent against paramilitary groups in Eastern Slavonia because it enjoyed the backing of NATO and the prospect of airstrikes against potential spoilers.[52] In limited conditions, then, the presence of even consent-based peacekeepers may make aggression physically more difficult or costly.

Raising the Benefits of Peace: Legitimacy, Aid, and Direct Economic Benefits

Peacekeepers can change incentives through carrots as well as sticks. Disarmament and demobilization of combatants has become a common and important function of peacekeepers; the Brahimi Report describes it as "key to immediate post-conflict stability and reduced likelihood of conflict recurrence."[53] But where peacekeepers do not have robust enforcement powers, peacekeepers cannot force reluctant belligerents to disarm.[54] How does the presence of peacekeepers induce the peacekept to give up their weapons and return to civilian life?

Many discussions of the deterrent value of consent-based peacekeeping imply a more abstract causal mechanism, citing symbolism or the moral authority of the UN. But how does this causal mechanism work? To what extent are combatants in civil war concerned with the moral suasion of world opinion? By shining the "spotlight of international attention" on a conflict, peacekeepers are thought to make aggression less likely. Durch, for example, writes that peacekeepers function, inter alia, as "a visible symbol of the outside world's continuing investment in peace."[55] Rotberg notes, somewhat skeptically, the "symbolic significance" of what he calls "type I" peacekeeping (what I term observation or interpositional peacekeeping) missions, the very presence of which "is meant to have a deterrent effect" even though they "are not expected physically to intervene to prevent the outbreak of renewed hostilities."[56] This symbolic effect is linked to the moral authority and legitimacy of peacekeeping. Diehl states that peacekeeping "provides a moral barrier to hostile action."[57] Hillen notes that, as traditional peacekeepers are not militarily capable of preventing aggression, "the UN force's role in deterrence was based on its moral and political authority."[58]

---

[52] On this case, see Howard 2008, chap. 7.
[53] UN Document A/55/305-S/2000/809, p. 7, par. 42. See also Rotberg 2000, p. 7.
[54] Durch 1996a, p. 23. This was the heart of the fiasco in Mogadishu in 1999.
[55] Durch 1996a, p. 17. See also Doyle and Sambanis 2000, p. 785.
[56] Rotberg 2000, p. 5.
[57] Diehl 1993, p. 10. See also Doyle and Sambanis 2006, pp. 14, 56.
[58] Hillen 2000, p. 102.

How peacekeepers' moral authority might change the incentives of battle-hardened combatants is not obvious on the face of it. James notes (in interstate cases) that censure by the UN and the possibility of withheld recognition might influence the peacekept by affecting soldiers' morale, encouraging a state's rivals and providing them with propaganda material, or causing doubts among its own public or its allies. He is generally doubtful that this will have a strong effect unless the state is fairly isolated, however.[59] Wesley is even more skeptical, contending that even if such moral suasion is effective for peacekeeping between states, it is much less so in civil wars. "Insurgent movements and embattled incumbent regimes, locked into a conflict for power and survival, are likely to be little affected by considerations of UN approval or the publicity of their non-compliance with a UN mission."[60] Or as Rotberg puts it, "The UN's legitimacy is not sufficient to convert warriors into compliant ex-combatants."[61]

Nonetheless, the stamp of legitimacy provided by peacekeepers can be valuable, both domestically and internationally, for parties to a civil war. Both government and rebel groups are often highly dependent on outside aid. If (and in some cases this is a large if) this aid is conditional on good behavior, then the peacekept will have a large incentive to cooperate with peacekeepers. If a peace deal was reached in part through pressure from the combatants' backers, and these backers continue to have an interest in peace, just such conditionality may apply.[62] Reports that a group is responsible for aggression or is dragging its feet in compliance can threaten economic, and perhaps military, aid. For example, during the peacekeeping mission in El Salvador, ONUSAL, UN undersecretary Marrack Goulding criticized the government of Alfredo Cristiani for delaying the demobilization process in a report to the Security Council. This "worked to embarrass the government internationally, and increased donor pressure on the Cristiani administration to comply with its commitments." Within a month the demobilization process was moving again.[63]

For rebel groups in particular, the chance to be treated as legitimate political actors, recognized by the outside world, is often a key benefit of a peace deal. Peacekeepers' reports of noncompliance can threaten that international legitimacy, providing an incentive against aggression. In Angola, the rebel group UNITA lost both international aid and legitimacy after it reneged on a peace supervised by UN peacekeepers.[64] While this

---

[59] James 1969, pp. 181–82, 195–96.

[60] Wesley 1997, p. 13. See also Mackinlay 1995, pp. 52–53.

[61] Rotberg 2000, p. 9.

[62] Boyce 2002.

[63] Howard 2008, pp. 115–16.

[64] UNITA had the dubious honor of being the first nonstate actor to come under UN sanctions. These sanctions were poorly enforced at first but were later tightened up considerably, particularly on the issue of "conflict diamonds." Howard 2008, pp. 38–41.

did not induce UNITA to remain at peace, it did contribute, eventually, to the rebel organization's military defeat. Similarly, the strategy of the UN mission in Cambodia (UNTAC) to marginalize the Khmer Rouge cost the rebels donor assistance and contributed to their eventual downfall.[65]

For both sides, if the peace deal includes an electoral process, peacekeepers' public judgments about each party's behavior may influence public opinion and voting. There are several ways, then, in which the peacekept might be very concerned about the judgment of peacekeepers about their behavior. In short, if collective disapprobation by the international community is costly, then the moral authority of peacekeepers might affect decisions made by the peacekept. The legitimacy of an international organization like the UN gives peacekeepers the ability to confer or withhold legitimacy from the peacekept. So while consent-based peacekeeping missions can only physically deter aggression in very limited ways, their presence may nonetheless provide an incentive against decisions to renege on a peace agreement or to go back to war.

The legitimacy of peacekeepers is important for this causal mechanism, but so is their neutrality, or at least their objectivity. In the fog of civil conflicts it may be quite difficult to tell "who started it" when conflict flares up. Both sides have an incentive to charge the other with aggression, so that neither side's claims are necessarily credible. The presence of monitors who can help differentiate between aggression and legitimate retaliation makes it less likely that an aggressor can get away with an attack by claiming that the other side started hostilities. The operation of international and perhaps domestic costs to violating a cease-fire thus depends to some degree on the monitoring and verification role of peacekeepers.[66]

Peacekeepers can also provide material incentives to maintaining peace. Peacekeeping missions often bring with them substantial resources into a war-torn country. The missions themselves often undertake civil engineering projects such as building schools or roads, and deliver basic humanitarian aid including food and medicine. Peacekeeping missions also provide substantial numbers of jobs (for drivers, maids, translators, secretaries, and so on).[67] Both the international attention and the increased security brought to a war-torn country by peacekeepers increase the amount of development aid directed to it. International nongovernmental organiza-

---

[65] Howard 2008, p. 154. On this case, see also Doyle 1995.

[66] For an analysis of impartiality in external support for negotiated agreements, see Schmidt, forthcoming.

[67] For arguments that meeting the basic needs of the peacekept through development and job creation is a way of enhancing the incentives to maintain peace, see Last 1997, p. 19; Doyle and Sambanis 2000, p. 782; Doyle and Sambanis 2006, pp. 59, 67; Diehl 1993, p. 10; UN Document A/55/305-S/2000/809, p. 7, par. 37. For an assessment of some of the downsides of peacekeepers' job creation effects, particularly an increase in prostitution and human trafficking, see Mendelson 2005.

tions and state-run development programs are likely to spend more on places where peacekeepers are present than where they are absent.[68]

There are also often more direct personal benefits and side-payments bestowed upon the peacekept by peacekeepers.[69] These may include payments to leaders to buy off potential spoilers directly.[70] Disarmament and demobilization programs generally include direct benefits for ex-combatants who lay down their guns. These include cash, farm and building materials, transportation, and job training.

If a civil war faction and its constituents benefit from the projects undertaken directly by peacekeepers, or indirectly by NGOs and development agencies because the mission is there, this can give peacekeepers substantial leverage over would-be spoilers. These economic effects can constitute a large "peace dividend" that may change the incentives of both the leaders of the parties to the war and individual soldiers. Leaders who benefit economically because of peacekeepers' presence will have less incentive to resume war if doing so will chase the mission away. And soldiers who benefit from demobilization schemes will have less incentive to follow leaders' call to take up arms again.

The effect of such positive inducements to maintain peace depend on the resources available to the peacekept, and to their economic incentives to wage war. If a group has independent access either to outside support or to natural resources (drugs or diamonds, say), then it will be less swayed by the prospect of disrupting the peace dividend.[71] But if the economic benefits of peace outweigh the often considerable economic benefits of fighting, belligerents are more likely to choose peace.[72]

In sum, if its threat to use force against aggressors is credible, an enforcement mission can deter decisions to resume war. The physical ability of consent-based peacekeeping to deter an attack is limited to making surprise attack more difficult to achieve, or serving as a trip wire for an enforcement mission. But the approval of even Chapter VI peacekeepers can have important effects on both the economic and political resources of the peacekept. To the extent that international aid and legitimacy are tied to

[68] There is often justifiable concern that these economic benefits will end when a peacekeeping mission ends, disrupting the economy. Thanks to Kim Marten for pointing this out. However, if peacekeepers leave a stable country (as opposed to pulling out because war has resumed), development agencies often stay on in a country long after peacekeepers have gone home.

[69] Durch 1996a, p. 24.

[70] Note, however, that attempts to buy off spoilers can create perverse incentives if more recalcitrant parties are "rewarded" with greater goodies to induce compliance.

[71] This suggests that peacekeeping should be less effective when a conflict is funded by contraband, a hypothesis that is tested empirically in the following chapter.

[72] Walter 2004a.

cooperation, the presence of peacekeepers monitoring behavior can change the costs and benefits of war and peace. The impact of a peacekeeping mission on the economy of a war-torn country, or more direct payoffs to the peacekept, may also alter their incentives, making peace preferable to war.

This is not to say that the presence of peacekeepers will stop all decisions to attack; no student of peacekeeping would make such a claim. If the status quo is sufficiently unpalatable, or if the gains from attack are sufficiently large, one side may decide that aggression is worthwhile despite the presence of peacekeepers. But if peacekeeping changes the cost-benefit ratio of decisions about war and peace at the margin, it can make peace more likely to hold.

Reducing Uncertainty and Fear about Actions and Intentions

NEUTRAL MONITORING

How might peacekeepers disrupt security dilemma spirals driven by the fears and insecurity of the peacekept? Many studies suggest that the presence of a peacekeeping mission helps to build trust and confidence among recent combatants.[73] It is not usually made explicit, however, how the presence of peacekeepers increases trust among deadly enemies. The literature emphasizes peacekeepers' role as monitors or supervisors of the peace process, arguing that such observation helps to "ensure" that parties live up to their agreements.[74] But the causal mechanism linking observation and more durable peace is not entirely clear; how does observation ensure compliance?

In addition to making a surprise attack more difficult, or informing outsiders whose aid is conditional on compliance with a peace agreement, monitoring can influence the decisions of the peacekept by affecting the information they have available about each other. In the atmosphere of mistrust after recent fighting, each side will worry that the other is cheating—failing to disarm, or mobilizing for another attack. The presence of neutral observers monitoring the cease-fire and each stage of a peace agreement's implementation can reassure each side that the other is acting in good faith, that its worst fears about the other are unfounded.[75]

There is some reason to think that the direct information-providing role of peacekeepers is limited. Hillen argues that many observer missions have not had the troop strength they need for effective monitoring. Rather, "It was hoped that [their] moral authority and responsibility would give all

---

[73] See, for example, Hillen 2000, p. 102; Durch 1996a, p. 17.

[74] Rikhye 1984, p. 15; Diehl 1993, p. 9. See, also Hillen 2000, p. 52; Doyle and Sambanis 2006, pp. 50, 54; Doyle 2001, p. 548.

[75] Doyle 2001, p. 532.

the belligerents the confidence that the other side was not flagrantly violating the accords of the peace settlement," thus building trust and helping to make permanent a temporary peace.[76] At the grossest level, belligerents do not need to be told by peacekeepers whether the other side is complying with the cease-fire; they know if they are under attack. And in some cases, even many minor violations may be noticed first by the other side, not by peacekeepers. In many cases, peacekeepers react to complaints of violations from the peacekept. In other words, they are often not telling the parties anything they do not already know. But much more so than in interstate wars, in which recently warring states are likely to have better intelligence than peacekeepers can provide, in civil wars, the belligerents may not have the technology or the manpower to monitor their own agreements effectively.[77]

The disarmament and demobilization process is particularly sensitive. As noted above, both sides have strong incentives to hedge their bets by maintaining armed forces. Knowing this, each side will require credible information that the other is cantoning its troops, that soldiers are turning in their weapons and disbanding. They will want to know whether troop numbers and numbers of arms turned in match estimates of force strength. In theory, the parties themselves might be able to devise a joint monitoring system to observe each other as troops are cantoned, lay down their arms, and demobilize. But in practice, there are several reasons self-monitoring may not work. Soldiers are likely to be understandably leery of coming out of hiding to areas supervised by their erstwhile enemies. Leaders may not trust each other not to exploit, for aggressive purposes, information gleaned by watching the disarmament process.[78] And perhaps most important, each side has an incentive to charge that the other is failing to disarm, so that such allegations are not necessarily credible if they come from the parties themselves. A neutral arbiter is thus often needed to pass judgment on this dicey aspect of the peace process. The presence of unbiased monitors providing all parties with reliable information about each other's actions can disrupt spirals of fear and misperception that might otherwise lead back to war.

---

[76] Hillen 2000, p. 51. He notes that "the use of the word 'hope' is common in UN documents related to peacekeeping" (p. 172). On transparency, see also Lindley 2007.

[77] Walter 2001, pp. 25–26. A well-known participant in the peace talks in El Salvador explained that "neither side trusted the other and no Salvadoran body could [verify implementation]. . . . [The UN peacekeeping mission] was a guarantee for each side." Quoted in Howard 2008, p. 103.

[78] In some cases, parties may have exaggerated their fighting strength as a bargaining ploy and will be reluctant to show just how poorly trained or equipped their forces really are. This can cause serious problems later as lower-than-expected turnout or weapons collection is likely to be interpreted by the other side as evidence of failure to disarm.

COMMUNICATION AND CREDIBLE SIGNALING

Peacekeepers may also make it easier for the peacekept to inform each other about their intentions. Spirals of fear and misperception can be ameliorated somewhat by improved communication. Talk is cheap, and there are incentives for the parties to argue that their own alleged violations do not in fact indicate malign intent. The belligerents may not believe each other when they talk, but there is a better chance of clearing up misunderstandings that would otherwise escalate if the parties can communicate than if they cannot. The political animosities between recently warring factions, and the fact that there can be high political costs even to expressing a willingness to meet and negotiate with the enemy, mean that a third party can play an important mediation role, allowing communication where it would not otherwise exist.

Peacekeepers can thus help the peacekept communicate their intentions to each other directly, but they can also play an important indirect role as a signaling device. Willingness to accept intrusive monitoring by peacekeepers sends a credible signal of commitment to peace. An actor that is just biding its time waiting for an opportunity to attack again will be less willing to accept monitors to verify that it is demobilizing on schedule. So giving consent to peacekeeping can serve as a costly signal that separates spoilers from those desiring peace. This signaling function continues after peacekeepers arrive. Those parties who cooperate willingly with inspections and monitoring are signaling benign intent, while those who become obstructionist cannot help but signal more malign aims.[79]

Critics might claim that this causal argument renders peacekeeping epiphenomenal. If peacekeepers are accepted only when belligerents intend to keep peace, then peacekeeping missions will be present only when peace would last in any case. This critique misses the importance, and the difficulty, of signaling intentions. If belligerents could easily signal their intent to maintain peace, then this causal mechanism would indeed be superfluous. But for well-known reasons, combatants cannot easily communicate their intentions to each other in a way that is credible.[80] Peacekeeping allows them to do so. Furthermore, the reason peacekeeping might serve a credible signaling role is that it actually makes aggression more costly (as outlined in the previous section). If it did not, then those intending to go back to war would be no less willing to accept intrusive peacekeepers than would those with benign intentions, and the signal would not separate "types." The role that peacekeeping plays in reassuring the peacekept

---

[79] A similar signaling mechanism is implicit in Doyle and Sambanis's (2006, p. 57) discussion of identifying spoilers.

[80] Farrell and Rabin 1996; Fearon 1992, 1997; Morrow 1999.

about each other's intentions is thus tied integrally to its ability to raise the costs of returning to war.

In a number of ways, then, the presence of peacekeepers can reduce the uncertainty of the peacekept about each other's actions and intentions. In doing so, peacekeepers can disrupt spirals of fear and misperception from leading back to war. Again, this is not to say that peacekeeping will always be able to surmount security dilemmas, but if these causal mechanisms operate, fear and mistrust will be less likely to cause resumption of war when peacekeepers are present than when belligerents are left to their own devices.

Preventing and Controlling Accidents and Involuntary Defection

The mere presence of peacekeepers is described as having "a calming effect" that can prevent escalation, or deter "spontaneous local violations" of a peace accord.[81] How the presence of blue helmets might calm belligerents or prevent local incidents is not spelled out, however. How can peacekeepers make it less likely that groups who desire peace will be carried back to war by the action of rogue forces or by accident?

The presence of peacekeepers can make "involuntary defection" by rogue forces less likely by monitoring the behavior of each side's military. In some cases, even if the peacekeeping force is too small or under too restricted a mandate to deter either side as a whole, it may be able to deter coups or aggression by splinter factions. For example, while the UN mission in East Timor, UNTAET, probably could not have deterred the Indonesian military from reentering the territory, it was able to push anti-independence militias out of East Timor.[82] By providing organizational or financial resources and information to moderates, peacekeepers may also be able to weaken hard-liners in ways that make spoiling less likely.[83] In other words, in addition to changing the incentives of a belligerent group as a whole, peacekeepers may be able to shift the power base within groups in a way that undermines or deters extremists who might otherwise disrupt a peace agreement.[84] This makes it less likely that those who are committed to peace will be thwarted by those within their ranks who are not.

In the tense aftermath of civil conflict, skirmishes, low-level incidents, and accidents are almost bound to occur. There are several ways in which

---

[81] Rikhye 1984, p. 16; Hillen 2000, p. 52.

[82] Howard 2008, p. 285.

[83] Doyle and Sambanis 2006, pp. 45, 50. See also Doyle 2001, p. 548, for examples.

[84] If a peacekeeping force is not seen as legitimate by the peacekept, this strategy can backfire. Outside support can make moderates look like puppets, weakening rather than strengthening them relative to hard-liners.

peacekeepers can reduce the frequency of these events, and more important, keep them from escalating back to war. In peacekeeping between two states, or between easily separated intrastate armies, the interposition of neutral troops to create a buffer zone can reduce the probability of hostile incidents simply be preventing direct contact between combatants.[85] But in the aftermath of civil wars, troops are rarely easily separated along a single clear cease-fire line.[86]

By facilitating communication between enemies, peacekeepers may be able to help the peacekept control low-level hostilities and to keep them from spiraling out of hand. But as discussed above, the parties' denial of responsibility for local violations or of malign intent may not be credible. Talking about the problem is certainly better than not talking about it, but it may not be enough.

Much of peacekeepers' day-to-day work consists of responding to reports of incidents and allegations of noncompliance. On-the-spot, low-level mediation and arbitration by peacekeepers may be able to nip local problems in the bud, before clashes or incidents escalate to more politically charged problems from which all sides will have a harder time backing down. And by taking on some responsibility for law and order (what Last refers to as "constabulary intervention")[87] peacekeepers can help control and minimize incidents such as rock throwing or mob behavior that might otherwise escalate and spark renewed conflict. In war-torn countries, local security forces (armies, militias, and police) are almost by definition biased toward one side and against the other. In the immediate aftermath of war, it is therefore very difficult for the peacekept to provide basic security in a neutral way, even if they wanted to. If combatants are left to their own devices, crime or local unrest, whether politically motivated to begin with or not, can exacerbate security fears and can quickly escalate to large-scale political violence. The riots in Kosovo in March 2004 indicate the danger of such a possibility. Had no peacekeepers been present, politically motivated arson might easily have spiraled to resumed warfare between Albanian and Serb populations.[88] By providing an international civilian police force, or by closely monitoring local forces, peacekeepers can help keep crime and public disorder from sparking escalation among polarized societies.

The reciprocity inherent in cease-fires makes them vulnerable to escalation. Violations of the cease-fire are met in kind, so that even small per-

[85] Diehl 1993, p. 10. Demilitarized buffer zones play a similar role in interstate wars. Fortna 2004c, esp. pp. 179–81.

[86] A recent exception is the peacekeeping and demilitarized zone in Côte d'Ivoire.

[87] Last 1997, p. 30.

[88] For an overview of events, and a critique of peacekeepers' role, see Human Rights Watch 2004.

ceived lapses can quickly unravel the peace process. One way in which peacekeepers can interfere in this cycle is by providing an alternative mechanism for responding to alleged violations. When no peacekeepers are present, each side has only two choices in the face of violations by the other: retaliate and risk escalation, or do nothing and risk looking weak, and thereby invite further encroachment by the enemy. If peacekeepers are present, however, there is a third option: report the violation to the peacekeeping mission for investigation.[89] This can provide a politically acceptable response that avoids retaliatory spirals. The effect of many peacekeeping investigations may thus have more to do with providing a face-saving response to the peacekept than with the actual information uncovered in the investigation.

There are thus a number of ways in which the presence of peacekeepers can help the peacekept avoid an accidental return to war. Even relatively small or consent-based peacekeeping missions may be able to deter rogue forces from disrupting the peace, or may be able to strengthen moderates relative to hard-liners. Peacekeepers can thus make involuntary defection less likely. Improving communication between parties who have a hard time meeting or speaking with each other, as well as low-level, on-the-spot mediation can prevent small problems from getting out of hand. By providing neutral policing, peacekeepers can also reduce the likelihood of polarized societies descending back to war because of crime or local violence. And by giving leaders a politically acceptable way to respond to small transgressions by the other side, an alternative to doing nothing or to escalating, peacekeepers can make reciprocal cease-fires more stable than they would be if no peacekeepers were present.

Preventing Political Abuse

With the advent of multidimensional peacekeeping in the 1990s, the literature began to focus more on the political and economic underpinnings of peace. These missions aim not just to keep combatants from each other's throats, but to help "implement a peace accord that addresses the causes of the underlying conflict."[90] The literature notes the new roles peacekeepers took on monitoring or running elections, monitoring and reforming institutions of law and order (police forces, and the judiciary), human rights monitoring[91] and training, and rebuilding (or in many cases building for the first time) state institutions.[92]

---

[89] Hillen 2000, p. 54.

[90] Durch 1996a, p. 4. See also Ryan 2000, p. 39; Ramsbotham 2000.

[91] For a much earlier argument that the UN should monitor the treatment of minorities, see James 1969, pp. 91–92.

[92] For example, Ryan 2000, p. 29.

The general argument is that these functions help to move conflicts from the battlefield to more peaceful institutions of dispute settlement.[93] James, for example, describes elections and human rights monitoring as part of a move toward "national reconciliation."[94] Where civil wars are the result of failed states (as in Somalia or Sierra Leone), building effective state administrations is arguably a mechanism for preventing the resumption of war.[95] It is eminently logical that dealing with the root causes of the first war will help prevent its recurrence. And there are plausible causal mechanisms linking the presence of peacekeepers monitoring elections or human rights, or retraining police forces, and so forth, to solving the underlying causes of conflict, but these mechanisms are not made explicit in the existing literature. How exactly do peacekeepers transform the treatment of minorities or build effective state institutions or promote good governance? Why might combatants be more likely to hold or to respect elections when peacekeepers are present? More broadly, how might the presence of peacekeepers prevent one side from excluding the other politically, thereby causing it to go back to war?

Perhaps the most obvious potential tool for political abuse is the security sector. As noted above, almost by definition in civil wars, armies and police forces are parties to the conflict, not neutral protectors of everyone's security. Rebel and opposition groups, often representing minorities or disenfranchised majorities, have good reason to fear that the government will use its security forces to harass and intimidate their members in postwar politics. Unless the country is partitioned, a unified army will have to be created, often composed of members of both sides in the civil war. By monitoring, or in some cases running the process by which soldiers are chosen for the new army, peacekeepers can help ensure that representation is fair. Similarly, civilian police monitors patrolling with local forces can deter the use of the police to harass, intimidate, or kill the government's opponents. For example, in Namibia, the large and visible presence of civilian police monitors as part of the UNTAG peacekeeping mission allowed Namibians to trust in the guarantee of freedom of political movement that was part of the accords. UNTAG's monitoring is credited with changing the relationship between society and the police; "people no longer feared the police."[96] International efforts to train newly constituted military and police forces, or to retrain and reform old ones, can help create

---

[93] UN Document S/2001/394, pp. 2ff.; Doyle and Sambanis 2006, p. 15.

[94] James 1994, pp. 10–11.

[95] Doyle and Sambanis 2006, pp. 14–15, 22–23, 59. On peacekeeping in failed states, see Herbst 2000. For an assessment of the UN's record at nation-building, see Dobbins et al. 2005.

[96] Howard 2008, pp. 74, 77.

forces less biased than their predecessors. Training and monitoring can both deter political abuse and help the population overcome mistrust of security forces.[97]

Human rights monitoring serves a similar purpose. In El Salvador, the UN exerted considerable pressure on the government to reform on human rights issues, "through shame, cajoling, and persuasion," as mediator Alvaro de Soto put it.[98] ONUSAL also took over policing duties in controlled areas during the transition to peace, until a reformed and unified police force could be created. Meanwhile, it pressured the Salvadoran government to transform the police from an instrument of state repression to a neutral provider of law and order.[99]

If, as is often the case in negotiated peace deals, elections are called for as part of the peace process, both sides are likely to be concerned that the other will use its influence to try to skew election results, and both will be tempted to do so. Control of the state apparatus gives the government an advantage in this regard, but if rebel groups have set up shadow administrations in territory they control, the problem may exist on both sides. Extensive international monitoring by peacekeepers of voter registration, campaigning, and polling can help deter electoral fraud, and at least as important, reassure both sides that elections will be free and fair.[100] Peacekeepers can also provide information to counter propaganda meant to sway elections. For example, in Cambodia, the UN mounted an information campaign to thwart attempts to intimidate voters into thinking their ballots would not be secret and they would therefore be vulnerable to retribution for their vote.[101] Similarly, in Namibia, the UN countered misinformation put out by South Africa about SWAPO's behavior.[102]

If the risks of political exclusion are high and an indigenous transitional government trusted by both sides cannot be created, the UN or another third party can provide a neutral administration to govern during the transition so that the powers of the state cannot be used against either side. The interim administrations in Bosnia and East Timor are examples of this approach.[103] But even short of taking over the entire administration of the

---

[97] On security sector reform in postconflict settings, see McCartney, Fischer, and Wils n.d.

[98] Quoted in Howard 2008, p. 103.

[99] Howard 2008, pp. 112–13.

[100] This is not foolproof, of course. Nothing short of winning the vote would have convinced Jonas Savimbi that the elections in Angola were free and fair.

[101] Howard 2008, p. 168; Doyle 2001, p. 545.

[102] Howard 2008, p. 83.

[103] For an analysis of such missions, see Chesterman 2004. Some have argued that the creation of an international interim administration tends to get in the way of development of a government with domestic legitimacy. Woodward 2004; see also Weinstein 2005.

country, the involvement of a peacekeeping mission, and specifically the special representative of the secretary-general (SRSG) (or the equivalent figure in non-UN missions), as an arbiter of state administrative decisions can help minimize use of the state to exclude parties deciding whether or not to go back to war.[104] The political efforts of the SRSG can help cajole parties into complying with the political aspects of a peace deal.

As with preventing outright aggression, all of these ways in which peacekeepers might deter the abuse of state (or shadow state) power to exclude opponents depend on the leverage of the peacekeeping mission and its SRSG. If the political head of the mission has the backing of important international donors, then he or she can wield significant influence over the peacekept by tying aid to good behavior. To the extent that the peacekept need the stamp of legitimacy provided by peacekeepers, the mission can have influence in the political game and can thwart exclusion. If peacekeepers control the timetable of the peace process, they can make some stages of the transition contingent on compliance with others. For example, the peacekeeping mission might insist that elections not be held until troops have been demobilized, so that groups that hope to win legitimacy through elections must first give up their guns. But if peacekeepers do not control resources (whether material or political) that the peacekept need, their influence will be minimal.

Peacekeepers can also play a role in helping military organizations, designed to fight on the battlefield, transform themselves into political organizations capable of competing at the ballot box.[105] This may be especially important for rebel groups who are likely to have little political experience other than waging war, but may also be important for government parties if they are facing electoral competition for the first time.[106] Helping the parties learn how to run a political campaign, by providing organizational resources, infrastructure (computers and fax machines, for example), and information will help reassure them that they will have a voice in the new system.

The civilian tasks of multidimensional peacekeeping, including human rights monitoring, civilian police monitoring and training, election monitoring, reform of judicial systems—the tasks that the UN refers to as peacebuilding and the United States refers to as nation-building—are all aimed at establishing a system in which political conflict can be managed peacefully. Building stable state institutions is an extremely difficult task, one

---

[104] Note that an emphasis on including parties who can credibly threaten to go back to war may shortchange legitimate, but less well armed, actors, and can create perverse incentives for the peacekept.

[105] Doyle and Sambanis 2006, p. 54.

[106] Söderberg Kovacs 2007.

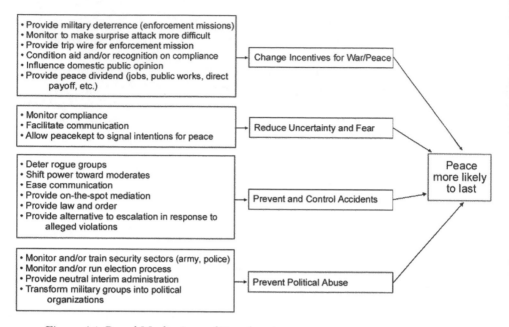

Figure 4.1 Causal Mechanisms of Peacekeeping

that took centuries in Western democracies, and peacekeeping missions have rarely succeeded in creating ideal states. But to the extent that peacekeepers can shape the political process during the transition to peace so that neither side can completely exclude the other, they will raise the probability that the peacekept have an incentive to play within the system, rather than upend it by going back to war.[107]

Conclusion

The foregoing sections have outlined a number of possible causal mechanisms through which the presence of peacekeepers might change the incentives of and information available to the peacekept. These are summarized in figure 4.1.

This is not to say that peacekeepers always have all or even any of these effects. As noted throughout, there may be reasons these causal mechanisms do not operate or have limited impact. The deterrence capability of

---

[107] Note that, to be stable, state institutions need not necessarily be democratic; they require only the acquiescence of those capable of taking the country back to war. Effective power-sharing arrangements often compromise democratic ideals.

peacekeepers is extremely limited. Even enforcement missions can only deter aggression if their threat to fight potential spoilers is credible. If the peacekept have access to their own resources, peacekeepers' leverage in terms of aid or international recognition will be limited. Peacekeepers often do not tell the peacekept much that they do not already know about the other side's actions. Even if peacekeepers facilitate communication, talk is cheap and may not be believed. The incentives for electoral fraud, or of using police forces or militias to exclude political opponents, may be greater than the incentives to cooperate with peacekeepers. And so on.

Moreover, different types of peacekeeping may operate through different causal mechanisms. Chapter VII missions will have more of a military deterrent effect, while Chapter VI missions' effects, if any, will operate through other mechanisms. Similarly, monitoring and interpositional missions will likely do less to prevent political abuse than multidimensional missions that are more extensively involved in postwar political institutions.

Determining whether peacekeepers do in fact have the effects outlined in this chapter is the task of the rest of the book. If these hypothetical causal mechanisms indeed operate, we should observe, first, that peace is more likely to last, all else equal, when peacekeepers are present than when belligerents are left to their own devices. This proposition is tested in chapter 5. Second, we should observe these causal mechanisms at work in the qualitative analysis of particular cases. Chapter 6 moves beyond the question of whether peacekeeping has an empirical effect, to test whether the causal mechanisms outlined here in fact account for that effect.

Five

PEACEKEEPING WORKS

EVIDENCE OF EFFECTIVENESS

NOW THAT WE HAVE SOME SENSE of where peacekeepers tend to go and a causal theory of how they might affect the prospects for peace, we can evaluate whether they are, in fact, effective in helping belligerents maintain peace. As we have seen, peacekeepers are not deployed to civil wars randomly, but rather tend to go where peace is otherwise most difficult to keep. To assess their effectiveness accurately we therefore need to control for other factors that shape the likelihood that peace will last. Statistical analysis, which allows for such multivariate evaluation, is thus necessary to answer the general question of whether peace lasts longer when peacekeepers are present than when belligerents are left to their own devices. Below I discuss the results of a number of statistical tests of peacekeeping's effectiveness. The quantitative evidence is overwhelming: peacekeeping works; it reduces the risk of another war dramatically. I then draw on the case studies for this project to evaluate whether the belligerents themselves view peacekeeping as an effective tool for helping them to maintain peace. In general, they do.

Peacekeeping and the Duration of Peace

Quantitative Evidence

To test whether peace lasts longer when peacekeepers are present than when belligerents are left on their own, I employ survival analysis, as described in chapter 1. In this analysis, peace is considered to "survive" until war resumes between the same parties, or if no war resumes, until the data are censored in 2005. Drawing on what we learned in chapter 2, I control for variables that may affect the ease or difficulty of maintaining peace as well as the likelihood that peacekeepers will deploy. As noted earlier, failure to do so would lead to misleading results.

Survival analysis yields hazard ratios rather than coefficients (such as those reported in chapter 2) that may be more familiar to some readers. Hazard ratios are interpreted relative to 1. Ratios significantly less than 1 indicate that a variable is estimated to reduce the hazard, or the risk, of another war, while ratios significantly greater than 1 mark an increased risk of another war. For example, if a dichotomous variable has a hazard ratio of 2, its presence is estimated to double the hazard, or risk, of war at any given time. A hazard ratio of 1.25 marks a 25% increase in the risk of another war. Similarly, a dummy variable with a hazard ratio of 0.5 is estimated to cut the risk of renewed warfare in half, a hazard ratio of 0.75 indicates a 25% reduction in the risk of war, and so on. In addition to hazard ratios (HR) and robust standard errors (RSE), the tables report the level of statistical significance for each finding $(P > |Z|)$.[1]

Table 5.1 shows the effect on the duration of peace of having any type of peacekeepers present (that is, it combines all types of peacekeeping into a single variable). Table 5.2 distinguishes between consent-based and enforcement missions, and table 5.3 breaks peacekeeping down even further, distinguishing between monitoring missions, interpositional (or traditional) peacekeeping, multidimensional missions, and enforcement missions. Table 5.4 shows the results of a less conservative, but probably more accurate, notion of peacekeeping's effects. It demonstrates that peacekeeping succeeds in establishing peace that holds even after peacekeepers leave. In each table, I show several models to give a flavor of some of the many robustness checks run to test how sensitive the findings are to particular model specifications. I discuss the findings for peacekeeping, our main variable of interest, first, then turn briefly to the results for the control variables. Finally, figures 5.1 and 5.2 show graphically the effect of peacekeeping on the risk of renewed warfare, in general and under specific conditions.

The results in these tables are striking. The hazard ratios (HR) for peacekeeping in the first three columns of table 5.1 range from 0.38 to 0.45 (column 4 is discussed below). In other words, having peacekeepers present reduces the hazard, or risk, of another war breaking out by 55%–62%, all else equal. This estimated effect is statistically very unlikely (less than 3% chance) to arise by chance alone, passing the standard test for statistical significance, and is quite robust to various specifications of the model.[2]

In the discussion of causal mechanisms in chapter 4, I argued that the effect of peacekeeping is diminished in cases where the rebels enjoy contraband financing. Access to easily "lootable" resources such as precious gems or drugs leaves belligerents much less beholden to the international com-

---

[1] These tables show a larger number of observations than the number of subjects because each subject (each case of a break in the fighting) may have multiple observations across time. This allows the data to reflect changes in independent variables over the course of a spell of peace, such as the arrival or departure of a peacekeeping mission.

[2] For example, it holds up when secessionist wars are controlled for, either in addition to or in place of the control for identity conflict, and when individual variables not significant in the fuller models (e.g., failed past agreements, rough terrain, Perm-5 colony, polity score, etc.) are included or omitted. Results not shown.

TABLE 5.1
Effects of Peacekeepers: All Missions Combined

	Model 1 Cox		Model 2 Cox		Model 3 Weibull		Model 4 Cox	
	HR (RSE)	P > |Z|	HR (RSE)	P > |Z|	HR (RSE)	P > |Z|	HR (RSE)	P > |Z|
All Peacekeeping	**0.38** (**0.12**)	**.00**	**0.45** (**0.16**)	**.03**	**0.43** (**0.17**)	**.03**	**0.37** (**0.14**)	**.01**
PK * Contraband							1.19 (0.87)	.81
Contraband	2.21 (0.67)	.01	3.55 (1.09)	.00	3.14 (0.85)	.00	2.08 (0.82)	.06
Victory	0.13 (0.06)	.00	0.12 (0.07)	.00	0.14 (0.09)	.00	0.13 (0.06)	.00
Treaty	0.28 (0.10)	.00	0.35 (0.15)	.02	0.32 (0.13)	.01	0.28 (0.10)	.00
Identity War	1.24 (0.36)	.46	1.50 (0.52)	.24	2.17 (0.84)	.05	1.25 (0.37)	.45
Deaths	1.15 (0.09)	.06	1.14 (0.10)	.15			1.15 (0.09)	.08
Factions	0.66 (0.18)	.13	0.84 (0.29)	.61	0.74 (0.22)	.30	0.69 (0.24)	.29
Democracy	0.98 (0.03)	.46	0.97 (0.03)	.19	0.96 (0.03)	.22	0.98 (0.03)	.46
Infant Mortality	1.005 (0.004)	.25	1.003 (0.004)	.42	1.005 (0.004)	.26	1.005 (0.004)	.25
Past Agreement	1.15 (0.44)	.72	1.10 (0.46)	.82	1.32 (0.54)	.49	1.14 (0.44)	.74
Government Army Size	1.000 (0.000)	.63	1.001 (0.001)	.05	1.000 (0.001)	.38	1.000 (0.000)	.62
Mountains	1.07 (0.16)	.67	1.19 (0.21)	.34	1.11 (0.20)	.55	1.06 (0.16)	.67
P5 Contiguity	0.55 (0.32)	.30	0.56 (0.32)	.32	0.39 (0.23)	.11	0.56 (0.31)	.30
Former P5 Colony	1.02 (0.41)	.96	1.37 (0.66)	.51	0.91 (0.36)	.82	1.02 (0.41)	.97
Duration of War	0.93 (0.02)	.00	0.92 (0.02)	.00	0.94 (0.03)	.02	0.93 (0.02)	.01
Neighbor Aids Rebels			1.04 (0.45)	.92				
P5 Involvement			0.70 (0.22)	.25	0.78 (0.29)	.50		
Shape Parameter P					0.62 (0.06)	.00		
Number of Subjects	92		81		88		92	
Number of Observations	128		107		123		128	
Log Pseudo-Likelihood	−202.69		−169.35		−133.50		−202.67	

munity and undermines the ability of peacekeepers to change the incentives facing the peacekept. This hypothesis is examined in column 4 of table 5.1. An interaction term marks cases in which there is both contraband financing and peacekeeping. As expected, contraband greatly reduces the positive effect of peacekeeping on stability, but peacekeeping also ameliorates the negative effect of contraband financing.[3] In other words, peacekeeping still contributes to peace, but much less so when rebels have independent and illegal sources of income.

Turning to table 5.2, we can see that both consent-based (Chapter VI) and enforcement (Chapter VII) missions have a strong effect on the duration of peace. Again, the hazard ratios in columns 1–3 indicate an estimated reduction of 55%–63% in the risk of another war. Interestingly, there is relatively little difference between the effects of these two types of mission. (The level of statistical significance is lower for enforcement missions, because of the relatively small number of cases of Chapter VII peacekeeping operations.)[4]

These findings suggest that the large emphasis the UN and the international community more broadly has placed in recent years on strengthening mandates and deploying more "robust" enforcement missions may be somewhat misplaced. Mandates to use force when necessary may be important in some cases, but unless these missions can prove their credibility, their ability to deter violence is limited. Meanwhile, the less militarily strong consent-based missions have had a clear and sizable effect improving the chances for peace.

---

[3] Because both parts of the interaction term in this case are dummy variables, the hazard ratios for peacekeeping, contraband, and the interaction between them can be interpreted as indicating the risk of another war, respectively for cases with peacekeeping but no contraband, contraband but no peacekeeping, and both contraband and peacekeeping, all relative to cases with neither peacekeeping nor contraband. Thus, we can see that in cases with no contraband, peacekeeping reduces the risk of another war by 63%. In cases with no peacekeeping, contraband more than doubles the risk of another war. Cases with both contraband and peacekeeping are, if anything, slightly less stable than cases with neither (though the difference is not statistically significant), but they are more stable than cases with contraband and no peacekeeping (the hazard ratio is much lower than for contraband alone) and less stable than cases with peacekeeping but no contraband (the hazard ratio is much higher than for peacekeeping alone).

[4] I find little difference between peacekeeping run by the UN and that done by other organizations or ad hoc groups of states. If anything, UN peacekeeping is more effective overall, although non-UN peacekeeping may have a slight edge when it comes to operating enforcement missions. Results not shown. These findings may be driven by the fact that non-UN operations combine missions undertaken by organizations considered to be quite capable, such as NATO, with missions by organizations that have lower military and organizational capacity, such as the OAU (now the African Union). For more on this question, see Sambanis and Schulhofer-Wohl 2007; Heldt 2004.

TABLE 5.2
Effects of Peacekeepers: Consent-Based versus Enforcement Missions

	Model 1 Cox		Model 2 Cox		Model 3 Weibull		Model 4 Cox	
	HR (HSE)	P > |Z|	HR (HSE)	P > |Z|	HR (HSE)	P > |Z|	HR (HSE)	P > |Z|
Consent-Based Peacekeeping	0.39 (0.14)	.01	0.42 (0.17)	.03	0.44 (0.15)	.02	0.39 (0.15)	0.01
Enforcement Peacekeeping	0.37 (0.22)	.10	0.37 (0.21)	.09	0.45 (0.28)	.20		
Enforcement Not Creating C.F.							0.65 (0.38)	.46
Enforcement Creating C.F.							0.000 (0.000)	.00
Contraband	2.21 (0.67)	.01	2.71 (0.61)	.00	2.59 (0.78)	.00	2.33 (0.81)	.02
Victory	0.13 (0.06)	.00	0.15 (0.06)	.00	0.12 (0.06)	.00	0.13 (0.06)	.00
Treaty	0.28 (0.10)	.00	0.38 (0.14)	.01	0.24 (0.10)	.00	0.27 (0.10)	.00
Identity War	1.24 (0.36)	.47	1.60 (0.55)	.17	1.36 (0.47)	.38	1.30 (0.38)	.37
Deaths	1.15 (0.09)	.06	1.22 (0.08)	.00	1.16 (0.10)	.08	1.15 (0.09)	.06
Factions	0.67 (0.19)	.15	0.72 (0.20)	.24	0.58 (0.18)	.08	0.61 (0.19)	.10
Democracy	0.98 (0.03)	.45	0.96 (0.02)	.15	0.98 (0.03)	.48	0.98 (0.03)	.39
Infant Mortality	1.005 (0.004)	.27			1.005 (0.004)	.28	1.004 (0.004)	.35
Past Agreement	1.15 (0.43)	.71			1.39 (0.57)	.42		
Government Army Size	1.000 (0.000)	.63	1.000 (0.000)	.47	1.000 (0.000)	.45	1.000 (0.000)	.67
Mountains	1.06 (0.16)	.68			1.06 (0.18)	.72	1.09 (0.17)	.56
P5 Contiguity	0.55 (0.32)	.30	0.61 (0.28)	.29	0.47 (0.29)	.21	0.56 (0.30)	.28
Former P5 Colony	1.02 (0.41)	.97			1.12 (0.48)	.80	1.04 (0.43)	.92
Duration of War	0.93 (0.02)	.00	0.94 (0.02)	.00	0.92 (0.03)	.01	0.93 (0.02)	.00
P5 Involvement			0.69 (0.21)	.22				
Shape Parameter P					0.62 (0.06)	.00		
Number of Subjects	92		88		92		92	
Number of Observations	128		123		128		128	
Log Pseudo-Likelihood	−202.68		−188.98		−139.41		−200.99	

Of the enforcement missions included in this study, a handful are cases in which the international community intervened militarily to bring about a cease-fire, one that the mission then stayed on to keep. The missions in Bosnia, Haiti, East Timor, Kosovo, and the Iraq-Kurd case fall in this category. Column 4 of table 5.2 distinguishes these cease-fire-creating missions from other enforcement missions. As explained in chapter 1, I do not directly examine the effects of such missions on bringing about peace in the first place, but these missions might have different effects on maintaining peace than other types of enforcement missions. Indeed, in none of these cases has full-scale war resumed.[5] Accordingly, the hazard ratio for these missions drops to zero. But once these cases are separated out, the other Chapter VII missions have a much smaller, and no longer statistically significant, effect on the duration of peace. When a peacekeeping mission has used force to bring about a cease-fire, it has proven itself to be a credible enforcer of the peace, whereas other enforcement missions, despite their Chapter VII mandates, are much less likely to provide a credible deterrent.

The relative effects of these types of missions should be treated with some caution, given the numbers of cases in each category, but we should certainly not conclude that if no large enforcement mission can be deployed, peacekeeping will be ineffective. Even militarily weak missions with mandates limited by the need to maintain consent have a clear stabilizing effect on peace. Meanwhile the effect of militarily stronger missions with beefier mandates depends on their credibility to use force. As we shall see, this finding supports the conclusions in the following chapter that nonmilitary mechanisms are often as important as the military aspects of peacekeeping. It also has important policy implications, as it runs contrary to the now conventional wisdom that peacekeeping should be made more robust militarily to improve its effectiveness.[6]

Table 5.3 shows a set of similar models, but with consent-based peacekeeping broken down by mission type to evaluate the effects of monitoring missions, interpositional peacekeeping, and multidimensional missions. Here we must be particularly careful in our inferences about the

---

[5] Despite considerable unrest in Haiti, the political instability and gang violence there does not qualify as resumption of war. See data notes.

[6] It is too early to tell whether the increased numbers of enforcement missions since 1999 will change this finding significantly. Note that some Chapter VII missions also have large multidimensional components, blurring the line between mission types. However, these data are coded such that missions are given the highest possible mission type. That is, a multidimensional mission with Chapter VII authorization is coded as an enforcement mission. This means that Chapter VII missions may be given some statistical credit for Chapter VI aspects. This should, if anything, make Chapter VII missions look more effective rather than less, making the finding of no strong difference between consent-based and enforcement missions all the more surprising.

TABLE 5.3

Effects of Peacekeepers: Comparing Monitoring, Interpositional, Multidemensional, and Enforcement Peacekeeping

	Model 1 Cox		Model 2 Cox		Model 3 Weibull	
	HR (HSE)	P > |Z|	HR (HSE)	P > |Z|	HR (HSE)	P > |Z|
Monitoring Peacekeeping	**0.41 (0.17)**	**.03**	**0.38 (0.16)**	**.02**	**0.38 (0.17)**	**.03**
Traditional Peacekeeping	**0.47 (0.20)**	**.07**	**0.58 (0.24)**	**.19**	**0.58 (0.24)**	**.19**
Multidimensional Peacekeeping	**0.14 (0.19)**	**.14**	**0.17 (0.22)**	**.18**	**0.20 (0.27)**	**.24**
Enforcement Peacekeeping	**0.35 (0.20)**	**.07**	**0.35 (0.20)**	**.07**	**0.44 (0.27)**	**.17**
Contraband	2.40 (0.67)	.00	2.97 (0.64)	.00	2.79 (0.84)	.00
Victory	0.13 (0.06)	.00	0.14 (0.06)	.00	0.11 (0.06)	.00
Treaty	0.30 (0.11)	.00	0.40 (0.15)	.01	0.24 (0.10)	.00
Identity War	1.27 (0.38)	.43	1.67 (0.59)	.14	1.41 (0.49)	.32
Deaths	1.17 (0.09)	.04	1.24 (0.08)	.00	1.17 (0.10)	.07
Factions	0.62 (0.18)	.11	0.67 (0.19)	.15	0.54 (0.17)	.06
Democracy	0.98 (0.03)	.48	0.96 (0.02)	.13	0.98 (0.03)	.46
Infant Mortality	1.005 (0.004)	.24			1.005 (0.005)	.25
Past Agreement	1.18 (0.45)	.66			1.41 (0.58)	.40
Government Army Size	1.000 (0.000)	.65	1.000 (0.000)	.46	1.000 (0.001)	.43
Mountains	1.06 (0.16)	.69			1.07 (0.19)	.71
P5 Contiguity	0.54 (0.31)	.28	0.60 (0.28)	.27	0.44 (0.27)	.18
Former P5 Colony	1.02 (0.42)	.97			1.10 (0.48)	.82
Duration of War	0.93 (0.02)	.00	0.94 (0.02)	.00	0.92 (0.03)	.01
P5 Involvement			0.68 (0.20)	.20		
Shape Parameter P					0.62 (0.06)	.00
Number of Subjects	92		88		92	
Number of Observations	128		123		128	
Log Pseudo-Likelihood	−202.03		−188.30		−138.87	

relative effects of different mission types—as the significance levels suggest, there are simply not enough cases in each category to reach strong conclusions (these hazard ratios are jointly significant, however). But the results suggest that multidimensional missions have the largest substantive effects on the duration of peace after civil wars. In this respect, recent trends in peacekeeping have been in the right direction. These missions, which combine military and civilian components of peacekeeping, have become the norm.

There is reason to believe that the results reported in tables 5.1–5.3 underestimate the positive effect of peacekeeping on the durability of peace. They measure the effect of peacekeepers only while they are deployed in the country, not any effect that they might have after they leave. These models use what is known as a *time-varying covariates* measure of peacekeeping. The peacekeeping variable is coded for a particular point in time, so that if a peacekeeping mission deploys and then departs, the measure changes over time. From the point of view of peacekeepers, the best outcome is to be able to depart without peace falling apart as soon as they leave. However, from the point of view of the statistical models (if they had points of view), this is a situation in which the ostensible cause of durable peace—peacekeeping—is removed but peace continues, suggesting that peacekeeping is not the real cause of peace. In the models reported above, such situations therefore count against the statistical finding that peacekeeping works. Peacekeepers are given no statistical credit for establishing peace that held after they went home in places like El Salvador, Mozambique, and Papua New Guinea. In other words, the most successful peacekeeping missions—those that do their jobs, go home, and leave lasting peace in their wake—are treated in the time-varying covariates statistical models as less successful than those in which peace fails soon after peacekeepers depart.[7] Substantively, what we really want to know is how well peacekeepers do at setting up a self-sustaining peace that lasts even after they go home.

There are two possible ways to handle this issue. One is to use a *time-constant* version of the peacekeeping variables. These variables mark whether peacekeepers were ever present in a particular case. The other is to include one variable that marks whether peacekeepers are deployed at a particular point in time, and another that marks peacekeeping missions

---

[7] An example is UNAMIR II, which was deployed in Rwanda until April 16, 1996, but had withdrawn before fighting between the RPF government and the Interhamwe in 1998. Note, however, that the statistical model does penalize the first UNAMIR mission for failure to prevent genocide because while most of the mission quickly withdrew, (*a*) this withdrawal came after the start of the genocide, and (*b*) there was still a small UNAMIR presence in Rwanda.

TABLE 5.4
Effects of Peacekeepers: Less Conservative Estimates

	Time-Constant Peacekeeping						Past and Current Peacekeeping		
	Model 1 Cox		Model 2 Cox		Model 3 Cox			Model 4 Cox	
	HR (RSE)	P > |Z|	HR (RSE)	P > |Z|	HR (RSE)	P > |Z|		HR (RSE)	P > |Z|
All Peacekeeping	0.24 (0.10)	.00					Current Consent	0.32 (0.16)	.02
Consent-Based			0.26 (0.14)	.01			Current Enforce	0.25 (0.15)	.02
Monitoring					0.40 (0.24)	.12	Past Consent	0.13 (0.14)	.06
Interpositional					0.35 (0.22)	.09	Past Enforce	0.000 (0.000)	.00
Multidimensional					0.06 (0.07)	.01			
Enforcement			0.18 (0.12)	.01	0.16 (0.10)	.00			
Contraband	2.35 (0.72)	.01	2.33 (0.71)	.01	2.89 (0.89)	.00		2.22 (0.70)	.01
Victory	0.11 (0.05)	.00	0.12 (0.05)	.00	0.11 (0.05)	.00		0.12 (0.06)	.00
Treaty	0.32 (0.12)	.00	0.33 (0.12)	.00	0.36 (0.14)	.01		0.30 (0.11)	.00
Identity War	1.14 (0.31)	.64	1.10 (0.30)	.73	1.04 (0.30)	.88		1.04 (0.28)	.90
Deaths	1.14 (0.08)	.07	1.14 (0.08)	.08	1.22 (0.10)	.01		1.14 (0.09)	.11
Factions	0.79 (0.23)	.42	0.84 (0.25)	.56	0.72 (0.26)	.37		0.88 (0.28)	.69
Democracy	0.99 (0.03)	.77	0.99 (0.03)	.74	0.99 (0.03)	.84		0.99 (0.03)	.82
Infant Mortality	1.007 (0.005)	.15	1.006 (0.006)	.23	1.007 (0.005)	.23		1.006 (0.005)	.21
Past Agreement	1.26 (0.51)	.57	1.28 (0.52)	.55	1.38 (0.55)	.42		1.25 (0.51)	.59
Government Army Size	1.000 (0.000)	.73	1.000 (0.000)	.68	1.000 (0.000)	.76		1.000 (0.000)	.64
Mountains	1.16 (0.18)	.36	1.14 (0.18)	.42	1.10 (0.20)	.61		1.11 (0.18)	.51
P5 Contiguity	0.41 (0.25)	.15	0.40 (0.26)	.15	0.40 (0.27)	.18		0.40 (0.27)	.17
Former P5 Colony	0.81 (0.33)	.61	0.79 (0.34)	.58	0.82 (0.36)	.64		0.81 (0.35)	.62
Duration of War	0.93 (0.02)	.00	0.93 (0.02)	.00	0.93 (0.02)	.00		0.93 (0.02)	.01
Number of Subjects	92		92		92			92	
Number of Observations	128		128		128			128	
Log Pseudo-Likelihood	−199.82		−199.66		−197.49			−198.69	

that have departed.[8] As we might expect given the bias discussed above, both approaches yield results that show much stronger effects for peacekeeping than in previous tables. Table 5.4 shows the results from these less conservative tests. Using the time-constant peacekeeping variable, we can see that peacekeeping reduces the risk of another war by over 75% (column 1). As before, enforcement and consent-based missions are similarly effective (column 2); and multidimensional missions have the largest substantive effect, cutting the risk of renewed fighting by 94% (column 3). We can have great confidence in these findings, as the levels of statistical significance indicate.

Coding for current and past peacekeeping missions (column 4) shows that having a peacekeeping mission present reduces the estimated risk of another war by about 70%–75%, all else equal, while having had one in the past that has done its job and gone home cuts the hazard of another war by 87%–100%.[9] (Note that the greater effect for past peacekeeping than for current peacekeeping may reflect the fact that peace gets easier to maintain the longer it holds—see below). In short, peacekeepers make an enormous difference to the prospects for peace, not only while they are present, but even after they depart. They are extremely effective at helping belligerents to set up self-sustaining peace.[10]

Figure 5.1 shows graphically the effect of peacekeeping on the risk of renewed warfare. The top portion, part A, shows the more conservative, time-varying effects; part B shows the less conservative but probably more accurate time-constant effects. In both graphs, the line indicating the hazard when no peacekeepers are present is substantially higher than the lines indicating the hazard when either consent-based missions or enforcement missions are present. This demonstrates the effect that peacekeepers have in reducing the recidivism rate. The graphs also indicate that there is little difference between consent-based and enforcement missions—these lines are quite close together. In sum, the risk of war is substantially lower when

[8] Thanks to Giacomo Chiozza for suggesting this method.

[9] There are only four cases in these data in which an enforcement mission departs in such a manner: in Croatia, Haiti, East Timor; and Tajikistan. In none of the periods after these enforcement missions departed did war resume. Hence the hazard ratio of 0. Most of these operations were replaced by Chapter VI missions, the effects of which are captured in the "current peacekeeping" variables.

[10] The models in table 5.4 may be preferable to those in tables 5.1–5.3 for another reason. Duration models assume "proportional hazards," that is, that the effect of each independent variable remains proportional and does not vary over time. Diagnostic tests reveal this assumption to be warranted for the peacekeeping variables in table 5.4, but not in all models in the earlier tables. (In the earlier tables, the effect of peacekeeping appears to increase over time, so our estimates overrate the impact of peacekeeping in the short term, but underrate it in the longer term.) The models in table 5.4 fit more accurately with the way peacekeeping works over time.

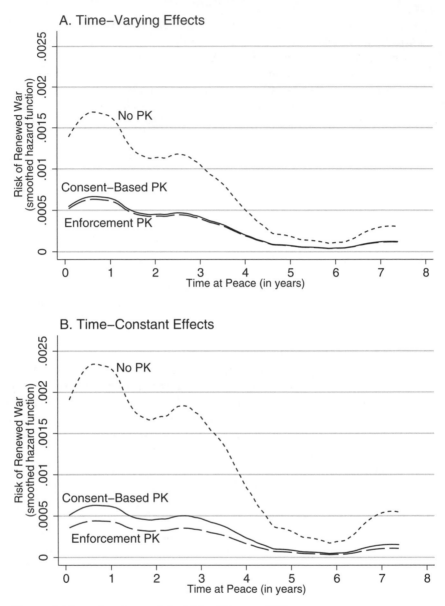

Figure 5.1 Peacekeeping and the Risk of Renewed War

peacekeepers are present, but there is little difference between consent-based and enforcement missions.[11]

One important caveat is worth noting. Simply controlling for other variables that shape the prospects for peace, as I do in tables 5.1–5.4, is not an ideal way to handle the endogeneity of peacekeeping. Two-stage analysis, or instrumental variable analysis, is often used to evaluate the effect of a variable, in this case peacekeepers, that is itself affected by (or endogenous to) other variables in the model. Unfortunately, it is not possible here, for several reasons. Some statistical techniques for dealing with endogeneity in duration models require assumptions about the selection process that cannot be sustained for peacekeeping.[12] More important, two-stage models require at least one variable that is a good predictor of where peacekeepers go that is uncorrelated with whether or not peace lasts. As discussed in chapter 2, most of the variables that shape whether or not peacekeepers are deployed are likely to be directly related to the ease or difficulty of maintaining peace. Variables such as whether the war ended in a clear victory for one side, the number of factions, whether rebels have access to contraband financing, and so forth, are included in this study precisely because they shape the prospects for peace as well as the probability that peacekeepers will deploy. Other variables found to affect where peacekeepers go might, in theory, serve as instruments. Factors that capture the relationship between the war-torn country and the permanent five members of the Security Council (Perm-5) seem likely candidates. Unfortunately, these variables turn out to be rather highly correlated with the durability of peace.[13] These relationships may or may not be causal, but they make these variables unsuitable as instruments for two-stage analysis.

The set of tests reported above controls for variables that affect both peacekeeping and the duration of peace in order to avoid the spurious findings that would result if we looked at the effect of peacekeeping without taking these other variables into account.[14]

---

[11] These graphs plot the hazard functions from the models in tables 5.2, column 1, and 5.4, column 2, respectively. All other variables are held at their mean or modal values. The scale of the y-axis is very small because it represents the probability of war resuming on a given day, assuming it has held to that point.

[12] For example, use of Vreeland's 2002 statistical technique would require the assumption that peacekeepers might equally deploy at any point over the course of the peace spell, an assumption that is empirically unsupportable. See also Vreeland 2003.

[13] In tests of the pre-1989 cases, similar to those reported in appendix B, former colonies of the Perm-5 and civil wars that have attracted great power involvement are associated with a higher risk of renewed warfare, while countries contiguous to former colonies of the Perm-5 are at a lower risk. Results not shown.

[14] Gilligan and Sergenti 2007 use a matching technique to handle the endogeneity issue. Their analysis suggests that, if anything, the technique used here *underestimates* the effect of peacekeeping on the duration of peace after civil war (though it may overestimate the effect

A second possible caveat concerns the "laundry list" nature of the control variables. Including many control variables can lead to problems if there are nonlinearities in the data.[15] There is thus a potential trade-off between including more controls, the better to handle the endogeneity of peacekeeping, and including fewer to minimize problems of nonlinearity. I have chosen to err on the side of the former. However, robustness checks that drop individual variables from the results reported here, while sometimes weakening the apparent effect of peacekeeping (as we would expect from the resulting omitted variable bias) do not show strong evidence of nonlinearity. That is, the peacekeeping results never shift dramatically or flip sign as one would expect if severe nonlinearity problems were driving results.

These caveats notwithstanding, the statistical evidence is overwhelming. In short, any way you slice the data, peacekeeping works. Peace is much more likely to last, and to last longer, when peacekeepers have deployed than when belligerents are left to their own devices. Conservative estimates suggest that peacekeeping reduces the risk of another war by at least 55%–60%, all else equal. Less conservative estimates suggest an even more dramatic effect, a 75%–85% reduction in the hazard of renewed warfare. Moreover, militarily weaker consent-based peacekeeping missions are no less effective than the more "robust" enforcement missions. In short, peacekeeping is an extremely effective policy tool for stabilizing peace in the aftermath of civil war.

Other Determinants of the Duration of Peace

While the other variables in tables 5.1–5.4 are included as control variables in the analysis of peacekeeping, they help answer the more general question of why peace holds in some cases but falters in others. Looking across these tables, it is clear that, as expected, whether a war ends in a clear victory for one side is an extremely good predictor of whether peace will last. Civil wars in which one side wins outright have about an 85%–90% lower risk of resumption than wars that end with only a truce or cease-fire (the omitted comparison category for the victory and treaty variables). But wars that end with a peace treaty are also much more stable than truces or cease-fires—treaties cut the risk of renewed fighting by 60%–75%. Both of these findings are quite robust to model specification and are highly statistically significant.

---

of intervention on creating peace in the first place—a question I do not address). Their results indicate that peacekeeping reduces the hazard of another war by about 80%.

[15] Achen 2005.

Two other strong predictors of the stability of peace are rebel access to contraband financing and the duration of the war. The involvement of rebel groups financed by drugs, diamonds, or other illicit trade increases the risk of another war by 100%–250%; that is, such wars are about two to three-and-a-half times more likely to resume than other wars. Long wars, on the other hand, yield more stable peace. Each additional year a war runs decreases the hazard of resumption by about 6%–8%, all else equal. Both of these finding are robust and strongly significant statistically. While longer wars yield longer peace, the same cannot be said for more deadly wars. Rather, peace is more likely to falter after more costly wars. This finding is relatively robust, but is sometimes only marginally significant.[16]

While rebel access to contraband financing is destabilizing, the support of neighboring countries for rebels has no negative repercussions for peace (table 5.1, column 2). Wars fought along identity lines appear to be in more danger of resumption, though this finding is not robust—both the size and the statistical significance of the hazard ratios for identity wars vary considerably across model specification. Surprisingly, wars that involve many factions are less likely to resume than are simpler wars fought between one rebel group and the government (though this effect is often insignificant). It is possible that wars involving many parties are harder to end, but that peace is more stable once reached.

The findings for democracy and infant mortality (as a proxy for economic conditions and standard of living) are in the expected direction, but never statistically significant. If anything, democracy makes peace more stable, and higher levels of infant mortality undermine peace, but we cannot place much confidence in these results.[17] Similarly, attempts to maintain peace after previous agreements have failed are, if anything, more likely to falter, but this effect also fails tests of statistical significance. In most model specifications, rough territory is detrimental to lasting peace, but this effect is not completely consistent, nor significant. The size of the government's army also has no clearly significant effect on the duration of peace.

Wars fought in or next to the territory of the permanent members of the Security Council (aka, great powers) may be less likely to resume than other wars. And peace appears to be more stable after wars in which the

---

[16] Note that this finding contrasts with interstate wars, in which more deadly conflicts yield more stable peace. Fortna 2004c, chap. 3. The difference may reflect the fact that in civil wars former enemies have to live with each other, so that the greater animosity built up in more deadly wars is destabilizing.

[17] The small size of these effects, with hazard ratios not far from 1, is partly the result of the scale of the measures. Other proxies for economic development (life expectancy, literacy rates, real GDP per capita) yield similar results but have more missing data problems.

great powers have been directly involved on one side or the other.[18] These effects are consistent across models, but fall short of statistical significance.[19] There is no consistent relationship between wars in former colonies of the Perm-5 and the stability of peace.

Note that because many of these variables affect whether or not peacekeepers deploy, models such as these that also include peacekeeping variables may bias the findings. Variables that otherwise make peace less stable but that make peacekeeping more likely may counteract their own effects, making them seem smaller than they really are. Meanwhile, variables that make peacekeeping less likely may appear to be more detrimental (or less helpful) for peace than they really are.[20] These findings should thus be interpreted with this possible bias in mind. It may account for the relatively weak findings for variables such as rough terrain, and perhaps even the counterintuitive result for the number of factions involved in the war.[21]

Nonetheless, these findings suggest that the best predictors of whether or not peace lasts, controlling for whether peacekeepers deploy, are the military and political outcome of the war—with truces much less stable than either clear victories or peace treaties, the length of the war fought, its death toll, and whether or not rebels have access to contraband financing.

Finally, the Weibull model's estimation of a shape parameter, P, provides an indicator of whether peace becomes more or less stable over time, given that it has lasted to date. As we would intuitively expect, but contrary to the expectations of an information-based account of warfare,[22] peace tends to be consolidated over time. (The generally downward trend of the lines

[18] This effect differs from the finding for wars ending before 1989, perhaps due to the bias introduced by including peacekeeping in the model. See below.

[19] A "by the book" statistical approach would be to conclude no effect for variables that do not consistently meet the standard .05 significance level. Because these are control variables, rather than the main variable on which my argument rests, I think it is more informative to discuss the most likely direction of an effect. While we cannot have strong confidence in these effects, neither can we have strong confidence that there is no effect.

[20] This is the reason I use the pre-1989 cases to estimate the difficulty of peace in chapter 2.

[21] Another important caveat pertains to these findings on the control variables. Diagnostic tests show that a number of them violate the proportional hazards assumption. For example, the effect of rough territory appears to diminish over time, while the effect of the previous war's duration increases over time. Testing the nonproportionality of these variables to explore how their effects change over time is an important avenue for future research on the stability of peace, but is unfortunately beyond the scope of this book. For a model of how to proceed with this research, see Box-Steffensmeier, Reiter, and Zorn 2003.

[22] In this perspective, the war itself reveals credible information about capabilities and resolve. As time passes and this information diminishes, renewed war should become more likely. Fearon 1995; Goemans 2000.

in figure 5.1 indicates the same thing.) The longer peace lasts, the more likely it is to continue to last. This may provide a partial explanation for why peacekeepers do not have to stay forever to help ensure lasting peace. They deploy during the most dangerous stage when peace is brand new. If they can help belligerents get over the early, most difficult stages of avoiding another war, peace takes on some momentum and becomes easier to maintain over time.

Figure 5.2 shows graphically the effects of the most important control variables, as well as the effect of peacekeeping missions as these factors vary. For comparison's sake, the first graph is the same as figure 5.1 part B (although the scale of the y-axis is different), showing peacekeeping's effect in a typical case in which all other variables are held at their modal or mean values. Part 2 shows what happens to the risk of war when rebels enjoy contraband financing. Parts 3 and 4 show effects when the war has ended in a victory and a treaty, respectively, rather than a truce. Parts 5 and 6 show effects in short and long wars, with war duration held at its tenth and ninetieth percentile values. Parts 7 and 8 show high- and low-cost wars, with the death toll held at its tenth and ninetieth percentile values. As in the previous figure, the difference between the lines shows the effect of peacekeeping (the risk for cases with no peacekeeping is higher than for consent-based or enforcement missions). Comparison between the graphs shows the effects of the control variables. For example, the risk is much higher when rebels enjoy contraband financing (graph 2). As we can see, long wars, treaties, and especially victories reduce the recidivism rate, while costly wars and contraband financing increase it. Under all of these conditions, peacekeeping reduces the risk of another war.

Peacekeeping and the Duration of Peace

Qualitative Evidence

The statistical tests reported here provide the best evidence that peace-keeping works. The case studies for this project were chosen to evaluate the causal mechanisms of peacekeeping (see the next chapter) not as representative cases suitable for evaluating the general question of whether peacekeeping works. But they nonetheless shed some light on this issue as well.

The remainder of this section discusses the views of the belligerents themselves in the Chittagong Hill Tracts, Mozambique, and Sierra Leone about whether peacekeeping makes a difference. At first glance, these cases provide only modest support for the central quantitative finding of this chapter, that peacekeeping has a strong positive influence on the prospects for peace in the aftermath of civil war. Peacekeeping was successful in Mo-

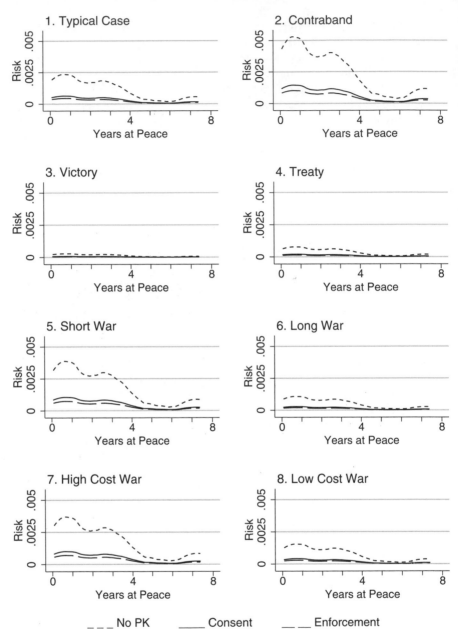

Figure 5.2 Peacekeeping and the Risk of Renewed War under Various Conditions

zambique, and eventually in Sierra Leone after Abuja, while peace faltered quickly in Sierra Leone's first cease-fire (Abidjan) with no peacekeepers deployed. But the presence of peacekeepers did not lead to lasting peace after the Lomé agreement, nor did the government of Bangladesh and the PCJSS require peacekeepers to maintain peace in the CHT. Even for the poster child of a successful mission, ONUMOZ, it is not immediately obvious to what extent peacekeepers were responsible for the transition from war to peace in Mozambique. Many accounts of the Mozambique case argue that there was strong "political will" for peace on both sides.[23] If the parties were committed to peace, perhaps the UN mission was unnecessary and the government and rebels could have avoided further conflict on their own.

However, taking a closer look at the cases and the specific causal mechanisms through which peacekeeping operates helps to clarify its effects. Here, I examine assessments made by the belligerents themselves and others in these war-torn countries of the overall effect of the presence or absence of peacekeepers. The following chapter then turns to more specific causal mechanisms. The presence of peacekeepers by no means guarantees that peace will last, but in many important ways, peacekeeping makes the resumption of war less likely.

Mozambique

This comes through most clearly in the Mozambique case. Everyone I talked to there expressed the view that some sort of international presence was necessary to bring peace to the country. While many also stressed the commitment of both sides to peace, no one thought that Renamo and Frelimo could have achieved it if left to their own devices.[24] Armando Guebuza (then Frelimo party leader, now president of Mozambique) explained:

> The accord worked well because both parties were committed to it, and more important, the people wanted peace. But still, the UN played an important role. People wanted peace 10 years [earlier], but it didn't happen. It takes more than just wanting peace; we also needed the international environment and partners.[25]

The atmosphere of mistrust built up during the fighting was too great for the parties to overcome on their own. As Renamo leader, José de Castro put it:

---

[23] For example, see Synge 1997, p. 6.

[24] As Howard 2008, p. 179, notes, the political will for peace was not necessarily evident at the outset of the peace process.

[25] Interview, Maputo.

After 16 years of war, there was great vengeance and hatred built up—
a bad atmosphere. It was impossible for it to be a national [as opposed
to international] process only.[26]

Teodato Hunguana, a Frelimo member of Parliament who served on the
Supervisory and Monitoring Commission, concurred. Despite seeing the
presence of the UN as an unfortunate infringement on the Mozambican
government's sovereignty, he allowed that

if we were left alone, the government and Renamo, even though the
people were anxious for peace, it would not have been enough.[27]

Some believed, especially in retrospect, that under the circumstances the
UN could have been just as effective with a smaller force or a mission made
up only of military observers rather than troops.[28] But it is easy to say in
hindsight that a mission that went relatively smoothly could have been
done with fewer resources. As the director of defense policy, Brig. Gen.
Paulino Macaringue, explained:

You couldn't have known at the beginning that this was too many UN
troops. There were a large number of combatants, over 100,000
armed people, trained and with guerilla experience. And it doesn't
take many to upset peace.[29]

In short, the peacekept in Mozambique believed that the UN presence was
instrumental in achieving peace.

Bangladesh

Because the war in the Chittagong Hill Tracts has not resumed, it is hard
to make the case that peacekeepers would have improved the chances for
peace. Two points bear remembering, however. First, this case was picked
precisely because it is an instance of peace that has lasted despite the absence of peacekeepers; it is exceptional rather than representative. And second, as explained in chapter 3 in the discussion of the selection process
that shapes where peacekeepers go, the problem of maintaining peace in
Bangladesh was less severe than in the other cases explored here. Nonetheless, there is at least mixed evidence that peacekeepers would have
smoothed the implementation of the peace agreement in the CHT.

Whether those I spoke to in Bangladesh thought peacekeepers would
have made a significant difference depended largely on which side of the

[26] Interview, Maputo.
[27] Interview, Maputo.
[28] Simpson interview, Maputo. See also Jett 1999.
[29] Interview, Maputo.

conflict they were on. The Bangladeshi government had refused international peacekeeping, and accordingly maintained that peacekeepers were unnecessary.[30] Similarly, a high-ranking embassy official from a donor country, assuming that the only threat to peace came from the rebel side, stated,

> There was no big need for peacekeeping in this case—the insurgents, PCJSS, were prepared to assist in fulfilling the accord.[31]

Representatives of the hill people, however, felt quite differently. As the Chakma king, Raja Devashish Roy, put it:

> The biggest problem with the agreement is the absence of neutral arbiters. . . . Neutral peacekeepers would have had a good effect.[32]

An "original" (i.e., not a settler) Bengali on the newly formed CHT Regional Council agreed.

> It would be better for everyone if there were outsiders to help implement the agreement, especially to provide good offices [i.e., to serve as mediators].[33]

The prospects for peace were relatively good in Bangladesh, making the resumption of war unlikely even without peacekeepers, but as we will see in more detail in the following chapter, the quality of the peace in the Hill Tracts leaves something to be desired.

Sierra Leone

In Sierra Leone, the history of attempts to make and maintain peace suggests both the importance and the limits of peacekeeping. The Abidjan agreement in 1996 fell apart within weeks when no peacekeepers were present. The withdrawal of the mercenary firm Executive Outcomes hired by the government gave the RUF a tempting military opportunity, while deep mutual mistrust between President Kabbah and Sankoh derailed the peace process.[34] Whether the presence of a peacekeeping mission might have made a difference is impossible to know for certain, but with no international presence to shift incentives or alleviate mistrust, war quickly resumed. Keen places part of the blame for the breakdown of Abidjan on

---

[30] Anonymous interviews, Dhaka.
[31] Anonymous interview, Dhaka.
[32] Interview, Rangamati.
[33] Alam interview, Rangamati.
[34] Hirsch 2001a, pp. 40, 54; Adebajo 2002, p. 86.

"weak international commitment" to the agreement, citing the underfunded DDR program and the lack of peacekeeping.[35]

The Lomé agreement provides a classic example of the limits of peacekeeping. The UN mission, UNAMSIL, was authorized under Chapter VII of the UN Charter, but in its initial incarnation was in no way prepared to enforce peace against the will of the peacekept. The RUF was recalcitrant from the beginning, and as soon as the ECOMOG force withdrew, attacked UNAMSIL troops, taking hundreds of them hostage. This latest example of the vulnerability of peacekeepers and their impotence in the face of determined aggression had the unanticipated effect of stiffening the backbone of the international community, particularly Great Britain. Sankoh and the RUF expected, understandably, that the international community would turn tail and withdraw, as it had done in Somalia and Rwanda, and as UNAMSIL's predecessor UNOMSIL had done earlier in the year when the RUF overran the capital.[36] This gambit backfired, however, triggering Britain's intervention and an enlarging of UNAMSIL, both in numbers and mandate.

By the time of the Abuja agreements in late 2000 and early 2001, the RUF was much weaker militarily and the international peacekeeping presence, UNAMSIL, backed by the British, was much stronger. The inability of ECOMOG and the early UN missions to stop the fighting makes clear that the arrival of peacekeepers does not by itself ensure peace. But despite peacekeeping's checkered record in Sierra Leone, there was a general consensus among those I interviewed that UNAMSIL was directly responsible for peace. Many people, including government leaders, ex-RUF leaders, UNAMSIL staff, and members of civil society, emphasized that peace would not have been possible without the UN mission, or that war would resume if it left too quickly. For example, the local (Sierra Leonean) commissioner for the demobilization, disarmament, and reintegration program in Magburaka said that the "peace process is possible because of the UN and the British rapid reaction force."[37] A former (or possibly current) RUF leader told me, "The withdrawal of UNAMSIL should not be too quick. [It is] needed to sustain the peace process."[38] Despite being critical of UNAMSIL in many ways, a prominent civil society activist in Freetown cred-

[35] Keen 2005, pp. 203–5.

[36] Sankoh referred to the peacekeepers as "paper tigers." And the West Side Boys maintained that "when we fire two shots, the whole of UNAMSIL will go away." Keen 2005, pp. 240, 263.

[37] Kamara interview, Magburaka.

[38] Interview with Moksin Sessay, Mile 91. It was unclear whether Sessay (no relation to Issa Sesay) had really quit the RUF as he claimed, or whether, as some UNAMSIL members suggested, he had "defected" strategically in order to help the RUF make contact with UNAMSIL after the April–May 2000 crisis.

ited the UN mission with "re-creating the [Sierra Leonean] state. . . . We became one nation because of the UN."[39]

The case studies thus generally support the conclusions of the quantitative section of this chapter. Not only is there overwhelming statistical evidence that peacekeeping contributes to longer-lasting peace, but the belligerents themselves, the peacekept, generally view peacekeeping as an important tool for helping them to maintain peace. Exactly how they thought it made a difference is explored at greater length in the following chapter.

Conclusion

The central question of this chapter, and one of the central questions of this book, is whether peacekeeping works to keep the peace. The answer is a resounding yes. Controlling for other factors that affect both where peacekeepers go and the prospects for peace, the statistical tests show clear evidence of a strong empirical effect. The hazard, or risk, of another war is significantly lower when peacekeepers are present than when belligerents are left on their own in the aftermath of war. Conservative estimates of this effect indicate that peacekeeping reduces the risk of war recurring by over half; less conservative estimates point to an even more dramatic effect, with the risk of another war dropping by 75%–85% or more when peacekeepers are present. These less conservative estimates provide an arguably more accurate notion of the "success" of peacekeeping, as they are based on the ultimate goal of this policy tool. That is, they reflect the ability of peacekeepers to foster self-sustaining peace, which holds even after peacekeepers go home. As noted in chapter 1, the coding decisions for the data used in this study are biased against finding peacekeeping effective. We can therefore be very confident that peacekeeping has at least as much of an effect as is reported here.

Evidence from interviews in the Chittagong Hill Tracts, Mozambique, and Sierra Leone support this general conclusion. It would not be surprising if peacekeepers maintained that they were effective, but by focusing on the views of the peacekept (or not peacekept in the Bangladesh case), this study provides evidence that belligerents themselves see peacekeeping as an effective tool for helping them to stay at peace.

An interesting and important finding from the analysis in this chapter is that Chapter VI consent-based peacekeeping is no less effective than more robust, Chapter VII enforcement missions. Enforcement missions are only effective if they can prove their credibility. This suggests that the recent

[39] Bangura interview, Freetown.

emphasis of the international community and especially the United Nations on beefing up the military aspects of peacekeeping may be overblown. This is not to say that stronger mandates are never important or desirable. Stronger military forces can help protect peacekeepers from awkward and often dangerous situations, but they do not necessarily make peacekeepers better at maintaining peace. As we shall see in the next chapter, the nonmilitary aspects of peacekeeping can be just as important.

In sum, in their central task of keeping peace, peacekeeping missions are extremely effective. Peacekeeping is not a silver bullet—there are cases where peacekeepers deploy yet peace falters. But compared to cases in which belligerents are left to their own devices, the chances that peace will last, and last longer, are significantly and dramatically improved when the international community deploys peacekeepers. Finally, and importantly, the salubrious effects of these missions last even after the peacekeepers have packed up and gone home.

Six

HOW PEACEKEEPING WORKS

CAUSAL MECHANISMS FROM THE
PERSPECTIVE OF THE PEACEKEPT

CHAPTER 4 LAID OUT A THEORY of how peacekeepers might improve the chances for lasting peace. It spelled out a number of causal mechanisms through which the presence of peacekeepers might (1) change the incentives of recent belligerents, making peace more desirable or war more costly; (2) reduce the uncertainty and fear that drive security dilemma spirals; (3) prevent or control accidents or the actions of rogue groups that might otherwise escalate back to war; or (4) prevent political abuse by one side (generally the government) that might cause actors losing the peace to take up arms anew.

Case studies are best suited to evaluating these causal mechanisms empirically. What do the cases of the Chittagong Hill Tracts in Bangladesh, Mozambique, and Sierra Leone tell us about how peacekeeping works? How did the presence or absence of peacekeepers affect whether peace would hold or war would resume? How did the peacekept (or in the Bangladesh case, the nonpeacekept) view the role of peacekeepers?

Changing Incentives

Mozambique

Consider the Mozambique case first. The vaunted "political will" for peace was by no means assured at the outset. Rather it was shaped, largely through economic incentives, by the peacekeeping mission. As a consent-based, Chapter VI mission, the deterrent value of ONUMOZ was necessarily limited. And while "there was some posturing and showing of military muscle" by the peacekeepers, "the UN would not have used force if the war had resumed."[1] Nonetheless, both sides expressed the view that the UN presence helped deter aggression to some extent. Frelimo leader

---

[1] Weimer interview, Maputo. Weimer noted that the Italian peacekeepers in particular capitalized on their macho reputation.

Teodato Hunguana noted that having the UN there was a "dissuading factor," and that this was particularly important because

> there was no military winner in Mozambique, it was a [military] equilibrium. It is very easy in that situation, in which both retain forces and capacity, to try to avail of the minimum opportunity to gain some points that they could not win during the war.

There were therefore strong incentives for aggression. He repeated that the presence of the international community was "a dissuading factor, because we knew that if we derailed the peace process, we would have a stronger force here." Hunguana thus suggested that a trip wire mechanism might have factored into calculations about whether to abide by the cease-fire.[2] But no one else expressed concern that the UN might deploy a larger or more robust force in the face of aggression by one side, and in the early 1990s, it is unlikely that the UN would have responded to a spoiler in this way.

Renamo hoped the international community would come to its defense if it were attacked by Frelimo: "That is why we wanted a big UN force, that is exactly why."[3] But Renamo probably expected international support rather than a strong military defense by UN troops. When asked what the UN would have done if Frelimo had attacked Renamo on a large scale, another Renamo leader, João Almirante, explained that it was hard to assess the counterfactual: "It didn't happen, so it is hard to answer, but there were small attacks in rural areas which were contained. . . . The UN was determinant in calming [things] down." He also noted that the UN presence protected Renamo leaders when they first came in from the bush to the hotel in Maputo that served as Renamo's headquarters during the transition.

> If Renamo came to the hotel, Frelimo could take them and shoot them. We needed an institution based in law, like the UN, for protection.[4]

The peacekeepers' presence may have altered the military costs of aggression slightly, but more important was the way in which international attention affected the belligerents' incentives. Aldo Ajello, the SRSG heading ONUMOZ, had significant leverage over the government of Mozambique because he had the international donors "in his hand."

> Mozambique is completely dependent on donors, so if you had the donors in line, you had Mozambique in line.[5]

---

[2] Interview, Maputo.
[3] De Castro interview, Maputo.
[4] Interview, Maputo.
[5] Interview with anonymous USAID official, Maputo.

Aggression by Frelimo thus risked Mozambique's lifeline of international aid, which was especially crucial during the drought in the early 1990s. According to an international NGO program officer who worked on reintegration programs for ex-combatants, Frelimo's experience in government over the years meant they knew the value of international reputation. "Having the UN there made them sit down and talk."[6] Renamo meanwhile was savoring its first taste of international legitimacy and respect.

> In some amorphous sense, having the eyes of the world, or part of the world, scrutinizing what was going on was a source of comfort for Renamo. . . . For Dhlakama, it meant a great deal to be taken seriously, to go to cocktail parties and be treated with respect. Through the UN he got the government to stop calling Renamo "armed bandits." It felt good to be wooed.[7]

For both sides the costs of being seen by the UN as the aggressor operated not just through the international audience, but the domestic one as well. According to the USAID official:

> You needed Ajello to have peace, to keep the parties in line. He held wide-open press conferences, and would say, "This week Renamo is dragging its feet" on such and such.[8]

This public pressure was used effectively on both parties to get them moving when there were delays in implementation of the peace process. One longtime international NGO worker in Mozambique argued that the "culture of transparency" cultivated by the UN was important for promoting democracy. In a country emerging from "a one-party system with a heavy propaganda machine" the UN provided reliable information. This was "highly appreciated by the local civil society."[9] It also gave the UN leverage to induce compliance from the two parties. For example, concern with being cast as a spoiler restrained Renamo when it learned that Frelimo hard-liners might be preparing to attack Renamo. João Almirante put it this way:

> We concluded [these] were only rumors; otherwise our soldiers would have left the cantonment centers. But because we had trust in the UN . . . that rumor didn't guide them [Renamo soldiers]. Otherwise we would have attacked, and Frelimo would have responded, and the UN would make negative reports on Renamo's side.[10]

[6] McDonald interview, Maputo.
[7] Simpson interview, Maputo.
[8] Anonymous interview, Maputo. See also Howard 2008, p. 203.
[9] Weimer interview, Maputo.
[10] Interview, Maputo.

When I asked him whether worries about such reports were important, Almirante brought up the importance of "a will for peace," but said that

> in some situations, the prospect of the reports was important. The verification commission was also preparing elections, and [there was concern with] influence on public opinion—the need to look good for the electorate.[11]

So the UN served as a neutral body that could either vouch for or undermine the reputation of the parties as they tried to woo the Mozambican public for votes.

The carrot side of the international community's leverage came in part from its provision of humanitarian aid. NGO workers stressed the general economic benefits of the "peace dividend."

> The UN brought with it money and employment. It brought in medical services, road repair, security. The UN affected people's purchasing power in a direct way, and spread it all over the country, not just in Maputo.[12]

> Just the fact that the UN spent so much money here had a huge effect contributing to peace . . . the economic burst of $1.5 billion over a couple years in a country with a GDP of maybe $3 billion a year.. The business community loved having the UN here—both because it brought in money, and because it provided security. It was grim in the countryside when the war ended; no one lived outside of the towns. The UN stationed troops along the road to South Africa, so this economic lifeline was opened. Trade and investment got going, and by 1995–96 this started flowing in.[13]

A former Renamo military leader also noted the connection between humanitarian aid and the "military part of the process":

> The humanitarian problem was in the rural areas, and the cantonment areas were in rural areas. . . . Humanitarian aid [was distributed] to the cantonment areas and to civilians. Transport of demobilized soldiers was also done by humanitarian agencies.[14]

Both Ajello and Boutros-Ghali threatened to withdraw international support if the parties dragged their feet in demobilizing troops.[15]

---

[11] Ibid.
[12] Weimer interview, Maputo.
[13] McDonald interview, Maputo.
[14] Ngonhamo interview, Maputo.
[15] Howard 2008, pp. 198, 200.

For government and rebel leaders and for rank-and-file troops, there were also direct economic benefits to the peacekeepers' presence. Frelimo benefited most from the economic windfall in Maputo, giving them a great stake in peace. As a rather cynical American observer of the peace process put it:

> So did the UN make a difference? Yes, to get lots of people rich, to pay Frelimo $3,000 [in rent] for their houses, to give them a stake in the process.[16]

(This effect brings new meaning to the term "rent-seeking" behavior.)

The co-option of the Renamo leadership was more direct, involving cold hard cash. The UN bought Dhlakama's cooperation with millions of dollars in a trust fund nominally set up to help Renamo transform itself into a political party.[17] According to one report, when a UN official offered Dhlakama a check for the first installment, he examined and returned it, saying he wanted it in cash.[18]

> In Mozambique, as you know, a lot of money was given to Renamo, to Dhlakama in particular. He got it after his last-minute threat to pull out of the elections, five million dollars. It was made sort of above board by setting up a UN trust fund. ... Only someone like Ajello could pull this off. He's a Sicilian after all. He understood what the game was all about.[19]

Another international observer of the peace process put it this way:

> The payments to Dhlakama helped keep him in power. He needed patronage to dole out, otherwise he would have been dead [literally].[20]

In addition to cash for Dhlakama, the trust fund provided Renamo with housing and a headquarters in Maputo at the Hotel Cardoso. The government promised in the General Peace Agreement to provide such resources, but was not terribly forthcoming. UN funds thus helped move things past this sticking point in the early days after the cease-fire.

The UN's role in training the new integrated army also helped reconcile Renamo military leaders to the peace deal by giving them jobs. A high-level Frelimo military official, Director of Defence Policy Brig. Gen. Paulino Macaringue, explained that the army accepted Renamo generals despite their lack of qualifications:

---

[16] Anonymous interview, Maputo.

[17] Reports of the total amount given to Renamo vary. Barnes 1998, p. 160, gives $13.6 million as the figure.

[18] Anonymous interview, Maputo.

[19] Anonymous interview with former UN official, Maputo.

[20] Anonymous interview, Maputo.

The UN helped with the training here. . . . These Renamo "generals" were accepted, and some of them are still there [in the army]. The idea was to forget about this, not worry about prior qualifications, but retrain. . . . [Now] there is no chance of Renamo regrouping for war, because the Renamo generals have been accommodated. They were let into the new army without qualifications. Some were even illiterate, but now some of them are getting an education.[21]

For rank-and-file soldiers, the peace dividend came in the form of financial incentives to disarm and demobilize. "There was a phased payment period for ex-combatants to keep them going, and to keep them peaceful."[22] Under the Reintegration Support Scheme (RSS), demobilizing soldiers received six months salary (half on the day they demobilized), transportation anywhere in Mozambique, and occupational training. The UN augmented this with a further 18 months' salary in two-month installments.

The UN support for demobilization meant that everyone wanted to go home. The allowance for two years was a big deal.[23]

The UN created incentives to disarm, gave money to these guys, ten to twelve million dollars in training projects. The projects were a joke, trying to get battle-hardened soldiers to do tailoring, etc., but the cold hard cash was important, and it was given over time with some follow-up.[24]

The RSS gave rank-and-file soldiers an incentive to demobilize rather than to fight, even if the leaders had ordered them back to battle.

Thanks to a generous redundancy package supplied by the donor community, demobilization was the preferred choice, even among the elite troops that both parties probably intended to keep back as a military contingency.[25]

Much of the unrest during implementation came from soldiers in cantonment areas clamoring to be given their benefits and sent home, rather than any threat to resume the war. The RSS "programmes were instrumental in the social pacification of this group in the critical pre- and post-election period."[26]

[21] Interview, Maputo.

[22] Weimer interview, Maputo.

[23] Macaringue interview, Maputo.

[24] Anonymous interview, USAID, Maputo.

[25] Synge 1997, p. 91. See also Howard 2008, p. 202.

[26] Barnes 1998, p. 173, Barnes notes that once the demobilization benefits, especially the cash payments, became known, 97% of soldiers wanted to be demobilized.

While peace in Mozambique was the result of the political will on both sides, to a large extent this will was bought by the international community. That is not to say that it was insincere, but that ONUMOZ and Ajello provided incentives, both for leaders and for soldiers, to make maintaining peace a distinctly better option for the belligerents than it would have been otherwise.

Bangladesh

In Bangladesh, the incentives for either side to restart the war were relatively weak, at least in the short term. Having recently lost India's support, the PCJSS was constrained militarily. Politically, too, the PCJSS was in a weak position to return to war. According to at least one observer, its constituents were war weary. Should they go back to arms, "They won't have the backing of the local population."[27] The PCJSS calculated it would fare better as a legitimate, peaceful political party. In part, this reflected a strategy espoused by Devashish Roy, the Chakma king: "Things will get better if we convince the government we are not a threat."[28] In part, it reflected the fact that the PCJSS leadership was happy with its newfound power (limited though it was) on the Regional Council. In response to a question about the PCJSS's incentives to go back to war, Abdur Rob Khan, research director of the Bangladesh Institute of International and Strategic Studies, said,

> Now PCJSS is a political force, this is empowering. They have a full-fledged Ministry of CHT with a hill person as minister, this is also empowering.[29]

For Shantu Larma and the PCJSS, to return to war would also require admitting that signing the agreement had been a mistake, validating claims made by the UPDF and thus undermining Larma's credibility. Meanwhile, the government of Bangladesh was happy with the status quo. It had granted limited autonomy, but the agreement required few other concessions, especially in the short term. The government thus had no reason to initiate a full-scale resumption of the war.

The military does, however, have incentives to maintain a certain level of instability, perhaps even low-level fighting. Continued instability helps the military budget and provides an excuse to remain in the CHT, where it has financial interests in logging and development contracts.[30] And while

---

[27] Anonymous interview with a foreign embassy official, Dhaka.

[28] Interview, Rangamati.

[29] Interview, Dhaka.

[30] Anonymous interview, Dhaka. For example, a Danish road-building project was taken over by the military after the kidnapping of Danish aid workers, allowing the military to skim

in the short term there was little reason for the PCJSS to take up arms anew, the longer-term prospects for the hill people's maintaining peace are less propitious. The Shanti Bahini did not fully disarm, and there have been accounts of a resurgence of Priti Kumar's hard-line faction of the PCJSS.[31] The fundamental issues of the conflict, the extent of the CHT's autonomy, and particularly the settler issue, have not been dealt with. Even Bangladeshi military leaders see the government's unwillingness to implement the terms of the agreement as a threat to peace.[32] In the CHT, the level of popular disaffection with the stalled implementation, and with the PCJSS leadership, is rising, while the more hard-line UPDF is gaining political strength. Instability in the region, in northeastern India and particularly across the porous border with Myanmar, means that arms are readily available, while the lack of law and order in the CHT fosters instability.[33] Thus, "Continuing frustration may provide incentives for regrouping and the resumption of violence."[34]

After the turnover in the Bangladeshi government from Hasina and the Awami League to Khaleda Zia and the BNP in 2001, India had less reason to play nice with Bangladesh and refrain from aiding a resurgent rebellion in the CHT. India still has concerns about large numbers of refugees, and about instability aiding rebels in its own northeastern states, but as Amena Mohsin put it, "There is support for coming to the aid of non-Muslims if they are persecuted."[35]

In this atmosphere, there are at least some incentives either for the UPDF to escalate its struggle against Bengali settlers, the military, and the PCJSS leadership that it sees as co-opted by the government, or for the PCJSS to renew its fight as a way of maintaining its mantle as protector of the hill people's interests. Larma has threatened as much on several occasions.[36] A journalist in the CHT explained:

> If the government doesn't implement the accord, the PCJSS will be forced to start the insurgency again—Larma has to satisfy the people of this region.[37]

10%–20% of the road budget off the top (anonymous interview with US diplomat, Dhaka). Others I interviewed made the same general point.

[31] Mohsin 2003, p. 67.

[32] Ibid, p. 59.

[33] Mohsin interview, Dhaka.

[34] Shelley, Khan, and Kabir n.d., p. 16.

[35] Mohsin interview, Dhaka.

[36] For example, at a rally in December 2002 marking the fifth anniversary of the accords. Kumar 2003; see also Mohsin 2003, p. 59. To date, these threats have not carried much weight.

[37] Huq interview, Rangamati.

At the same time, there are hard-liners within the BNP who would like to renounce the agreement, or to push the issue of Bengalis' rights to settle in the CHT. While none of these moves have been taken yet, any of them could lead to a resumption of conflict. The most likely scenario is continued low-level instability in the CHT with no real resolution of the underlying issues—an uneasy peace. But a decision by one side to renew the war is not beyond the realm of possibility.

To what extent has the absence of peacekeeping contributed to this incentive structure? A UPDF leader put it most directly: "There is nobody to put pressure on either side to comply."[38] It is possible that India plays a role in deterring aggression by either side. On the rebels' side, to launch and maintain an effective insurrection without assistance from India would be difficult. On the government side, there seems to be at least tacit understanding that India provided the PCJSS with something of a guarantee when it pressed Larma to settle the conflict. A retired Awami League official involved in the CHT negotiations told me that "India must have given a guarantee to the PCJSS, but only to the PCJSS [i.e., not to the government]."[39] But the secrecy surrounding the existence of this promise and its terms would make it easy for India to disavow it if need be, undermining its credibility.[40]

The counterfactual nature of the speculation notwithstanding, there are reasons to think that peacekeepers might have had a fairly strong influence on both sides' decision making in this case. Both sides desire recognition and respect from the international community, and both are dependent on outsiders for support, material and political.[41] The PCJSS, and the hill people more generally, have struggled to get the outside world to pay attention to their plight, knowing that international pressure is one of the few levers they have with the government.[42] Larma raised the issue of the moral force of the international community. When I asked him why he was willing to trust the government enough to disarm, he answered, "We signed the agreement in the presence of the whole world."[43] Unfortunately for the

[38] Anonymous interview, Dhaka.

[39] Anonymous interview, Bangladesh.

[40] Several of those I interviewed would discuss this guarantee only off the record, even if they were otherwise willing to be quoted, and then only in vague terms.

[41] The desire for the resumption of development aid, and the ability to skim some off the top, was one of the incentives to sign an agreement in the first place. Interview with anonymous US diplomat, Dhaka.

[42] The easy access I was granted to the highest levels of the PCJSS leadership and to royalty in the CHT is testament to their wish to have their story told internationally.

[43] Larma interview, Rangamati. Whether Larma was naive enough to believe this would carry much force on its own or not is unclear. When I pushed, arguing that governments break agreements, as my own had done countless times with Native Americans, and saying I would not have trusted the government had I been in his shoes, he just smiled.

hill people, with no peacekeeping presence, the "whole world" barely knew that the CHT existed, let alone that a peace agreement had been signed, or whether it was being implemented.

The aid dependence of Bangladesh and the CHT gives the international community some leverage even without peacekeepers, and there have been attempts to make aid conditional on implementation of the peace agreement.[44] But the only aid so affected has been that in the CHT itself, not in the rest of the Bangladesh. This has put the hill people in a bind; they want the international community to pressure the government to implement the agreement, but cutting off aid hurts them more than the government. And with little good information coming out of the CHT, it is hard for donors to hold anyone accountable. It is not clear to outsiders, and sometimes even to insiders, who is responsible for the unrest and kidnappings in the CHT. Even basic compliance with the terms of the agreement is unclear. The government claims that is has implemented 98% of the provisions of the treaty, while the PCJSS claims that 98% has been left undone. The number of military camps withdrawn is similarly disputed.[45] Were peacekeepers on the ground monitoring implementation, the international community could more easily exert pressure.

The generally high level of instability and crime in the CHT also sheds light on what occurs when disarmament, demobilization, and reintegration (or lack thereof in this case) happen without outside help. Unlike in Mozambique and Sierra Leone, there have been no payoffs to ex-soldiers returning to civilian life. According to Larma,

> [After disarming,] some Shanti Bahini could not go home because of the presence of settlers (for example, some who live near here in the Rangamati area). They are leading a miserable life. The agreement calls for rehabilitation, socially and economically, but the government hasn't done it. They may turn to crime as a way to live. They are trying to survive, and we are hoping employment projects will come through. The European Commission [Union] has offered some money for this, but they have been discouraged to come for security reasons.[46]

Not only has there been no international help to reintegrate ex-soldiers, a job often taken on as an integral part of a peacekeeping mission, without peacekeepers helping to maintain law and order, it has been too dangerous for other aid groups to help out.

---

[44] For example, a European Union delegation in Dhaka declared in 1999 that it would not give aid for projects in the CHT unless the accord was implemented. SAHRDC 1999.

[45] Shelley, Khan, and Kabir n.d., p. 6.

[46] Larma interview, Rangamati. The issue of unemployed insurgents contributing to law-and-order problems in the CHT was also raised by Prof. Aftab Ahmed. Interview, Dhaka.

As far as material incentives for the leadership, there is an interesting contrast between the Bangladeshi and Mozambican cases. In both instances rebel leaders were successfully bought off with some power (as opposition members of Parliament in Mozambique's case, and as leaders of the Regional Council in the CHT) and the economic perks that go with it. But because this co-option was done by the Bangladeshi government rather than by the international community as in Mozambique, the PCJSS has been open to the charge of selling out to the enemy, an accusation that the UPDF has exploited. So while the incentive structure was affected in similar ways for Renamo and the PCJSS, in Bangladesh the process has led to a strengthening of hard-liners rather than moderates.

This suggests that while co-option arrangements can be worked out between the belligerents themselves, the implications of such strategies for peace are quite different than when peacekeepers are involved.[47] Having outsiders, who are considered relatively neutral and legitimate by both sides, provide the resources for economic incentives is more conducive to peace than if these resources come from the parties themselves.

Sierra Leone

The Sierra Leone case shows most clearly how the use or demonstration of force can alter incentives. With no peacekeepers present, there was nothing to stop either side from resuming the fight after the Abidjan agreement. Whether peacekeepers could have prevented this resumption is an open question, but the RUF's refusal to countenance peacekeepers suggests that they felt they would be constrained.[48]

In its early incarnation after Lomé, UNAMSIL did not present a credible deterrent, certainly not one capable of thwarting the combined forces of the AFRC and the RUF. While technically authorized under Chapter VII, UNAMSIL's original mandate fell "short of authorizing a full-fledged enforcement operation."[49] It arrived in "dribs and drabs" and did not take on a robust force posture initially.[50] Moreover, the creation of a security vacuum during the changeover from ECOMOG to UNAMSIL "provided an opportunity for those wanting to test both the capabilities and resolve of the newcomers."[51] This credibility gap was made worse in UNAMSIL's

---

[47] For more on co-option as a strategy for ending civil war, see Byman 2002.

[48] Because the Abidjan agreement faltered so quickly, information on the decision making of belligerents for this case is sketchy.

[49] Hirsch 2001b, p. 157.

[50] Malan, Rakate, and McIntyre 2002, p. 14; Kai-Kai and Hagoss interviews, Freetown.

[51] Bright 2000, p. 1.

early days by bickering between the Nigerian and Indian contingents.[52] The RUF saw its opportunity and took it.[53]

The failure to keep peace in 2000 is a perfect example of the limits of peacekeeping's deterrent role. But responding both to new thinking within the UN (embodied in the Brahimi Report) about the need to present a credible deterrent to deal more strongly with spoilers, and with events on the ground in Sierra Leone, UNAMSIL shifted its strategy significantly after the May 2000 crisis. The expansion of UNAMSIL's mandate included authorization to "deter and, where necessary, decisively counter the threat of RUF attack by responding robustly to any hostile actions or threat of imminent and direct use of force."[54] This was interpreted to include forward deployment into RUF areas and preemptive action.[55] Even in this later incarnation, UNAMSIL might not have been able to enforce peace were there not other important changes. But the RUF was significantly weakened militarily by the split with the AFRC and internal fracturing, by reduced support from Charles Taylor, and by battles with Guinean forces.[56] The much larger UN mission, now demonstrably willing to fight back, was strong enough to deter a weakened RUF.

The fact that Britain had intervened when UN forces were overrun, and the perception that Britain would do so again, gave UNAMSIL much greater deterrent force.[57] UNAMSIL's presence made the prospect of aggression much more costly both because it proved it would fight if necessary and because it served as a trip wire for the British "over the horizon force." UNAMSIL and Britain have created "peace through superior firepower."[58] As the paramount chief in Magburaka put it,

> The RUF had to stop [fighting and disarm] because they didn't see a way through. They were stopped militarily by a stronger force: the UN presence and the British.[59]

UNAMSIL's influence, however, was not the result of military force alone, nor was it directed only at restraining the RUF. Because the peacekeepers' mandate was to support the elected government of Sierra

[52] Hirsch interview, New York.

[53] The head of the CDF told me it was only a matter of "forbearance" on his part that the CDF did not also attack the UN at this point. Norman interview, Freetown.

[54] UN Document S/2000/832, p. 1.

[55] UN Document S/2001/228, p. 9.

[56] Sadry interview, Freetown.

[57] Kamara and Hagoss interviews, Magburaka and Freetown. A British military official seconded to UNAMSIL told me, "UNAMSIL in its original form was totally ineffective. . . . It was a blessing that they [the RUF] took hostages, because then the British intervened" and put things right. Anonymous interview, Freetown.

[58] Douglas interview, Freetown.

[59] Khiolfa interview, Magburaka.

Leone, and because the RUF had attacked the UN, spoiler management was directed mostly at the RUF. But UNAMSIL also played a role restraining progovernment forces. There were a number of incidents, after the RUF was weakened militarily, in which the British-backed SLA or CDF Kamajor units mobilized to go on the offensive but were restrained by UNAMSIL.[60]

> There was lots of dealing and wheeling to keep things cool. After the RUF got drubbed, the progovernment forces wanted to go into Kambia and started mobilizing for that. The UN had to restrain them.[61]

There was considerable tension, particularly in the period from November 2000 to March 2001, between the Sierra Leone government and the British on one hand, and the UN on the other, about how to deal with the RUF. The former preferred simply to defeat the RUF militarily, while the UN pressed for a strategy of carrots and sticks,[62] and negotiation to bring the RUF into the political process.[63] While this lack of strategic coordination might under other circumstances have been disastrous,[64] in this case it was fortuitous. It led to something of a "good cop/bad cop" dynamic that gave the UN greater leverage with the RUF. RUF leaders were more willing to cooperate with UNAMSIL knowing that the alternative was the more aggressive strategy favored by the government and the British. Opande described playing this card to convince RUF leader Issa Sesay to cooperate with the peace process:

> I said, "Yah, mon, one day you will go to Freetown and you will need me." Now he [Sesay] lives in Freetown [under UNAMSIL military protection]. He asked, "When you disarm me, who will provide for my security?" I said, "I will." He said, "Will you?" I said, "I will provide protection for you." And we did.[65]

Many of the people I interviewed emphasized that it was not just UNAMSIL's military force that mattered, but its willingness to negotiate and to come in with a robust but nonaggressive stance. UNAMSIL's approach

[60] Opande and Sadry interviews, Freetown.

[61] Sadry interview, Freetown.

[62] Ali interview, Freetown. Or, in the Sierra Leonean idiom, a strategy of "salt and pepper—I hold out the salt to you, but I can throw pepper in your eyes." Kamara interview, Magburaka.

[63] Malan, Rakate, and McIntyre 2002, pp. 25, 63; Adebajo and Keen 2007; Ali interview, Freetown.

[64] CDF leader Chief Hinga Norman thought that it was this confusion about the international community's strategy, especially as UNAMSIL was taking over for ECOMOG, that led to the crisis in May 2000. Interview, Freetown.

[65] Opande interview, Freetown.

was "amicable but firm."[66] For many, this distinguished UNAMSIL's approach from that of ECOMOG, and made it more successful.[67]

The nonmilitary resources brought to Sierra Leone by UNAMSIL also gave it some clout. The sheer size of the mission had an impact.[68] The UN provided helicopters and planes to shuttle leaders to the negotiations, rebuilt roads, and brought in food, while UNICEF immunized children. As one UN administrator put it, "Cumulatively [this] gives you gravitas to be a central player."[69] The Security Council also took the mission more seriously because it was so large. Members of the Security Council came to visit in October 2000, signaling to Sierra Leoneans a commitment to making peace work.[70] UNAMSIL built up a great deal of goodwill with the people of Sierra Leone, by providing humanitarian aid, rebuilding schools and mosques, providing medical care, and so forth. Several UNAMSIL officials told me that the people then put pressure on faction leaders to cooperate with the UN.[71] As in Mozambique, there is some evidence that the international presence and the peace dividend it provided influenced electoral politics. Kabbah gained votes from those who noted the international community's support for him and what it would mean for ongoing aid: "If Kabbah go, white man go, UN go, money go."[72]

Cooperating with the UN provided political leaders on both sides with international legitimacy. The government remains quite dependent on international aid, while the RUF (now the RUF-P) craves international respectability.[73] While it is hard to know for sure, the UN's ability to bring resources into Sierra Leone probably helped it to restrain the government from launching an offensive against the RUF. And once militarily weakened and fracturing politically, RUF leaders such as Sesay seem to have decided that working with the UN was their best option.

As in Mozambique, there was a large effort in Sierra Leone to disarm, demobilize, and reintegrate ex-combatants, though here the program was conducted by the government through the National Commission for Demobilization, Disarmament, and Reintegration (NCDDR) with UN assis-

---

[66] Ali interview, Freetown.

[67] Khiolfa interview, Magburaka; Opande, Adetuberu, and Massaquoi interviews, Freetown. See also Keen 2005, pp. 272-73.

[68] Lecoq interview, Freetown.

[69] Hagoss interview, Freetown.

[70] Ibid.

[71] Alam and Sarwardy interviews, Magburaka. In a war in which all sides treated civilians brutally, this may have carried only limited weight. It is true, however, that Sankoh's complete alienation of civil society in 2000 led to his arrest in Freetown. Adetuberu interview, Freetown.

[72] Quoted in ICG 2002, p. 3.

[73] See Bright 2000, p. 2.

tance and oversight rather than run by the UN directly.[74] In a conflict fueled by disenfranchised and unemployed youth becoming soldiers as a way to survive, the DDR process is arguably critical. The reintegration program has been hampered by the low level of economic development and high level of unemployment in Sierra Leone. Even with training, there are few job opportunities for ex-combatants or any one else.[75] Whatever the ultimate success of the "R" part of the program, the DDR opportunities provided to RUF soldiers contributed to the rebels' collapse as a fighting force. During the military offensive against the RUF after the crisis in 2000, UNAMSIL set up DDR centers so that those not willing to die for the RUF had somewhere to go.[76] As in Mozambique, the international community provided direct material incentives to soldiers to disarm. Ex-combatants received a transportation allowance and $150 for going through the DDR process.[77] Rather than "push the rebels against the wall and force them into submission," the UN chose a different approach, "according the RUF equal status amongst the factions, gradually persuading them to disarm, offering DDR incentives."[78]

The Sierra Leone case provides further evidence that co-option of belligerents into a peace process is more effective when the resources come from outside. In the Lomé agreement, an attempt was made to buy off Sankoh and the RUF, in large part by granting Sankoh control of the Commission for the Management of Strategic Resources (including diamonds). The commission was never constituted, however, and Sankoh continued to fund RUF activities through his diamond-mining proceeds.[79]

[74] Humphreys and Weinstein 2007 argue that there is little discernable difference at the micro level between those who went through the DDR process and those who did not in terms of reintegration into Sierra Leonean society. They are agnostic, however, as to whether DDR had a macro-level effect.

[75] This has also hampered other development projects undertaken by peacekeepers. In Mile 91, I was shown several projects started by the Bangladeshi contingent, such as a bakery, a soap factory, and a school, that had faltered because residents could not afford the products and teachers had not been paid.

[76] Over 75,000 combatants were disarmed, and 54,000 had received reintegration benefits by the end of March 2001. Zongwe 2001; UN Document S/2004/536, p. 7. These numbers include members of the SLA, AFRC, RUF, and CDF. While the CDF militias have been formally disbanded, most observers judged they could be remobilized quickly, as their command structures remain intact. Ali interview, Freetown; ICG 2002. By 2003, the ICG was less pessimistic about the prospects for the CDF remobilizing to threaten the peace. ICG 2003, p. 14.

[77] Note, however, that unlike Mozambique, this has not been a staged process that would allow for ongoing oversight of ex-combatants' behavior.

[78] Ali interview, Freetown. DDR incentives had been available after the Lomé agreement as well, but according to Keen 2005, p. 254, much of the RUF rank and file were not told about these benefits by commanders who wanted to keep a loyal fighting force available.

[79] Bright 2000, p. 3.

This gave peacekeepers no leverage over the RUF and gave Sankoh no incentive to cooperate with peacekeepers to maintain his source of funding. In fact, it was the UN's attempt to deploy into diamond-mining regions that sparked the crisis and renewed warfare in 2000.[80]

The presence of diamonds in Sierra Leone meant that peacekeepers had much less economic leverage relative to the belligerents than they did in Mozambique or would have had in the CHT. This limited the ability of peacekeepers to use nonmilitary means to alter incentives. After the Lomé agreement, the UN thus had little ability to prevent a return to war. Its military presence was weak and lacked credibility, while the carrots it could offer were relatively valueless to those with access to contraband financing. A similar dynamic limited peacekeepers' ability to co-opt the belligerents in Angola. A former UN aide who had worked on the negotiations between UNITA and the Angolan government in 1993–94 told me that the Angolans knew about the trust fund that was set up for Renamo in Mozambique, but because UNITA had access to diamonds, it would take much more to buy them off.

> Meanwhile, we in the negotiations in Angola were following these developments in Mozambique. Once a UNITA delegate pulled me aside at a break and let it be known, subtly, that if my boss [the SRSG for Angola, Alioune Blondin], Beye, was thinking along these lines, $5 million would be thrown back at the UN [as not nearly enough]. It would take ten times that, plus. . . . That amount would do for them [in Mozambique] but not for us.[81]

It was only after peacekeepers could provide a reliable military deterrent in Sierra Leone, thanks in large part to the British intervention, as well as changes in UNAMSIL's strength and force posture, that efforts to alter incentives in nonmilitary ways bore fruit. After the RUF was neutralized as a potent military force, the nonmilitary causal mechanisms through which peacekeepers can change the costs and benefits of war kicked in. The UN's ability to provide physical protection to former RUF leaders such as Sesay, legitimacy and economic aid to the politically weak government, and resources for the DDR process to give rank-and-file soldiers an incentive to disarm gave all sides in Sierra Leone greater incentives to maintain peace.

In sum, the cases examined here support most of the hypotheses outlined in chapter 4 about ways in which the presence of peacekeepers can shape the incentives of the peacekept. In relatively rare circumstances, peacekeepers can provide a credible deterrent against those considering renewing the

---

[80] Some argue that Sankoh had little incentive to upset the apple cart after Lomé, and that local commanders were responsible for the breakdown of the agreement. Keen 2005, p. 263.

[81] Anonymous interview with former UN official, Maputo.

war. This requires a large enforcement mission, not merely mandated under Chapter VII of the UN Charter, but a robust force posture and the willingness to prove it will fight if necessary.[82] In Sierra Leone, the credibility of this deterrent also required the backup of the British "over the horizon" force. Even where peacekeepers do not provide a credible deterrent themselves, they can serve as a trip wire leading to enforcement against attackers. In the early part of the 1990s the international community often failed to respond when the wire was tripped (with Rwanda being the most egregious example). This has changed in recent years; Sierra Leone is a prominent example of a new ethos in this regard, though it is too early to tell whether the pendulum will swing back. In any case, it is more likely that a robust response will be forthcoming, if only through embarrassment, if peacekeepers have been overrun than if no peacekeepers were present in the first place, and there is some evidence of a trip-wire deterrent in Mozambique even in the early 1990s.

But many of the ways in which peacekeepers affect incentives are through nonmilitary mechanisms. While there is little evidence from these three cases that peacekeepers prevented surprise attacks, Renamo leaders clearly believed that UN monitoring protected them from Frelimo hostilities in the early days of the Mozambican peace process. Mozambique and Sierra Leone also provide examples of peacekeeping missions using international aid and recognition as levers of influence and of providing massive peace dividends in the form of development aid, public works, and direct payoffs to both leaders and rank-and-file soldiers. The Sierra Leone case suggests, as expected, that the nonmilitary causal mechanisms, particularly the use of economic carrots, depend on the belligerents' access to independent financing such as diamonds. In Bangladesh, in the absence of peacekeeping, the international community has had much less ability to influence either side to maintain its commitments to peace.

Furthermore, in Bangladesh, the fact that financial incentives for the rebels to cooperate came from the government, not from a neutral party such as the UN, has strengthened hard-liners at the expense of moderates. Similarly, in Sierra Leone after the Lomé Accords, the attempt to co-opt rebels with control of the ministry that ran diamond mining was not conducive to peace. The contrasts in the process of co-option in these cases indicate a causal mechanism not anticipated in chapter 4. When peacekeepers control the resources used to buy belligerents into the peace process, co-option is much more effective than when the belligerents themselves use internal resources to try to cement peace.

---

[82] UN missions may be more likely to fit this description than they once were, in the aftermath of the Brahimi Report (UN Document A/55/305-S/2000/809), but this is still not the UN's modus operandi.

Reducing Uncertainty and Fear

Mozambique

Most of the people I talked to in Mozambique noted the importance of the UN peacekeeping presence for building confidence in an atmosphere of deep mistrust. Renamo and Frelimo could have reached a "consensus" on their own, "but to build really trust [*sic*] could be very difficult for Mozambicans alone."[83] Lt. Gen. Ngonhamo argued that Mozambicans needed a neutral representative to serve as "godfather" to the peace:

> Trust has to be constructed. During the negotiations, the signing of the AGP, Ajello's coming, this was the period of construction of that trust. Since the parties gave their trust to the UN in this period, this means that each gives its trust to each other.[84]

There was consensus that the UN's presence made it easier for both sides to trust each other. In a general way, this helped ameliorate the concerns each side had about the other's intentions. More specifically, we can see evidence for the causal mechanisms hypothesized above to disrupt the security dilemma. Both Renamo and government leaders noted the role of the various commissions to verify the disarmament process, though they tended to stress their own discovery of the other side's failure to comply more than the UN role in monitoring compliance. But as Mark Simpson put it, UN observers were necessary because "you needed people to track movements, to do head counts" of demobilizing troops and so on.[85] One example involved the UN's monitoring of elite troops the government "hid" in the Presidential Guard (part of the police force) as a hedge.[86]

> In the military field, Ajello asked the UN police forces to do surprise inspections of the Presidential Guard. The government was furious, but there were suspicions that demobilized soldiers were secretly being transferred to the Presidential Guard and trained [in violation

---

[83] Forquilha interview, Maputo.

[84] Interview, Maputo.

[85] Interview, Maputo.

[86] One government official admitted to this, without putting it in so many words: "One can't give up all your [*sic*] weapons knowing the other side didn't give up all of its. We're still discovering arms and ammunition [in Renamo caches]. I'm not prepared to tell you that the government kept weapons, but it probably found ways, because it is responsible for law and order. The police remained the only legal body with arms, and it was in the hands of the government. The police were stronger than they had been." Anonymous interview, Maputo.

of the accords]. This was discovered by the UN; things were called what they were.[87]

The UN presence was also important to provide security for both sides during the demobilization process, the process during which the security dilemma is most acute. Both Renamo and Frelimo military leaders made this point:

If the UN hadn't been here, we would not have given up our guns. We would not [have given arms] to the enemy without the UN. With the UN we had assurance that the guns will be safe, that they wouldn't go back to Renamo or Frelimo.[88]

The UN helped overcome the stalemate. No one knew what was happening, there were incidents reported initially. . . . No one was taking the initiative [to get the peace process going]. For Renamo the issue was, "If I give up my army, how important will I continue to be?" And the same thing for the government.[89]

Having the UN present and monitoring the process at the cantonment and demobilization centers allowed both sides to overcome this security dilemma. It was also important for local commanders.

You need military observers to sit down with local commanders, to explain the stages of disarmament, etc. the calendar, the various steps, what they have to get their men to do. They can't just tell that to each other. The rebels aren't going to believe what the government tells them. So you need someone neutral for transparency.[90]

Hunguana echoed the importance of having a neutral referee to identify aggression:

If they violate the agreement, it's not enough for us [Frelimo] to say it. You need someone else to say it.[91]

Facilitating communication between Frelimo and Renamo also helped dampen spirals of mistrust:

You have to assume zero trust between the belligerents. So you need someone neutral. You can't expect them to communicate with

---

[87] Weimer interview, Maputo. He also used this example to explain why ONUMOZ could not have been just a unarmed observer mission. "[Ajello] needed military backup for this; he sent the [UN] police to inspect the Presidential Guard."

[88] Ngonhamo interview, Maputo.

[89] Macaringue interview, Maputo.

[90] Simpson interview, Maputo.

[91] Interview, Maputo.

each other, even to have communication systems that are compatible. You need to give a radio to each side, say, "Okay, we talk on this channel. If you have a problem, you call the UN. We'll try to resolve it. If not, we'll send it to the next level up [for deliberations] etc." For guys coming out of the bush, communication is crucial; they need to know what's going on. The trouble starts when they are left in the dark.[92]

Ongoing UN mediation also made it easier for the parties to work out details of the implementation process that were not specified in agreements:

In Rome we signed principles to orient [guide] peace. But in Maputo we had to work out the details. In the cease-fire supervisory commission and the commission for the new army, the UN was the mediator between Renamo and Frelimo in these commissions. The enemies had no trust either in themselves [within each party] or in each other.[93]

Hunguana argued that the UN presence helped keep parties from reopening subjects for negotiation that they'd already agreed to:

There was a structure for supervision of implementation. The government and Renamo were equal partners, with the UN presiding. This reduced Mozambique's sovereignty, but the government had to accept this compromise. This was important because if you don't have this mechanism, there is a risk of rediscussing and quarreling that could derail the process.[94]

The role of the UN in helping the parties move past their mistrust is particularly apparent in the commission for the reintegration and training of the new army. ONUMOZ was not involved in this commission at the beginning. Until it was, the commission was immobilized by the parties' fear of each other's intentions.

It took two to three months for most of the commissions to begin operating, [but] the one for the new army was still not operating. It was not meant to be chaired by the UN, and it got hung up on who would be chair, and how to manage a cochairmanship [between Renamo and Frelimo], how things should be done, the procedures for selecting troops into the new army, etc. So the UN was obliged to take the lead in chairing the sessions, and then the two parties began to feel more confident in each other.

[92] Simpson interview, Maputo.
[93] Ngonhamo interview, Maputo.
[94] Interview, Maputo.

So the two parties gave back [delegated] some of their own power [over things they were supposed to control] to the UN in that area, because of the element of mistrust, especially on implementing military aspects [of the agreement]—what structures, what kind of training for which units, etc. The agreement was too vague on these points. The agreement said the two sides would make these decisions on their own, but they were not able to do so without the UN.

Initially the stress was too high on the military—each side was keeping it own things [equipment, troops], watching to see what the politicians would do on the commission, and time was going by, nothing was happening on reintegration. This worried the UN, and even the leadership of each side. They were not making progress, even when meetings were held, there weren't direct meetings between Frelimo and Renamo. So the UN took the initiative.[95]

As the weaker (and less savvy) party politically, Renamo in particular required an international presence to have confidence in the peace process. It needed the government to signal its commitment to peace by consenting to peacekeepers. Several Frelimo leaders stressed the point that Renamo would not trust the government unless there was an international presence, explaining that that was why they overcame their concerns about Mozambican sovereignty to allow a UN presence:

> The invitation for the UN to come in came from the government— it was the government's understanding that sovereignty would be best protected if peace prevailed. We knew that Renamo would not feel secure if no one was there, no international presence. Renamo didn't want to sit with us with no one present. So the UN was present in the negotiations in Rome, and during implementation.[96]

> It is hard to find a country that will easily invite the UN in . . . but when we negotiated with Renamo, they said they didn't have confidence in us, said they needed someone to oversee it [the process]. We realized the UN could have a positive role.[97]

Renamo was particularly mistrustful because of "the high differences between Renamo and Frelimo: material, financial resources, training."[98]

Ajello saw that the government was the stronger side, so he helped Renamo a little, to establish equilibrium, as a guarantor of the agreement. It was hard for the government to see this as a good-faith

---

[95] Macaringue interview, Maputo.
[96] Guebuza interview, Maputo.
[97] Hunguana interview, Maputo.
[98] Forquilha interview, Maputo.

move [by Ajello], and meanwhile Renamo was suspicious of the UN because the UN is made up of governments. The Mozambican government is a member, so they thought it would support the government. So there was a climate of suspicion. There was always a mix: confidence and suspicion, suspicion and confidence.[99]

Because willingness to accept a peacekeeping mission provided a credible signal of intent, the peacekeepers had an effect even before most of the mission had fully deployed. When I asked about incidents that occurred in the days just after the peace agreement was signed, Renamo leader de Castro noted that the UN presence calmed things down. I observed that ONUMOZ was barely in Mozambique at that point, and he responded:

But Ajello was here, and his political representatives in the provinces were here. That situation, that the SRSG was here and the UN was coming, signified that the war was over.

Bernard Weimer also listed as one of the most important ways the UN made a difference that "it tested the instrument," meaning that the UN presence tested the government's willingness to make peace.[100] This was particularly true since the government believed accepting the UN's infringement on its sovereignty was a major concession.[101] Almirante noted that while Renamo was reassured somewhat by the government's commitment to peace in the "declaration of intentions" during the negotiations, he was emphatic that Renamo would not have agreed to peace if Frelimo had refused a UN force.

Q: If the government had refused the UN force, would you have agreed to peace?
A: *No!* It [peacekeeping] is a warranty.
Q: Of what exactly?
A: Of security, specifically.

Consenting to a peacekeeping mission was thus a crucial way for the parties to signal their intentions.

Mistrust and the possibility of security dilemma spirals were arguably the biggest threat to peace in Mozambique. For the peacekept, the importance of the causal mechanisms that disrupt this causal pathway—monitoring, facilitating communication, and allowing them credibly to signal benign intent—were evident.

[99] Hunguana interview, Maputo.
[100] Interview, Maputo.
[101] Barnes 1998, p. 160. This infringement was still felt keenly a decade later, making the subject sensitive for many of the government officials I interviewed.

Bangladesh

As discussed in chapter 3, the level of mistrust and mutual fear was much lower in Bangladesh than in the other cases examined here. It was a much less intense conflict, with fewer killed and much less abuse of civilians. Some have also argued that the hill people tended, by nature, to be rather trusting of others. The government of Bangladesh was not overly worried that the Shanti Bahini did not disarm fully.

> Disarmament was incomplete. Shanti Bahini tucked some arms away, but the Bangladeshi government and military aren't too worried about it. They accepted the turn-in of weapons as complete, even though everyone knows it wasn't.[102]

And relative to other conflicts, the PCJSS did not worry much (critics would say not enough) about whether the government would hold up its end of the bargain once the Shanti Bahini disarmed.[103] Larma put it simply:

> The government committed to implement the agreement, and we trusted the government. That's why we could deposit our arms before the accord was fully implemented.[104]

Nonetheless, in the aftermath of deadly fighting and decades of perceived injustice, there was some level of mistrust and uncertainty to contend with, both among ordinary people in the CHT (between Bengali settlers and hill people), and at the leadership level between the government and the PCJSS.[105] An international diplomat in Dhaka noted that even years later the "lack of understanding between the two sides is still immense."[106] Leaders of the hill people and government military leaders concurred:

> There is a lot of tension, memories of wrongs committed during the conflict. Many settlers were trained as militia and attacked hill people, and they also suffered atrocities committed by the Shanti Bahini. . . .

[102] Anonymous interview, international diplomat, Dhaka.

[103] Kalparanjan Chakma interview, Dhaka. Shafriqul Islam, a Bengali official in the Ministry of CHT Affairs argued that the Shanti Bahini had gained confidence in the government as "the government has gone softly in pressing its issues." Interview, Dhaka. The PCJSS would doubtless disagree with that characterization, however.

[104] Interview, Rangamati.

[105] Mohsin 2003, p. 59; Kaiser interview, Chittagong.

[106] Anonymous interview, Dhaka. He argued that confidence-building measures were necessary to bridge this gap, but the PCJSS secretary for international relations, Rupayan Dewan, argued that while ambassadors and donors were pushing confidence-building measures, "From the PCJSS view, the settlers are supposed to leave, so it's ridiculous to talk about reconciling with them." Interview, Rangamati.

So peacekeeping would have been helpful to ease these tensions, manage the disputes, etc.[107]

The former military commander in Rangamati district argued that the government's mistrust of the Regional Council under PCJSS leadership was a reason the military was reluctant to withdraw from the CHT as stipulated in the agreement:

> If there is a resurgence of the insurgency, how will you regain these positions? A military tries to gain and *hold* ground. The military feels we gave lives to get these positions. And there was a communication gap between Hasina and the military. The presence of the military (except for border control) in the CHT [is supposed to be] up to the Regional Council, but what if the Regional Council misbehaves?[108]

In other words, the military was reluctant to implement the terms of the agreement because it was uncertain of the PCJSS's intentions, particularly whether it would use limited autonomy to push for secession. Ibrahim later noted that a lack of trust could lead to resumption of the conflict,

> maybe in two to three years. The young people [in the PCJSS] still have their camps, etc. And complete trust isn't there yet.[109]

Without neutral monitors to verify the Shanti Bahini's disarmament and the military withdrawal, the two sides have bickered about basic levels of compliance with the peace agreement.[110] Abdur Rob Khan noted that India's role was "crucial in creating trust" for the parties to reach an agreement, and whatever guarantee India provided the PCJSS presumably alleviated its worst fears.[111] But with no international monitors on the ground providing information about each side, the government's uncertainty about whether the hill people will push for secession is making a military withdrawal unlikely. Meanwhile, the hill people's suspicion that the government will never implement the agreement fully is contributing to disillusionment and frustration that makes maintaining the status quo less palatable.

Mistrust and security dilemma spirals have not (at least not yet) led to the resumption of war in the CHT. But relative to Sierra Leone (as we shall see) and especially to Mozambique, where peacekeepers were present, it is remarkable how little movement there has been in establishing trust

---

[107] Roy interview, Rangamati.

[108] Ibrahim interview, Dhaka.

[109] Ibid.

[110] Shelley, Khan, and Kabir n.d.. There is uncertainty, for example, about whether the settler paramilitaries had disbanded. A. R. Khan interview, Dhaka.

[111] A. R. Khan interview, Dhaka.

between the two sides since the peace agreement. In Bangladesh, the level of mistrust was much lower to begin with, but there has been almost no improvement over time. In contrast, in the cases where peacekeepers monitored compliance and assisted with communication and signaling, the great mistrust at the end of the fighting has been significantly reduced.

Sierra Leone

Because deterrence has been so important in Sierra Leone, the people I interviewed put relatively less stress on reassurances about intentions or confidence-building. But problems of mistrust were clearly an obstacle to peace in Sierra Leone. Keen describes a spiral of mistrust between the RUF and the CDF as largely responsible for the failure of the Abidjan agreement. Progovernment forces' fear of an RUF offensive led to preemptive Kamajor attacks against RUF bases in North Kailahun. The RUF stepped up its own attacks in response. Sankoh explained that Kamajor attacks after Abidjan proved that the government was not ready for peace, "So we prepared for the worst."[112] Without peacekeepers present, "It was hard to rein in the Kamajors or to reassure RUF combatants, in particular, about their future safety."[113]

Similarly, while the RUF's aggressive intentions certainly played a role, even a current government minister attributes the breakdown of peace after the Lomé agreement to security dilemma spirals driven by "profound levels of mistrust."[114] The relatively weak UN peacekeeping presence in this period did little to overcome this problem. RUF combatants were afraid to disarm without the CDF being disarmed as well.

> Sankoh was pointing to renewed kamajor activity and to the still mobilized government troops as reasons for not demobilising. In these circumstances, it was difficult for a weak UNAMSIL with a limited protection mandate to reassure RUF combatants that they would not be mistreated on surrendering their weapons, or, for that matter, to reassure the civil defense forces that they could be safely disbanded.[115]

In contrast, there is evidence that after Abuja, UNAMSIL played a role in reducing uncertainty about intentions and security dilemma dynamics. Sierra Leone's diamond-mining areas are the most likely flashpoints for renewed fighting. Peace faltered in May 2000 when peacekeepers at-

---

[112] Keen 2005, pp. 196-97. More generally, Keen attributes the RUF's incentives to renege on the Abidjan agreement, for both leaders and rank and file, to fear of punishment (arrest or execution) by progovernment forces (pp. 193ff.).

[113] Keen 2005, p. 203.

[114] Bright 2000, pp. 1, 4.

[115] Keen 2005, p. 261.

tempted to deploy to diamond-rich regions, and even in 2002 the security situation was palpably more tense in towns like Koidu where diamonds are plentiful than in towns like Magburaka where they are not. Control of diamonds and other easily exported resources translates directly into military strength, into guns and recruits.[116] It is thus no wonder CDF and RUF forces faced a security dilemma in diamond-rich areas. Neither side could allow the other access to these resources without endangering its own survival. On several occasions (e.g. May 2001, near Koidu in Kono) UNAMSIL was able to step in to stop the fighting, disarm both sides, and to station forces as a buffer in these areas.[117]

The UN played a similar role in reducing the vulnerability inherent in the disarmament process. For example, to allay the CDF's fears that they would be vulnerable to attack if they disarmed in Bo before nearby RUF-controlled areas were disarmed, UNAMSIL deployed in the no-man's land between the factions.[118] In contrast to the process after Lomé, in which "weaknesses [in peacekeeping and DDR] exacerbated the anxieties of combatants about demobilization,"[119] Keen credits the beefed-up mission with being able to reassure RUF combatants, who came to see UNAMSIL "as a source of security rather than a threat."[120] By interposing themselves between opposing forces in strategically important territory, or during periods of high vulnerability caused by disarmament, peacekeepers were able to alleviate each side's quite reasonable concerns about the other.

UN monitoring was also crucial to alleviating mistrust. UNAMSIL pushed to have the RUF and AFRC represented on the NCDDR, and the UN monitored the process and provided security at DDR sites throughout the country. Even seriously weakened as it was, the RUF would not have handed over any of its guns voluntarily without this international oversight.[121]

The local commissioner for DDR in Magburaka attributed the turning point in the peace process in May 2001 in part to the UN's demonstration of force, but also to the reassurances UNAMSIL gave RUF combatants about disarmament. He described UNAMSIL's most important activity as

encouraging ex-combatants to disarm—explaining the process to them, being friendly to the RUF. . . . Combatants were given incentives [to disarm], but they were afraid. When they saw that the

[116] Bangura 2002; Hirsch 2001b, p. 151; Lord 2000, p. 3.
[117] Malan, Rakate, and McIntyre 2002, p. 38; Opande interview, Freetown.
[118] Malan, Rakate, and McIntyre 2002, pp. 47-48.
[119] Adebajo and Keen 2007, p. 259.
[120] Keen 2005, p. 272.
[121] Malloy and Massaquoi interviews, Freetown.

peacekeepers had good intentions and wouldn't attack them, they gained confidence.[122]

Interestingly, having unarmed UN monitors along with armed peacekeepers helped in this process. The chief of staff of UNAMSIL's military observers unit noted that

> some combatants came to us [and disarmed] because we were unarmed and neutral. They were scared of anyone who had military force. So sometimes you have credibility and access if you are unarmed that you wouldn't have if armed, so long as you have some sort of umbrella of protection.[123]

The head of the NCDDR agreed that UNAMSIL's presence alleviated mistrust both in general and particularly in the disarmament process.

> [During the DDR process] they provided umbrella security. Also, DDR is a military operation, so you need military [UN soldiers, as opposed to civilians] to participate, to identify weapons, etc.[124]

As a UN official involved in the DDR process put it,

> It was important to have UNAMSIL as a neutral party for the DDR process. It doesn't often work when just the NCDDR says how it's going to work—until the UN says it, people don't believe it.[125]

The UN presence also eased communication and provided a signaling device. UNAMSIL was reportedly crucial in overcoming mistrust in negotiations between the RUF and progovernment forces in Sierra Leone, using its "good cop" image to facilitate talks. It helped reestablish contacts after the 2000 crisis, providing "a neutral go-between."[126]

> Peacekeepers create an atmosphere for negotiations. [Whether or not to make concessions] becomes a point of pride—it's a human trait. So you need a mechanism that allows negotiations without losing dignity and pride. The UN is that mechanism.[127]

As both RUF and government officials explained, UNAMSIL also helped with ongoing negotiations after Abuja:

> One of the other key issues [roles of the UN] was to speed up the tripartite meetings. If there are any problems in those meetings, you can iron it out with the UN there.[128]

---

[122] Kamara interview, Magburaka.
[123] Douglas interview, Freetown.
[124] Kai-Kai interview, Freetown.
[125] Malloy interview, Freetown.
[126] Adetuberu interview, Freetown.
[127] Malloy interview, Freetown.
[128] Massaquoi interview, Freetown.

The presence of the UN was importance for confidence—they could talk to both sides. They stayed as neutral as possible, even though they were really here to protect the government in place.[129]

The UN held monthly meetings providing

an opportunity for expression and exchange of ideas about the process. They focused on the disarmament process, but were also a forum for other issues—not just technical problems but political problems. The UN played an important broker role, and it gained credibility over time.[130]

That agreeing to peacekeeping provides a credible signal of intentions can be seen in the breach in the Sierra Leone case. In the Abidjan accords, both sides agreed to a Neutral Monitoring Group, but Sankoh then balked, refusing to allow its deployment. This contributed to the mutual mistrust that helped bring down that agreement.[131] After Lomé, the RUF agreed to UNAMSIL, but refused to allow it into areas under its control, particularly those containing diamond mines. In both cases, this sent an unmistakable signal of malign intent and contributed to the RUF's reputation as a group that signs agreements only for tactical purposes rather than through any commitment to peace.[132]

In both Mozambique and Sierra Leone, then, peacekeepers were able to prevent mistrust from driving spiraling fears over security by monitoring disarmament and facilitating communication, and in the Sierra Leone case by physically interposing itself in strategic locations. These cases also illustrate how agreeing (or not) to peacekeepers credibly signals intentions. Where peacekeepers were not present, after the Abidjan accord in Sierra Leone and in the CHT, mistrust has hampered efforts to maintain peace. In other words, the cases provide evidence for the causal mechanisms for reducing uncertainty outlined in chapter 4.

Preventing and Controlling
Accidents and Involuntary Defection

Mozambique

While war is unlikely to resume purely by accident, in the tense atmosphere immediately after a cease-fire, accidents can easily escalate. Peacekeeping can make this less likely. Interviews with the peacekept in Mozambique

---

[129] Kai-Kai interview, Freetown.
[130] Lecoq interview, Freetown.
[131] Hirsch 2001a, p. 54; Keen 2005, p. 195.
[132] ICG 2001.

indicate that the causal mechanisms on accident prevention and control discussed in chapter 4 were indeed at play. Both sides in the Mozambique conflict told me that ongoing communication and mediation by peacekeepers helped prevent accidents from spiraling out of control. For example, Frelimo leader Hunguana argued that, without an international presence,

> we wouldn't have had confidence in each other. The minimum difficulty or quarrel would have been enough to grow to a big difficulty. It was important to have someone to mediate within the process of implementation.[133]

Renamo leaders agreed. José de Castro responded to a question about whether the UN was really necessary for peace by saying:

> I don't agree that the UN wasn't necessary. For example, in those attacks four days after the AGP, Ajello had to mediate. This whole mechanism was necessary. If the UN hadn't been here those attacks would have flared.[134]

In response to a follow-up question about ONUMOZ helping to calm things down and "contain" incidents and "small attacks [by Frelimo] in rural areas," Almirante pointed to on-the-spot verification and reporting by peacekeepers.

> **Q:** How did the UN calm things down?
> **A:** Reports in the place [on-site reporting]—ONUMOZ took a report, found the cause of the small conflict, took this to the commission for verification, [consisting of] Renamo and Frelimo and UN representatives. That report from the field was discussed, and the commission would go to verify it. For example [some problems were caused by] missing food, [lack of] security, trust, because in that period there was much hate and [desire for] revenge.
> **Q:** Could the verification commission have done that on its own, without the UN?
> **A:** No, it needed a neutral party to create stability between the belligerents.[135]

Frelimo leaders also maintained that the UN presence helped it control hard-liners within the party who might otherwise have taken the country back to war. There were those within Frelimo who believed that Renamo's acceptance of the peace deal and disarmament signaled its weakness and

---

[133] Interview, Maputo.
[134] Interview, Maputo.
[135] Interview, Maputo.

that Frelimo should thus press for a military victory. ONUMOZ helped
deter aggression by hard-liners within the military:

> On both sides, you could have [aggressive] intentions, not necessarily
> the government, but the army—[the government doesn't exercise]
> control to the last general, there are temptations. Having an inter-
> national presence with expertise to oversee what was going on was
> important for the government vis-à-vis our own military. This is
> not to say that we had an undisciplined army, but ... If we had a
> coup d'état, with the UN here, the coup leaders would face not just
> Renamo and the government and part of the army, but also the inter-
> national community.[136]

There is also some evidence that ONUMOZ provided a mechanism for
responding to violations that offered an alternative to escalation. In response to a question about whether Renamo thought the UN presence
restrained Frelimo, de Castro referred to the system for responding to
perceived violations:

> Yes, it restrained Frelimo. For example, if Renamo had supporters in
> a rural area and they created a disturbance, Frelimo could make a
> report to Ajello. He was the mediator between Dhlakama and [Presi-
> dent Joaquim] Chissano. He would talk to Dhlakama, Dhlakama
> would give a comment [an order] to stop the problem. And same the
> other way, if Frelimo caused problems.[137]

In Mozambique, the UN also helped provide law and order to prevent
general instability.

> Once the commissions got going, there was a phase in this country
> when the government formally disbanded the armed forces, and Re-
> namo did the same. But Renamo didn't have responsibilities for secu-
> rity, [so it was a problem that the government disbanded]. There was
> nothing to replace this immediately—there was a power vacuum that
> could have been very dangerous. In a country that had been at war,
> there was nothing to rely on. For the population, who is taking care
> of security?[138]

But providing law and order was important less to prevent incidents among
an embittered population that might spiral out of control than to prevent
abuse of police powers by Frelimo. That is, in Mozambique this role fell

[136] Hunguana interview, Maputo.
[137] Interview, Maputo.
[138] Macaringue interview, Maputo.

more under the fourth category of causal mechanisms (discussed below) than under the heading of accident control. Rather, peacekeepers prevented accidental or involuntary escalation by facilitating communication, by monitoring and reporting on the spot, and by deterring potential action by hard-liners within the military.

Bangladesh

In the Chittagong Hill Tracts, there has been little concern with the possibility of war resuming through purely accidental escalation, but some worry about hard-liners or spoilers taking the region back to war even if mainstream leaders on both sides are content with peace. Despite a good deal of frustration with the postaccord situation in the CHT and basic incompatibilities in their views of the settlement, both the PCJSS leadership and the government of Bangladesh seem relatively content with the status quo. "The best possible outcome for them is to just muddle through with peace," commented one US diplomat.[139] But there are extremists on both sides who do not feel the same way. Not only does their disgruntlement create pressure on both sides to take a harder line, it also raises the possibility of rogue elements restarting the war.

On the government side, the agreement has been a point of contention between the Awami League and the BNP. And even within the BNP there are divisions between soft-liners and hard-liners. Prime Minister Zia has said she will not renounce the agreement, but many within her own party oppose it on the grounds that it helps India, and opens the door to greater autonomy for the CHT. The CHT is generally a low-salience issue for most Bangladeshis, but there has been pressure on Zia from within her own party to reevaluate some of its provisions, and there is little incentive to speed up implementation. Several interviewees also expressed concern about a government policy of "Islamicization" in the CHT that would prove destabilizing.[140]

Within the military, there are hard-liners who have resisted withdrawal from the CHT, and as noted above, there are financial incentives for the military to stay engaged in the region. One observer described civilian control over the military as strong enough that it is unlikely elements in the military would restart the war, but there have been allegations that the military gives at least tacit support to the UPDF, as a certain level of instability is in both groups' interest.[141]

---

[139] Anonymous interview, Dhaka.
[140] A. R. Khan interview, Dhaka; Larma interview, Rangamati.
[141] Anonymous interview, Dhaka.

On the other side of the conflict, the largest threat to the peace clearly comes from hard-liners: "The UPDF was formed after the agreement for the express purpose of opposing it. . . . Their raison d'etre is to oppose the agreement."[142] And according to observers of the peace process, the UPDF is gaining political strength as the hill people grow more frustrated with the government's unwillingness to implement the agreement.[143] This is reportedly creating divisions within the PCJSS, and there are reports of a resurgence of the hard-line faction of the organization led by Priti Kumar.

Assessments of whether the UPDF will or can start a full-scale war differ.[144] And we can not know whether the presence of peacekeepers in this conflict would be able to deter rogue elements from either side from destabilizing the CHT. It does seem likely, however, that the international recognition (and aid) that accompanies peacekeeping missions would have strengthened the position of moderates, particularly within the PCJSS. Having monitors present to keep tabs on the military and on the UPDF would, at the very least, improve information about collusion, and the possibility of preparations for a resumed insurgency.

Furthermore, the rather precarious state of law and order in the CHT has created an environment conducive to extremists, and has provided the military with an excuse to stay deployed in the region, rather than withdraw in accordance with the peace agreement. Kidnapping is a frequent occurrence in the CHT, and drugs and arms trafficking are on the rise. The line between criminal activity and politically motivated violence is often blurry.[145] Concerns about politically motivated violence against Bengali settlers were the reason a military withdrawal was delayed. As former Minister of the CHT, Kalparanjan Chakma explained,

> after the agreement, withdrawal of the military was up to me as CHT minister. I thought it best to move slowly, phase-wise, to see if there were disturbances as the military started to withdraw. Bengali settlers would be vulnerable and there was the danger of communal disturbances from either side, a hue and cry.[146]

Had peacekeepers been present, there would have been someone other than the Bangladeshi army to help protect civilians in the CHT.

While neither accidents nor rogue action by spoilers have taken the CHT back to war, there is at least some evidence that the absence of peacekeepers has made the chances for such an outcome more likely.

---

[142] Anonymous interview with international embassy official, Dhaka.

[143] Sen interview, Dhaka.

[144] For example, Sen was concerned about this, while Shafriqul Islam and Kaiser saw little threat. Interviews, Dhaka and Chittagong.

[145] Mohsin 2003, pp. 67-68.

[146] Interview, Dhaka.

Sierra Leone

There is also evidence that the UN's presence in Sierra Leone helped prevent smaller incidents and accidents from escalating out of control.[147] NCDDR commissioner Kai-Kai noted that it was crucial to have neutral forces present during the DDR process.

> People from the bush turn back to their old behavior very quickly. There was unrest, riots, etc. [in the DDR camps] and it was good to have neutral forces to quell them. Observers also helped to identify problems.[148]

For government officials to have reacted to these incidents would have provoked greater unrest, but UNAMSIL was seen as sufficiently neutral to calm things down. A former RUF leader made a similar point:

> There were hiccups in the disarmament process. There were clashes between the RUF and the CDF, and the UN helped iron it out.[149]

Maintaining order in the diamond-mining areas has been particularly important, as violent incidents there are most likely to spark larger conflict.[150] Force Commander Opande provided a pertinent example.

> When the Kamajors came in from Guinea, they were advised wrongly that they could come in and take Kono easily. They came in and there was a fight. I decided to go in between and stop it because it wouldn't be easy for [progovernment forces], and this fight would have scuttled the whole [peace] process. Either we had to do what was expected of us or the whole thing would crumble. The only way to save the situation was to get in between. . . . We had to stave off this tension. UNAMSIL took control so that no one else can—we will have it, so don't bother fighting for it.[151]

There was particular concern about the possibility of incidents among organized youth groups, including groups of ex-combatants, with easy access to arms setting off wider fighting in the strategic diamond areas. The commander of the Pakistani battalion stationed in Kono gave examples of times the UN had to stop clashes between organized groups before they got out of hand.[152] And members of these groups shared these concerns themselves, stressing the need for the UN to stay in Sierra Leone because

[147] Ijawazan interview, Koidu.
[148] Interview, Freetown.
[149] Massaquoi interview, Freetown.
[150] Malloy interview, Freetown; Hasan and Kono Youth League interviews, Koidu.
[151] Interview, Freetown.
[152] Hasan interview, Koidu.

of tensions and the potential for clashes between groups. Members of the Kono Youth League, for example, described incidents of fighting in the area that the UN had stepped in to stop.[153] As noted above, there was a much more palpable sense that violence could easily break out in Koidu, a diamond-mining town, than in other towns I visited in Sierra Leone.[154]

Peacekeepers in the field in Sierra Leone certainly felt that accident control was a central part of their contribution to peace. In a follow-up question to a discussion about the UN's role in facilitating negotiations, I asked why a military presence was necessary as part of the peacekeeping mission. Brig. Gen. Ijawazan answered,

> You need a large military presence for security for ordinary people. It was not a conventional war. It was hard to identify the enemy or the target, so everyone was a target. If there was no sizable contingent [of peacekeepers] to ensure security and deter troublemakers . . . small incidents would escalate.[155]

He also cited the problem of involuntary defection.

> Rebels lower down [as opposed to leaders] took the opportunity, even if the leaders agree to peace. You need to create a sort of barrier, need deterrence, between the two [sides].[156]

He attributed command and control problems to RUF recruiting methods, often forcing soldiers to kill members of their own families, "so their fighters were half-mad, violent, and it was very hard to control."[157]

Dynamics between hard-liners and moderates were partly responsible for the failure of early efforts at peace in Sierra Leone. The government's attempt to consolidate peace with a breakaway faction of the RUF after Abidjan is cited as one of the reasons for RUF participation in the May 1997 coup.[158] Whether peacekeepers would have had better luck is an open question, but UN peacekeepers after Abuja were able, for example, to support the leadership of Issa Sesay, generally considered a relative moderate.[159]

---

[153] Group interview, Koidu.

[154] In Koidu, I was accompanied by armed UN guards who kept their guns at the ready, and the assessment of people there about the fragility of peace was markedly more pessimistic than elsewhere.

[155] Interview, Koidu.

[156] Ibid.

[157] Ibid. The prevalence of drug use among combatants presumably also worsened leaders' ability to control their forces once peace was agreed to.

[158] Keen 2005, p. 195.

[159] Adebajo and Keen 2007, p. 267. This effort was undermined somewhat by Sesay's indictment by the Special Court. By this time, however, the RUF presented little military threat. Keen 2005, p. 274.

Across the three cases, then, we see evidence from the peacekept that the presence of peacekeepers can make involuntary defection or accidental escalation less likely to take a country back to war. By shifting power toward moderates, facilitating communication, providing law and order, and even taking control of sensitive territory (such as diamond-rich areas), peacekeepers make accidents or rogue action less likely to occur in the first place, and less likely to spark renewed warfare when they do occur.

Preventing Political Abuse

Bangladesh

There is a stark contrast between the CHT and the other two cases on the issue of political abuse by one side (generally the government in power). In Bangladesh, there was no international pressure on the government to live up to the terms of the peace agreement. Many of the ongoing tensions in the region reflect the state's use and abuse of power. One of the largest unresolved issues in the CHT is the settlement of competing claims to land between hill people and settlers. Like several other key issues, this was glossed over in the peace accord.[160] Devashish Roy explained that these disputes tend to get settled in the Bengalis' favor because of the Bangladeshi military's political influence.

> The presence of Bengali settlers means there are tensions and land disputes between hill people and settlers, and the military gets involved. . . . The army folks here are senior in rank to the civilian authorities, so they wield a lot of political influence when disputes come up.[161]

More generally, the hill people do not trust the institutions of state power to treat them equally. The agreement calls for a local police force, but this has not been set up yet, and the existing police force is made up of Bengalis whose sentiments favor the settlers. And, of course, the military is considered highly biased. Roy argued that international peacekeepers would have helped to keep the military in line and protect the interests of indigenous people:

> After such a long conflict, with ethnic and religious, especially ethnic, overtones, you can't expect the military to be neutral.[162]

---

[160] Ataur Rahman Khan Kaiser described this as one of the biggest sticking points in the negotiations. Interview, Chittagong.

[161] Interview, Rangamati.

[162] Ibid.

With no outsiders pressuring the government to resolve these issues or to implement the terms of the agreement, there is a risk that the insurgency will resume. This view was shared by outside observers, hill people, and at least some Bengalis:

> The government could go a long way by implementing just a little more than they have so far—close a few more camps, resettle some Bengali plains folks. Many of the settlers would like to go back.[163]

> The UPDF is getting more chances. If the agreement is not implemented, they will get their chance politically.[164]

The hill people's feelings of vulnerability at the hands of the state are strengthening the UPDF. This has at least the potential either to enable the UPDF to raise their level of resistance from low-level violence to full-scale rebellion, or to push the PCJSS to return to war in order to maintain its position as the defender of hill people's rights. While the threat of resumed warfare in the CHT remains relatively low, this potential remains the greatest danger.

It is, of course, a counterfactual assessment that the presence of peacekeepers would have made a difference in this regard. But as discussed above, there are good reasons to think that had peacekeepers been deployed to the CHT, there would have been considerable pressure on the government to comply with the political terms of the agreement. This, of course, is one of the reasons the PCJSS wanted peacekeepers and the government resisted them.

The peacekeeping mission in El Salvador, where land reform was a similarly difficult issue, provides a useful comparison. In that case, the government dragged its feet on implementing a land transfer program agreed to in the peace deal, and disputes between "landowners," generally supportive of the government, and "landholders," who occupied land during the war and were generally supportive of the FMLN rebels, threatened the ceasefire. Mediation and "active verification" by UN peacekeepers of the land reform program put pressure on the government to comply and "succeeded in defusing potentially serious [land] disputes before they became violent."[165] A peacekeeping mission like ONUSAL in El Salvador would likely have made a big difference in this regard in the CHT.

Moreover, Bangladesh's dependence on international development aid would give a peacekeeping mission significant leverage with the government, and had peacekeepers deployed to the CHT they would have had a

---

[163] Anonymous interview with international embassy official, Dhaka.
[164] P. B. Chakma interview, Dhaka. Alam made the same point. Interview, Rangamati.
[165] Howard 2008, pp. 118-21.

large stake in full implementation of the peace agreement, including with-drawal of the army. Moreover, if the peacekeeping mission followed the typical model for operations in this period, it would likely have included police monitoring and human rights monitoring that would have gone a long way to alleviate concerns about political abuse.

Beyond this counterfactual assessment, however, the role of peacekeepers in preventing political abuse comes through most clearly in a comparison of the CHT case with how peacekeepers affected this issue in Mozambique and Sierra Leone.

Mozambique

The UN's presence was clearly an important factor limiting the ability of the Mozambican government to abuse state power to the detriment of Renamo. As Renamo did not trust the national police, there was significant concern about the provision of security.

> The UN presence was important for law and order—[security] was a joke in this country. And Dhlakama didn't want the national police in his areas, so the UN did it.[166]

Not surprisingly, the extent of the UN's role in policing the country was an issue in the negotiations. The government, citing sovereignty concerns, pushed for a minimal UN role, while Renamo, fearing abuse at the hands of government-controlled police forces, pushed for a larger civilian police (CIVPOL) component.[167]

Concerns about abuse of political power during the elections were also an issue for Renamo. In addition to ONUMOZ observers monitoring the electoral process, the UN trained 8,000 Mozambicans who were deployed throughout the country to guard against foul play. A number of interviewees noted that the UN's oversight of elections helped prevent fraud.[168]

> Electoral observation, running the elections, this was an important confidence-builder.[169]

> Another institution for peace was the STAE [Technical Secretariat for Electoral Administration], which was made up of 25% ONUMOZ, 50% Frelimo, 25% Renamo.[170]

---

[166] Interview with anonymous USAID official, Maputo.

[167] Howard 2008, p. 206; Guebuza interview, Maputo.

[168] Less was made of this than one might have expected. It tended to come up in passing in interviews, perhaps because the government had no incentive to bring attention to the issue (as it was the party most capable of engaging in fraud), while Renamo continued to have a political stake in claiming that fraud did occur.

[169] Weimer interview, Maputo.

[170] De Castro interview, Maputo.

One of the reasons Renamo wanted a large UN peacekeeping mission was to help it keep tabs on Frelimo in the run-up to elections:

> It's a big country—for Renamo it was impossible to have a representative in each province, especially on the STAE.[171]

Some Renamo officials did not believe the UN had successfully ensured fair elections, and that fraud explained their loss at the polls.

> If votes hadn't been stolen, Renamo would have won, but boxes disappeared. Some were buried, some were dumped in the ocean.[172]

More generally, however, Renamo gave the UN credit, at least where it had a large presence, for preventing abuse of power by the state during the transition to peace.

> These things happened, the government abused its power, but not in the south, mostly in the center and the north—Renamo members were imprisoned, tortured by the police. The reason it was worse in the center and the north was that in the south there was a massive UN force, embassies, and NGOs, so you only had abuse of power in small dimensions, but in the center and north it was much, much worse, and these were the areas where Renamo was strong. Frelimo tried to intimidate voters in Renamo strongholds.[173]

Almirante complained that the UN did not investigate Renamo complaints aggressively enough, particularly Frelimo's use of patronage to control people.

> In the cities, the UN understood [what Frelimo was up to] and so could prevent abuse. The UN knew what happened in the cantonment centers, how many men and women there were, how much food they needed, etc., but didn't know how things were going in the villages. . . . They would say it was impossible [to investigate in rural areas] because of [land] mines, or because there were no roads. And Renamo didn't have a map [of the mines] to say it was okay [to convince them it was safe to travel].

Renamo's fear of electoral fraud nearly derailed the peace. Dhlakama threatened to withdraw from the elections on the first day of voting. However, Ajello's intervention was instrumental in keeping peace on track. Ajello mobilized the diplomatic corps to assure Dhlakama the voting would

---

[171] De Castro interview, Maputo.
[172] Ibid.
[173] Almirante interview, Maputo.

be watched carefully for fraud, and he created an ad hoc committee to investigate any and all of Renamo's allegations. Dhlakama was persuaded not to withdraw, and crisis was averted.[174]

More generally, the UN served as a watchdog over the state using its power to shut out Renamo, in part by

> question[ing] the predominant role of Frelimo and the government [in security affairs], in a transparent way. Ajello briefed the press every week, made no bones about it. . . . [The UN] called things what they were because they had their own observers, they could call the government's bluff.[175]

Because Renamo was the weaker side, UN pressure on the government was particularly important:

> The UN will oblige the government to fulfill [its promises] and tell the government, "We will side with Renamo [if you renege]," make them understand [they have to comply].[176]

Frelimo leaders recognized this influence and its reassuring effect on Renamo:

> For Renamo, they knew that if the government overuses its power, they can go to ONUMOZ with a complaint.[177]

Last, but certainly not least, ONUMOZ was instrumental in helping Renamo transform itself from a guerilla movement into a viable political party. This entailed providing everything from fax machines and office equipment to administrative know-how and even clothing:

> Eric Lubin, Ajello's assistant in charge of Renamo, held Dhlakama's hand through the peace process. When Dhlakama said, "We need suits [for the negotiations]," Lubin got them suits.[178]

Augustinho Zacarias notes that the UN mission in Mozambique played a crucial role in "coaching" the politically unsophisticated Renamo on becoming a viable political party.[179] Renamo officials were understandably a bit sensitive about this issue, arguing that Renamo was already a "political force," but admitted that the UN helped it to organize:

---

[174] Howard 2008, pp. 215-16.
[175] Weimer interview, Maputo.
[176] Forquilha interview, Maputo.
[177] Hunguana interview, Maputo.
[178] McDonald interview, Maputo.
[179] Interview, New York.

After the AGP, Renamo left the bush and the fields and went to the city. There the UN helped to *organize*, not to transform, Renamo. We didn't know how to manage a political force. Renamo needed offices, computers—all that was also important—but helping to organize the management of a political party, administrative [capacity], was most important. I want to underline that during the war, we knew how to manage military logistics—the guns go here and there, etc., but how to administrate politically, how to set up an office, etc., was different. Political logistics were new to us.[180]

This hand-holding, coaching, and cajoling during repeated crises helped convince Renamo to stick with the peace process. Ajello's strategy was to bolster Renamo politically so as make them more likely to compete at the ballot box rather than on the battlefield.[181]

Sierra Leone

In a case like Sierra Leone where the roots of the war lie in state failure, the challenge is to prevent political abuse while rebuilding state authority. While the RUF was the most important spoiler in Sierra Leone in the short term, it has now largely disintegrated and does not pose the greatest long-term threat. However, as Behrooz Sadry put it, though the RUF is gone, there are still "twenty-three other letters in the alphabet."[182] Other groups will spring up if the root problems of state capacity are not solved.[183]

While it is too early to evaluate the long-term effect of the international community's efforts in this regard, UNAMSIL and Britain have placed extraordinary emphasis on state-building. Some of these efforts have focused on the provision of social services such as health and education, but the primary focus has been on the military and the police.[184] In other words, the first priority has been the extension of the government's monopoly on the use of force. Britain has taken responsibility for rebuilding, retraining, and reforming the Sierra Leone army through the International Military Advisory Training Team (IMATT). IMATT operates independently from UNAMSIL and remains in Sierra Leone even now that the UN mission has withdrawn, but the two missions were closely connected.[185]

---

[180] Almirante interview, Maputo.

[181] This was also the approach taken initially in Sierra Leone, though as the RUF disintegrated politically and militarily, this strategy was dropped.

[182] Sadry interview, Freetown.

[183] Civil society activist Zainab Bangura made the same point. Interview, Freetown.

[184] Malan, Rakate, and McIntyre 2002, p. 11.

[185] IMATT has indicated it will continue to train RSLAF until at least 2010. UN Document S/2005/777, p. 6.

UNAMSIL's drawdown was explicitly tied to growth in the military's capability to provide security. A 2002 UN report notes that the Republic of Sierra Leone Armed Forces (RSLAF) "is now a much-improved force and is effectively patrolling both the border areas and Sierra Leone's waters. . . . Although RSLAF self-confidence is growing, the general public is yet to be fully convinced of the long-term reliability of the armed forces."[186] Over several years, UNAMSIL gradually returned responsibility for security over to Sierra Leonean forces. Retraining and reforming the RSLAF has been particularly important given this institution's shaky track record of heeding civilian control or loyalty to the state.[187] The new army is intended to be 15,500 strong, with up to about 15% recruited from ex-RUF and ex-CDF ranks as a measure of reconciliation and to keep some of these ex-combatants gainfully employed.[188] The UN influenced the government to include its erstwhile enemies in the army.

> We got a full colonel [from the RUF] onto the commission to form the army, to make sure that all three, CDF, RUF, and former SLA, will have an equal opportunity. We took the RUF to see how it was working [on the ground], and they saw we weren't taking them for a ride.[189]

The police forces in Sierra Leone were reduced by almost one-third during the war. Approximately 900 policemen were killed, and many were amputated.[190] UNAMSIL's CIVPOL division and the Commonwealth Safety and Security Project (CSSP) both worked to strengthen police capacity in Sierra Leone.[191] The UN Development Program (UNDP) provided support for a police-training school,[192] and by the time UNAMSIL withdrew in December 2005 the UN had trained some 4,000 police personnel. Deployment of police to the provinces has been impeded by lack of housing and police stations, however. In the UN's assessment, the Sierra Leone police force now seems capable of maintaining basic law and order

---

[186] UN Document S/2002/1417, p. 4.

[187] ICG 2003, pp. 6-8. A UN commander argued that weak and unprofessional militaries spawn rebel groups, noting that both Sankoh and Taylor came from military ranks. Shawkat interview, Magburaka.

[188] Malan, Rakate, and McIntyre 2002, p. 63. The final UN report on UNAMSIL notes efforts to reduce the size of the armed forces to 10,500 by 2007. UN Document S/2005/777, p. 6.

[189] Opande interview, Freetown.

[190] This chilling expression became common in the grim grammar of Sierra Leone's atrocities.

[191] CIVPOL and CSSP had a somewhat ambiguous relationship, but the former operated mostly in Freetown, the latter in the hinterland. Malan, Rakate, and McIntyre 2002, p. 67.

[192] UN Document S/2003/321, p. 4.

in the face of localized disturbances, but is "likely to be seriously challenged, however, particularly in the districts, in the event of a countrywide crisis, because of their deficiencies in communication and transport."[193] The UN tried to have ex-RUF participate in the police forces, but only a few met the job qualifications. According to UNAMSIL's civilian police commissioner, the "number of RUF that have high enough qualifications is only in the tens. Some were absorbed into the military where the qualification is more liberal [i.e., lax]."[194]

The justice system in Sierra Leone was also in a shambles as the country emerged from war, both in terms of the infrastructure of prisons and judicial personnel. Help on this front has come primarily through UNDP. The most visible judicial developments in Sierra Leone have been the establishment of a Special Court to try war criminals and a Truth and Reconciliation Commission to take statements from those victimized during the war. In March 2003, the Special Court indicted former RUF, AFRC, West Side Boys, and CDF leaders including: Foday Sankoh, Johnny Paul Koroma, Sam Bockarie, Issa Sesay, and Hinga Norman.[195] Of those indicted, all but Koroma and Bockarie were taken into custody. Liberia, under pressure to turn over Bockarie, later reported that he had been killed. Koroma also died, reportedly after fleeing to Liberia. Sankoh died in prison while awaiting trial. Hinga Norman died during his trial, apparently of heart failure.[196]

UNAMSIL's Civil Affairs division assisted the government in restoring administrative representatives throughout the country. In about 70% of the country there has been no government representative for 20 years.[197] The March 2003 secretary-general's report notes that the process of deploying government officials in all districts had almost been completed, and that the process of filling paramount chief vacancies had been completed, but "logistic and infrastructure constraints" meant that many of these officials "lack the basic facilities for the discharge of their functions."[198] Since then, local councils have been elected, but similar resource constraints also inhibit their ability to provide services.[199]

Nonetheless, there is clearly much more of a state apparatus in Sierra Leone than there would have been without the UN's presence. While critical of UNAMSIL's impact in Sierra Leone in many ways (including causing

---

[193] UN Document S/2005/777, p. 7.

[194] Dankwa interview, Freetown.

[195] Many I interviewed were skeptical that these efforts at postconflict justice would foster reconciliation. However, as I interviewed mostly leaders who were presumably implicated in atrocities, they were probably biased.

[196] BBC News 2007.

[197] Malan, Rakate, and McIntyre 2002, p. 30.

[198] UN Document S/2003/321, pp. 6-7.

[199] UN Document S/2005/273, p. 5.

prostitution, spreading HIV, and creating an artificial economy), the Sierra Leonean head of a good-governance NGO credited the UN with reestablishing the state.

> We could have ended up like Somalia. We had to pay the price [of having the mission here]—UNAMSIL brought us together. . . . It took UNAMSIL almost a year to deploy [throughout the countryside]. The government couldn't have done it. UNAMSIL broke the ice, opened up access, helped in re-creating the state, ensured freedom of movement. . . . They gave us back [our country]. It was like we had taken our last breath. The UN literally re-created the state—the UN went in [to RUF and CDF areas] and then the government followed up.[200]

The government of Sierra Leone has also made some progress in restoring control over diamond mining. Official exports have increased from $10 million to $130 million, but uncontrolled mining and illicit trade continue to be rampant, with over half of diamond mining in the country still unlicensed at the end of 2005.[201]

The problem of uneducated and unemployed youth, many of them now with fighting experience, arguably remains the largest threat to peace in Sierra Leone and the region. Fighting, and the looting that goes with it, remain one of the more viable occupations available to young Sierra Leoneans. After Abuja brought peace to Sierra Leone, ex-combatants reportedly moved to both Liberia and Côte d'Ivoire to fight in those countries' civil wars.[202] Ex-combatants themselves noted that it would not be difficult, once UNAMSIL leaves, for fighters to come back to Sierra Leone.[203] A new rebellion would find easy recruits, and if the diamond areas are not secured, a new cycle of war in Sierra Leone is frighteningly easy to imagine.[204] State-building and economic development are thus key to Sierra Leone's long-term prospects for peace.

Given the history of poor government in Sierra Leone, the trick for the international community has been to support the extension of state authority while maintaining pressure for fair and accountable government. As in Mozambique, the UN was instrumental in ensuring relatively free and fair (and peaceful) elections, and has made good governance a priority in Sierra

---

[200] Bangura interview, Freetown.

[201] UN Document S/2005/273, p. 6; UN Document S/2005/777, p. 7.

[202] One UN official told me of reports that Liberia's rebel group LURD was offering $200 for Sierra Leonean ex-combatants to sign up. And an RUF leader confirmed that ex-RUF forces were regrouping in Liberia. Anonymous interviews.

[203] Interviews with Kono Youth League and Kono Ex-Combatant Development Organization, Koidu.

[204] Hirsch interview, New York.

Leone. The peacekept in Sierra Leone saw the government's treatment of the opposition as a key to stability. A local religious leader noted, "If the government marginalizes the [electoral] loser, this is a threat to peace."[205]

The UN's presence clearly influenced Kabbah's government. Ex-RUF members in particular saw UNAMSIL's role in this regard as quite important for peace.

> The presence of the UN is helping reform, bringing law and order, stability. Now we only have to fight corruption. It's important that the UN stays because Kabbah's government is full of guys from the old government. . . . With a neutral force, things will go in a neutral way, not in a corrupt way.[206]

How the government will fare in this regard in the long-term remains to be seen, especially now that UN peacekeepers have left. One UN official was skeptical of the long-term impact: "Without the attention of the international community, I'm not sure the government will maintain its openness."[207] RUF leaders agreed with this assessment. After complaining about corruption and lack of justice in the Sierra Leonean government, former RUF spokesman Gibril Massaquoi said, "Some things are moving [getting better] because the UN is here, but when the UN leaves, it will come back to square one."[208]

Whatever the long-term prospects for inclusive government in Sierra Leone, it is clear that the UN was successful in the short term in influencing the government to limit political abuse of the types that can easily lead back to war. Sierra Leone is by no means out of the woods, but assessments of the risk of the country sliding back into war have become significantly less pessimistic over the last several years.[209]

As all three cases suggest, the chances for political abuse and exclusion are much lower when peacekeepers are present than when belligerents are left to their own devices after civil war.

Conclusion

These cases illustrate specific ways in which peacekeepers shape belligerents' choices about returning to war or maintaining peace. When they can prove their credibility, peacekeepers can have a direct military effect, deter-

[205] Group interview with religious leaders (imams and priests), Mile 91.

[206] Razaq interview, Freetown.

[207] Lecoq interview, Freetown.

[208] Massaquoi interview, Freetown.

[209] This is evident in the periodic reports of the secretary-general on UNAMSIL. See UN documents listed in the references.

ring aggression. When they are not strong enough relative to the parties themselves, they can sometimes act as a trip wire for more robust intervention by others. But notwithstanding the fact that peacekeeping is a job done primarily by soldiers, its effects operate at least as much through political and economic mechanisms as through military ones. The presence of peacekeepers changes the incentives of the peacekept by allowing the international community effectively to condition aid on compliance, by influencing domestic public opinion, and by providing a peace dividend, sometimes in the form of cold hard cash, for both rebel and government leaders and rank-and-file soldiers.

The use of economic leverage in particular depends on the resources available to the peacekept, but as the comparison between Mozambique and the CHT shows, having a legitimate outside party play a role in coopting leaders into the peace process is more effective than attempts by the belligerents themselves to do so. Internal attempts have the potential to strengthen hard-liners at the expense of moderates.

Peacekeepers can also reduce the uncertainty and mistrust that can lead even parties without aggressive intentions back to war. By monitoring compliance, peacekeepers can reassure each side that the other is acting in good faith. Peacekeepers can also facilitate communication between actors who have a difficult time politically even meeting face to face. And because agreeing to peacekeepers is costly, particularly for those who intend to renege on an agreement, just the possibility of peacekeepers allows belligerents credibly to signal their intentions to one another.

The presence of peacekeepers can shift power toward moderates, making it less likely that hard-line groups will be able to disrupt peace. Facilitating communication, providing law and order, especially in sensitive areas, and providing an alternative complaint mechanism to escalation can help prevent accidents from spiraling back to war. And last, but not least, by monitoring and retraining security forces, helping military organizations become viable political parties, and rebuilding effective state institutions, peacekeepers can help to ensure that state power is not abused in ways that make the resumption of war more likely.

These causal mechanisms overlap in practice, and they are by no means deterministic. They do not guarantee that peace will last in every case. But evidence from the belligerents themselves shows that peacekeepers can have a causal impact, improving the prospects for stable peace in war-torn societies.

Seven

CONCLUSION AND IMPLICATIONS

THIS BOOK ASKS three empirical questions: Where do peacekeepers go? Does peacekeeping work? And if so, how does it work? This chapter summarizes the answers to these questions, drawing out implications for our understanding of the problem of recidivism after civil wars, and especially for policymakers trying to reduce it.

The first question is important for evaluating the other two, but it is also interesting in its own right. While existing studies of this question have focused on choices made by the international community, I argue that choices made by the belligerents themselves are as important, at least for the consent-based missions that make up the bulk of peacekeeping. Not surprisingly, peacekeeping is a matter of both supply and demand. That peacekeeping is unlikely in civil wars within or next door to the permanent five members of the Security Council is testament to a supply-side effect. But the fact that peacekeeping is generally more likely when rebels are relatively strong (but not strong enough to win outright) reflects dynamics on the demand side. The case studies illustrate this point well. Whether or not consent-based peacekeeping happened in Bangladesh, Mozambique, and Sierra Leone was the result of choices made by the belligerents, and particularly by the relative bargaining strength of rebels and the government.

For the purposes of the rest of the analysis, the most important answer to the question of where peacekeepers go, is that they are much more likely to deploy when the danger of war recurring is particularly high. That is, peacekeepers select into the hardest cases. This finding flies in the face of policy admonitions that peacekeepers should only go where the chances of "success" are relatively good. A policy of sending peacekeepers only to the easy cases would help international organizations avoid embarrassment, but would ensure that peacekeeping was less useful than it could be. If peacekeepers only went where peace is likely to last in any case, they would render themselves irrelevant. Fortunately, however, this policy advice has apparently been ignored. As both the quantitative and qualitative evidence in chapters 2 and 3 makes clear, the higher the risk of recidivism in a particular case, the more likely peacekeepers are to deploy. In particular, peacekeeping is most likely when neither side has won outright, where mistrust is high, and where refugee flows threaten regional peace. Chapter VI consent-based peacekeeping is more likely where rebel groups are relatively strong and in countries with lower living standards. Chapter VII enforcement missions are more likely in less democratic states and where the war involves multiple fighting factions. In short, peacekeepers are most likely to be sent where they are most needed, where the job of maintaining peace is most difficult.

The answer to the question of whether peacekeeping works is a clear and resounding yes. To see this, it is crucial to control for the fact that peacekeepers select into the difficult cases. But once this selection is accounted for, the statistical evidence is overwhelming. Chapter 5 cuts at the data in many different ways, but the conclusion is always the same; the risk of war resuming is much lower when peacekeepers are present than when belligerents are left to their own devices. Estimates of the size of this effect depend on how conservative one wants to be. If one sets up a particularly difficult test, in which peacekeepers are only given credit for keeping peace while they are actually deployed, not for peace that lasts after they leave, peacekeepers reduce the risk of another war by 55%–60%, all else equal. If peacekeepers are given credit for cases in which peace survives even after they go home (which, after all, is their main goal) estimates of the beneficial effects of peacekeeping are much more dramatic, suggesting that the risk of recidivism falls by at least 75%–85% relative to nonpeacekeeping cases. The evidence from interviews with rebel and government decision makers also supports this general conclusion that peacekeeping works. The belligerents themselves view peacekeeping as an important and effective tool that has helped them maintain peace.

Several other findings emerge from the analysis of peacekeeping's effects. One of the most important for peacekeeping policy is that Chapter VI consent-based missions are empirically just as effective as the militarily more robust Chapter VII enforcement missions. Much of the discussion within policy circles in the last several years has been about the importance of beefing up the mandates of peacekeeping missions. There are certainly cases in which an enforcement mandate may be necessary. More robust military capabilities can help peacekeepers protect themselves and others if peace begins to falter. And if the aim is to deter aggression militarily, then a Chapter VII mandate is needed. But it is not enough. Only enforcement missions that prove their willingness to fight, as missions that intervene to create a cease-fire by force have done, can deter effectively. Otherwise, a Chapter VII mandate does not a credible deterrent make. Thus, UNAMSIL's Chapter VII mandate meant little until British intervention and a robust force posture convinced the RUF that the international community was serious about enforcing peace.

However, the findings of this study show that peacekeeping is worthwhile even under consent-based mandates. Large and relatively well armed troop deployments are not necessarily essential for peacekeeping to work;

even small, unarmed or very lightly armed missions significantly reduce the likelihood that peace will break down. Given that consent-based missions are typically much less expensive, and that it may be easier to find countries willing and able to contribute troops for them, this is an important finding. Robust Chapter VII–mandated peacekeeping may be the safest option, but the international community should not shy away from smaller, less robust Chapter VI peacekeeping if that is all that is possible politically. In other words, we should not conclude that the mission's mandate does not matter, but rather that even peacekeeping missions with limited mandates and constrained military power can be extremely effective. This is because many of the mechanisms through which peacekeepers have an effect are political and economic in nature and do not depend on robust mandates or strong military force (more on this below).

Among consent-based operations, multidimensional missions are most effective. The dearth of cases in each category makes it harder to reach strong conclusions about the relative effects of different types of Chapter VI missions, so this finding should be treated with some caution. But the available evidence suggests that the civilian aspects of peacekeeping that go into multidimensional missions—election monitoring, human rights training, police reform, and so on—do contribute to its general effectiveness. More of the causal mechanisms through which peacekeeping operates, particularly those relating to political exclusion, are at play in these multidimensional missions than in other types of peacekeeping.

Peacekeeping is not a cure-all. Beyond the task of maintaining peace, the international community increasingly aims to foster democracy in the war-torn societies in which it intervenes. While stable peace may be a requisite for the growth of democracy, and as we have seen here, peacekeeping promotes stable peace, outside intervention may in other ways undermine or crowd out democratization. So, while peacekeeping is clearly effective at maintaining peace, it has not necessarily left significantly more democratic societies in its wake.[1] Nonetheless, if the aim is simply to keep the peace, to keep civil war from recurring, then peacekeeping is an extremely effective policy tool.

While the answers to the first two questions addressed in this book can be summarized quickly—peacekeepers go where peace is hardest to keep, and yes, peacekeeping works to keep peace—the answer to the third question, how does peacekeeping work, is a bit more complicated. Peacekeeping works along multiple causal pathways. To understand the causal mechanisms of peacekeeping, we must consider the reasons belligerents who have recently been fighting each other might return to war. This work identified

---

[1] See Fortna 2008.

four analytically distinct, but in practice overlapping pathways: aggression, fear and mistrust, accident or the actions of rogue groups within either side, and political exclusion. I hypothesized particular ways that the presence of peacekeepers might block these potential causal pathways; that is, ways peacekeepers might (1) change the incentives for aggression relative to maintaining peace, (2) alleviate fear and mistrust so as to reduce security dilemmas, (3) prevent or control accidents or "involuntary defection" by hard-liners, and (4) dissuade either side (and particularly the government) from excluding the other from the political process.

An empirical evaluation of the specific causal mechanisms through which peacekeepers might achieve these results requires paying attention to the perspective of the peacekept. The peacekeeping literature tends to be a bit narcissistic. It pays attention mostly to the peacekeepers, to their functions, the particulars of mandates, troop deployments, command and control, relationships between headquarters and the field, "best practices," and so, while largely ignoring the peacekept. But it is the peacekept who must choose between war and peace. Only if peacekeepers change something for the peacekept can they have a causal impact on this choice. This project has tried to rectify this shortcoming in the literature by examining how the belligerents themselves viewed the situation they faced, and particularly how they thought the presence or absence of peacekeepers mattered in their case.

The evidence from interviews with the peacekept (or not peacekept in the Bangladeshi case) indicates a number of ways in which the presence of peacekeepers can shape belligerents' choices. In large enforcement missions, this shift can entail military deterrence, although, as stressed above, to be effective, a deterrent force must establish the credibility that all deterrence entails. Where peacekeeping will depend on military deterrence, the international community must expect to have to prove its credibility on the ground. Enforcement missions may actually have to fight to convince the peacekept that peacekeepers are willing to use force. Smaller missions and consent-based peacekeeping might serve as a trip wire for more robust intervention, but again, would-be spoilers must believe that the international community really will respond with a large-scale intervention. The conditions under which peacekeeping has a strong military effect are therefore fairly narrow. But many of the ways in which peacekeeping changes belligerents' incentives are nonmilitary in nature.

Peacekeepers can have a causal impact by changing economic incentives. For rank-and-file soldiers, this generally entails the material benefits of going through a demobilization, disarmament, and reintegration (DDR) process. For leaders, it can entail the general boost to the economy that a peacekeeping mission brings, a boost that political elites are often in a position to capitalize on. Or it may entail more direct forms of co-option.

The Mozambique case provides examples of both. Co-option can happen without peacekeepers, of course. But as the CHT examples shows, if one side buys off the other, as the Bangladeshi government did the PCJSS by granting control of local budgets (and the opportunities for corruption that go with it), this leaves the co-opted open to charges of selling out. Co-option done by a peacekeeping mission, as a more neutral and acceptable body, is less likely to strengthen hard-liners at the expense of moderates than is co-option among the belligerents themselves.

Because altering economic incentives can be crucial to maintaining stable peace, contraband financing for rebels is not only a powerful factor in civil war recidivism, it also reduces peacekeepers' leverage. As shown in chapter 5, peacekeeping still helps when parties have independent and illegal sources of funding, but its effect is diminished. Co-option will be more expensive, perhaps prohibitively so, in these cases. Alternatively, as was the case in Sierra Leone, attempts to alter economic incentives may work in conjunction with military deterrence when contraband financing is an issue.

Beyond economics, peacekeepers can influence the incentives of the peacekept by influencing perceptions of the parties' legitimacy, both internationally and domestically. In many civil wars, recognition as a legitimate political actor is itself a valuable and sought-after good, as well as one that may translate into international economic or other aid. Internally, pronouncements by peacekeepers about who is or is not cooperating with a peace process may affect parties' electoral prospects.

In short, while peacekeeping may deter aggression through military means in some cases, its effects on the incentives facing belligerents are largely economic and political. There are policy implications of this for peacekeepers. Peacekeeping strategy should focus at least as much on identifying the points of economic and political influence in a particular case that will provide the most leverage over belligerents' decision making as on beefing up the mission's military strength. Similarly, the allocation of scarce resources (money, personnel, etc.) should be directed at least as much to making peace profitable and politically viable for the peacekept as to the creation of militarily effective peacekeeping forces. Where possible, an attempt should be made to control or eliminate contraband sources of funding for belligerents.[2]

By alleviating fear and mistrust, peacekeeping also increases the chances that belligerents will maintain peace. It does this, in part, by helping erstwhile deadly enemies to communicate with one another. Thus, as the inevitable problems and glitches in the peace process arise, peacekeeping mis-

---

[2] The Kimberly Process Certification Scheme to combat the trafficking of "blood diamonds" from conflict zones is an important step in this direction.

sions should emphasize ongoing mediation. They can also support peace by monitoring each side's compliance with a cease-fire. It is here, perhaps, that the military nature of peacekeeping is most important. Peacekeeping missions should include military personnel, not because they can fight (in fact, unarmed military observers may be most effective in some cases), but because they have the expertise to monitor demobilization and disarmament, and because they can garner the respect of the soldiers they monitor and the commanders they work with.

Peacekeepers also alleviate fear and mistrust, to some degree, merely by existing. To the extent that agreeing to peacekeeping allows the parties to signal their intentions to each other, it is less what peacekeepers actually do than whether the parties have asked for them or not that makes a difference. But for this signaling mechanism to work, it has to be credible, and to be credible, it has to be costly. Specifically, it has to be costly for a party that intends to resume fighting. Peacekeeping missions should thus be designed to be as intrusive as possible as a way of testing the credibility of this signal. Peacekeeping, particularly UN peacekeeping, traditionally proceeded on an assumption of good faith on the part of the belligerents. Lessons learned, usually the hard way, during the 1990s have tempered this assumption, with more attention now paid to the possibility of spoilers. But the signaling function of peacekeeping should be used proactively. Peacekeeping strategy should focus on identifying and insisting on things that those intending to go back to war or renege on a political deal would object to, but that those committed to peace would not necessarily mind. And because intentions can shift over time, peacekeepers should be intrusive not just when they first deploy, but over the life of the mission. This is not to say that they should go out of their way to antagonize the parties to the conflict, but rather that missions should be designed so as to maximize the clarity of the signal that consent and ongoing cooperation with peacekeeping provides to the other side.

Peacekeeping can make the resumption of war less likely by preventing hard-liners or rogue factions from inciting violence, and by helping to prevent or control accidents from sparking renewed conflict. Peacekeepers should work with moderates on each side to identify hard-liners within their own group who might pose a threat to peace. Peacekeeping strategy should determine whether these would-be spoiler splinter groups can be deterred militarily (something even relatively weak peacekeeping forces may be capable of), and how they can be weakened politically. By facilitating communication, peacekeeping can nip accidental conflagrations in the bud. This provides another reason peacekeepers should spend time and energy on continuing mediation between the parties, both among leaders and among local commanders, dealing with problems on the spot.

Providing security or basic law and order can help accidents from starting in the first place, so peacekeeping missions should continue to invest in policing, perhaps especially in identity conflicts where the actions of the general population might provide sparks for the fire. Similarly, providing security in particularly tense phases of the peace process (such as disarmament) or in particularly contested territory (diamond-mining areas, for example) can forestall problems that could easily escalate. Finally, peacekeeping missions should establish a formal mechanism for handling disputes over compliance. This gives both sides an alternative to, on the one hand, doing nothing in the face of perceived violations by their antagonists, and on the other, responding in kind and risking escalation. These dispute resolution mechanisms can appear irrelevant. Their formal findings may not tell either side anything it does not already know. But often it is not their role in providing information to the various parties that is important, but rather their existence as a political mechanism that allows the parties to save face by taking nonescalatory action in response to alleged violations.

Last, but certainly not least, peacekeepers can make peace more likely to endure by preventing either side from shutting the other out of a political process in a way that makes the political loser choose war. In most cases this entails pressuring the government, which can use the trappings of state power to influence political outcomes, not to abuse its position. There is a stark contrast in this regard between the Chittagong Hill Tracts conflict, where the absence of peacekeepers has given the Bangladeshi government a relatively free hand to disregard key elements of the peace deal, and Mozambique and Sierra Leone, where considerable pressure was brought to bear on the government to be inclusive. Beyond general political pressure (with international aid and legitimacy providing leverage), peacekeepers can minimize abuse by monitoring security forces and by monitoring or running electoral processes. They can help military groups (especially rebels) transform themselves into viable political parties, sometimes with the expenditure of relatively small amounts of money or other resources. (In some cases, computers and new suits can go a long way.) After some conflicts, peacekeepers may temporarily take over the entire administration of the country to prevent either side from dominating the political process during the most dangerous phases of the transition to peace. Again, peacekeeping strategy should be formed with an eye toward these mechanisms.

In short, peacekeeping intervenes in the most difficult cases, dramatically increases the chances that peace will last, and does so by altering the incentives of the peacekept, by alleviating their fear and mistrust of each other, by preventing and controlling accidents and misbehavior by hard-line factions, and by encouraging political inclusion.

Beyond its answers to these questions about peacekeeping and its effects, this study also makes both theoretical and empirical contributions. It builds on a theory of international cooperation developed for interstate conflict, extending it to the realm of internal warfare.[3] It provides further support for the notion that while cooperation is often extremely difficult, perhaps nowhere more so than among deadly enemies who have just fought a war, deliberate efforts by the belligerents themselves and by outsiders can often overcome the obstacles to peace.

It also helps us to understand the more general issue of recurrent civil war. Interstate war has, thankfully, become relatively rare since the end of the Cold War. This has left internal conflicts as arguably the greatest security problem facing the world as a whole.[4] Countries that have been torn apart by civil war face a significant recidivism problem—those who have had a civil war are especially likely to have another. The empirical findings of this study help us understand the nature of that problem. They point to particular factors (such as military outcomes, or contraband financing for rebels) that make civil wars particularly likely to recur. But they also show that this "conflict trap" is not inevitable.[5] The conclusions of this project are therefore fundamentally optimistic. The problem of maintaining peace in the aftermath of civil war is a serious one, but it is not a hopeless one. Parties to civil war, together with the international community, can use the tool of peacekeeping to reduce dramatically the risk of another war.

Peacekeeping is not free. It costs money and personnel on the part of the international community and the countries that contribute troops. It also entails political costs for the peacekept, not least of which is the infringement on a country's sovereignty. Policymakers may decide peacekeeping is not worth these costs in a particular instance. But relative to the cost of recurrent warfare, peacekeeping is an extremely good investment. Peacekeeping is not a panacea, nor a silver bullet. It cannot guarantee that peace will last. But contrary to the views of many who think only of well-publicized failures, peacekeeping is an extremely effective tool for maintaining peace—a tool that the findings of this study will, I hope, make even more useful.

[3] Fortna 2003, 2004c.

[4] Other threats, such as terrorism or the proliferation of nuclear weapons, may be of greater concern to particular countries at particular moments. Civil wars may also be on the decline, but continue to pose a significant threat to the lives and livelihoods of millions.

[5] See Collier et al. 2003.

APPENDIX A

THE DATA

THE MAIN ANALYSES in this project use data encompassing cease-fires in civil wars between January 1, 1989, and December 31, 1999.[1] Civil wars are messy affairs, and information on them is often ambiguous or simply unavailable. Creating a data set such as the one used here requires numerous, often arbitrary, coding decisions. Wherever possible, I have tried to make these decisions in such a way as to weaken the evidence for my central argument. Imperfect as these data are, we can thus be confident that peacekeeping is at least as effective as this book indicates.

The list of cases is adapted from the Doyle and Sambanis (D&S) data on civil wars; however, as explained in chapter 1, I have added short-lived cease-fires excluded in the D&S data.[2] I include all cease-fires lasting at least one month. I coded key variables for this study, including cease-fire dates, the dates of renewed warfare (if any), peacekeeping missions, and war outcomes, from numerous sources and data sets, including: *Blue Helmets* (UN 1996a); Doyle and Sambanis 2000, 2006; and Sambanis's "Civil War Coding Notes" for Sambanis 2004; Dubey 2002; Fearon and Laitin 2003; Fearon 2004; the UN's peacekeeping website;[3] the Uppsala Conflict Data Program (UCDP);[4] and research on individual cases.[5]

I code peace as failing if D&S code a new war in the same country and research indicates that it involved the same or similar parties, or if UCDP code a restart to a war they consider previously terminated, or if my own research provided evidence of full-scale fighting after the date of a cease-fire. If it was ambiguous whether fighting should be considered a full-scale return to war, I coded cases in a way that would cut against the argument that peacekeeping is effective. In other words, if peacekeepers were present, I erred on the side of coding a resumption of war, and if

---

[1] Data for cases from 1945 to 1988 were used for the analysis described in appendix B. Data for these earlier cases are from Doyle and Sambanis 2000.

[2] While the revised (2006) D&S list of cases is more comprehensive and systematic, the original (2000) version of their data suits my purposes better. The original data emphasized peacebuilding attempts, and therefore coded more short-lived cease-fires. The new version combines episodes of fighting in stop-and-start wars into single cases. My list of cases thus builds on the 2000 list, with revisions made according to the revised D&S data as well as other sources.

[3] http://www.un.org/Depts/dpko/dpko/index.asp.

[4] UCDP n.d.; Harbom 2004.

[5] With special thanks to Megan Gilroy for research assistance.

TABLE A.1
List of Cases

Case Name	Cease-Fire	Fail Date	Outcome	Peacekeeping[a]
Afghanistan—Mujahideen	25 Apr 1992	10 Aug 1992	Victory	None
Afghanistan—Taliban	07 Mar 1993	15 Apr 1993	Treaty	None
Algeria—FIS/AIS	15 Oct 1997		Truce	None
Angola	31 May 1991	11 Oct 1992	Treaty	Monitoring
Angola	20 Nov 1994	04 Dec 1998	Treaty	Multidimensional
Azerbaijan–Nagorno Karabakh	31 Aug 1993	05 Oct 1993	Truce	None
Azerbaijan–Nagorno Karabakh	16 May 1994		Truce	None
Bangladesh—CHT	01 Aug 1992		Truce	None
Bosnia	01 Jan 1995	01 May 1995	Truce	Interpositional
Bosnia	14 Dec 1995		Treaty	Enforcement
Cambodia	23 Oct 1991		Treaty	Multidimensional
Central African Republic	25 Jan 1997		Treaty	Interpositional
Chad	11 Aug 1994	15 Mar 1997	Treaty	None
Congo-Brazzaville	30 Jan 1994	25 Jun 1997	Treaty	None
Congo-Brazzaville	15 Oct 1997	15 Aug 1998	Victory	None
Congo-Brazzaville	29 Dec 1999	15 Mar 2002	Truce	None
Congo, Democratic Republic/Zaire	17 May 1997	02 Aug 1998	Victory	None
Croatia[b]	30 Mar 1994	15 May 1995	Truce	Multidimensional
Croatia	12 Nov 1995		Truce	Enforcement
Djibouti	28 Feb 1992	19 Jul 1992	Truce	Interpositional
Djibouti	26 Dec 1994		Treaty	None
Egypt	15 Sep 1997		Truce	None
El Salvador	16 Dec 1992		Treaty	Multidimensional
Ethiopia-Eritrea	21 May 1991		Victory	None
Ethiopia—ideology	21 May 1991		Victory	None
Georgia—Abkhazia	27 Jul 1993	16 Sep 1993	Truce	None
Georgia—Abkhazia	14 May 1994		Truce	Interpositional
Georgia—Ossetia	14 Jul 1994		Truce	Interpositional
Guatemala	26 Apr 1991	15 Dec 1991	Truce	None
Guatemala	20 Mar 1996		Treaty	Interpositional
Guinea-Bissau	26 Aug 1998	31 Oct 1998	Truce	None
Guinea-Bissau	02 Nov 1998	31 Jan 1999	Treaty	None
Guinea-Bissau	03 Feb 1999	06 May 1999	Truce	Monitoring
Guinea-Bissau	07 May 1999		Victory	Monitoring
Haiti	18 Sep 1994		Truce	Enforcement

[a] Operations listed are time-constant, showing the highest mission type deployed.
[b] See also Yugoslavia.

TABLE A.1 (continued)
List of Cases

Case Name	Cease-Fire	Fail Date	Outcome	Peacekeeping[a]
India—Assam	20 Apr 1991	15 Sep 1991	Truce	None
India—Assam	17 Dec 1991	01 Jan 1994	Truce	None
India—Sikh	31 Dec 1993		Victory	None
Indonesia—Aceh	31 Dec 1991	15 May 1999	Victory	None
Indonesia–E. Timor	25 Oct 1999		Victory	Enforcement
Iraq—Kurds	01 Mar 1993	15 Mar 1995	Victory	Enforcement
Iraq—Kurds	15 Oct 1996		Victory	Enforcement
Iraq—Shia	15 Dec 1993		Victory	None
Israel—Palestinians	13 Sep 1993	28 Sep 2000	Treaty	None
Lebanon	13 Oct 1990		Treaty	Enforcement
Liberia	28 Nov 1990	15 Oct 1992	Treaty	Enforcement
Liberia	17 Aug 1996	15 May 1999	Treaty	Enforcement
Mali	06 Jan 1991	15 May 1991	Treaty	None
Mali	31 Mar 1995		Treaty	None
Moldova–Trans Dniester	21 Jul 1992		Treaty	Enforcement
Morocco–W. Sahara	06 Sep 1991		Truce	Monitoring
Mozambique	04 Oct 1992		Treaty	Multidimensional
Myanmar—Karen	28 Apr 1992	01 Jun 1995	Truce	None
Myanmar—Karen	15 Jun 1995	15 Feb 1997	Truce	None
Myanmar—Kachin	15 Oct 1993		Truce	None
Namibia	01 Apr 1989		Treaty	Multidimensional
Nicaragua	19 Apr 1989		Treaty	Interpositional
Pakistan—Mohajirs	15 Oct 1999		Truce	None
Papua New Guinea	15 Mar 1990	15 Sep 1990	Truce	None
Papua New Guinea	21 Jan 1991	15 Apr 1991	Truce	None
Papua New Guinea	10 Oct 1997		Truce	Monitoring
Peru	31 Dec 1996		Victory	None
Philippines—Communists	31 Dec 1995	15 May 1999	Truce	None
Philippines—Mindanao	07 Nov 1993	22 Dec 1993	Truce	None
Philippines—Mindanao	31 Dec 1990	01 Jan 1993	Truce	None
Philippines—Mindanao	02 Sep 1996	15 Nov 2001	Treaty	None
Romania	23 Dec 1989		Victory	None
Russia—Chechnya	01 Jun 1996	07 Jul 1996	Truce	None
Russia—Chechnya	23 Aug 1996	15 Sep 1999	Truce	None
Rwanda	31 Jul 1992	01 Jan 1993	Truce	Monitoring
Rwanda	04 Aug 1993	06 Apr 1994	Treaty	Interpositional
Rwanda	18 Jul 1994	01 Jan 1998	Victory	Interpositional

[a] Operations listed are time-constant, showing the highest mission type deployed.

TABLE A.1 (continued)
List of Cases

Case Name	Cease-Fire	Fail Date	Outcome	Peacekeeping[a]
Senegal	08 Jul 1993	01 Jun 1995	Truce	None
Sierra Leone	30 Nov 1996	15 May 1997	Treaty	None
Sierra Leone	07 Jul 1999	02 May 2000	Treaty	Enforcement
Somalia	27 Jan 1991	05 Sep 1991	Victory	None
South Africa	26 Apr 1994		Treaty	None
Sri Lanka–Tamil	07 Jan 1995	19 Apr 1995	Truce	None
Sri Lanka–JVP II	29 Dec 1989		Victory	None
Sudan	01 May 1989	31 Oct 1989	Truce	None
Sudan	28 Mar 1995	15 Aug 1995	Truce	None
Sudan	15 Jul 1998	15 Feb 1999	Truce	None
Sudan	15 Apr 1999	15 May 1999	Truce	None
Tajikistan	27 Jun 1997		Treaty	Enforcement
Turkey—Kurds	20 Mar 1993	24 May 1993	Truce	None
Turkey—Kurds	01 Sep 1999		Victory	None
Uganda—Kony	15 Feb 1989	15 May 1989	Truce	None
Uganda—LRA	15 Jul 1992	15 Jan 1995	Victory	None
United Kingdom– N. Ireland	31 Aug 1994	15 Feb 1996	Truce	None
United Kingdom– N. Ireland	10 Apr 1998		Treaty	None
Yemen	10 Jul 1994		Victory	None
Yugoslavia-Croatia[c]	03 Jan 1992	22 Jan 1993	Truce	Interpositional
Yugoslavia-Kosovo	12 Oct 1998	01 Dec 1998	Truce	Monitoring
Yugoslavia-Kosovo	09 Jun 1999		Victory	Enforcement

[a] Operations listed are time-constant, showing the highest mission type deployed.

[c] See Croatia cases.

no peacekeepers were present, I erred on the side of coding no failure of peace. If peace held through December 31 2004, the observation is censored at that point.

Peacekeeping mission types follow D&S categories, but were checked and recoded. I thus distinguish between no peacekeeping; monitoring missions; interpositional missions (aka traditional peacekeeping); multidimensional missions; and enforcement missions.[6] A dummy variable groups the four types of mission together, and a separate variable distinguishes enforcement missions from the other three. In some cases more than one peacekeeping mission is present at one time. Both missions are coded, though the statistical analyses use the highest mission type present. The

[6] I do not include small peacebuilding missions as peacekeeping, though these operations are noted in the data.

TABLE A.2
Control Variables

Variable	Description	Source
Contraband	Contraband financing for rebels	Fearon & Laitin 2003
Deaths	Natural log of deaths in war (civilian and battle)	D&S 2000
Democracy	Polity IV score, year before cease-fire	Marshall and Jaggers 2002
Duration of War	(In years)	D&S 2000
Factions	More than two factions	D&S 2000
Former P5 Colony	Former colony of Perm-5 member (US, Britain, France, China, Russia)	Gilligan and Stedman 2003
Government Army Size	(In thousands of troops)	D&S 2000
Identity War	Ethnic, religious, or identity conflict	D&S 2000
Infant Mortality	Rate at war start, as proxy for economic development	D&S 2000; WDI
Mountains	Mountainousness of the country's terrain	Fearon & Laitin 2003
Neighbor Aids Rebels	Neighboring country intervenes on side of rebels	Regan 2002
Oil Exporter	More than one-third of export revenues from fuels	Fearon & Laitin 2003
P5 Affinity	Max "affinity" score with Perm-5 member in year war starts	Gartzke and Jo 2002
P5 Alliance	Ally with Perm-5 member	Bennett and Stam 2003; COW alliance data
P5 Contiguity	Geographic contiguity with Perm-5 member (by land or up to 150 miles of water)	Bennett and Stam 2003
P5 Involvement	Perm-5 participation in war. Direct intervention or "extensive political support"	D&S 2000
Past Agreement	A past war or round of fighting (since 1945) ended in a truce or settlement	
Secession	Secessionist Conflict	Sambanis and Zinn 2003
Treaty	War ends in settlement (not truce or victory)	Author
Victory	War ends in victory (not truce or settlement)	Author

peacekeeping variables can change over time as peacekeeping missions come and go.[7] Time-constant versions of the peacekeeping variables code the highest mission type deployed.

Dummy variables indicate whether the war ended in victory for one side, treaty (settlement), or truce. Truces include cease-fires, agreements on a

---

[7] Peacekeeping operation dates go by authorization dates, unless I have information that a mission actually deployed much later, in which case I use deployment dates.

peace process that do not themselves settle underlying political issues, interim arrangements that leave final status negotiations on major issues unsettled, and cases in which the fighting ends with a unilateral cease-fire or just a fizzling out of the violence. The settlement or treaty category requires agreement on fundamental political issues. Outcome can change over time within cases as truces are replaced by settlements.

Other control variables come from existing data sets, as shown in table A.2. Missing data were filled in, where possible, with research on individual cases.

APPENDIX B

PREDICTING THE DEGREE
OF DIFFICULTY OF MAINTAINING PEACE

DRAWING ON THE EXISTING literature on the duration of peace after civil wars,[1] I examine the effects of the following variables on the stability of peace: economic development, democracy, the cost of war,[2] its military outcome, and whether a peace treaty was signed, whether it was an identity conflict, whether it was a secessionist conflict, the number of factions involved, contraband financing for rebels, and a neighboring country's support for rebels.[3] I estimate a Weibull model of the duration of peace, from a cease-fire to another war between the same parties or until the data are censored by the end of the data set in December 2004.[4] The universe of cases is cease-fires in civil wars, as defined by Doyle and Sambanis (2000), between 1945 and 1988. As described in chapter 2, these pre-1989 cases provide a useful "counterfactual" because peacekeeping was not used in civil wars with any frequency until after the end of the Cold War. The estimates of effects on the degree of difficulty of maintaining peace are thus not biased by the potential presence of peacekeepers. War resumes in 29 of the 61 cases in this time period.

Table B.1 presents the model, run on pre-1989 cases, used to generate predictions of the degree of difficulty for post-1989 cases (column 1). Because the neighbor support for rebel variable is missing for a substantial

---

[1] For a concise summary of the quantitative findings of this literature, see Walter 2004b. See also Downs and Stedman 2002, pp. 55–57.

[2] Note that the cost of the war used here includes both deaths (battle and civilian) and those displaced by the fighting as refugees and internally displaced persons (IDPs), while the measure used in chapters 2 and 5 includes only those killed. Measures including only deaths performed slightly less well in the 1945–88 period, while the more inclusive measure of costs had more missing data for the post–Cold War period.

[3] Downs and Stedman 2002 include three additional factors in their list of what makes peace difficult to implement. One of these, the likelihood of spoilers, is probably not knowable a priori. As they themselves suggest, potential spoilers are almost always present. Whether they disrupt the peace depends on the incentive structure—something that is shaped by the presence (or absence of peacekeepers). They argue that two other factors, a collapsed state and the number of soldiers, affect the size of the job peacekeepers are faced with (in terms of rebuilding institutions, monitoring and demobilization, etc.) rather than the probability that war resumes. I also tested the effects of duration of the war (measured in months) but found it to have no discernable effect, so dropped it from the analysis.

[4] Results are much the same if a Cox nonproportional hazards model is estimated.

TABLE B.1
Determinants of Durable Peace, 1945–88

	Model 1 Weibull		Model 2 Weibull	
	HR (RSE)	P > |Z|	HR (RSE)	P > |Z|
Infant Mortality	1.01 (0.01)	.45	1.01 (0.01)	.29
Democracy	0.95 (0.05)	.37	0.97 (0.03)	.33
Identity War	1.63 (1.25)	.52	2.82 (1.62)	.07
Secession	0.38 (0.35)	.29	0.34 (0.20)	.07
Deaths and Displaced	1.12 (0.13)	.35	1.22 (0.11)	.03
Victory	0.11 (0.09)	.01	0.27 (0.19)	.07
Treaty	0.66 (0.63)	.66	0.76 (0.53)	.69
Contraband	8.46 (6.46)	.01	3.97 (1.53)	.00
Neighbor Aids Rebels	3.44 (2.06)	.04		
Factions	0.47 (0.53)	.50	1.33 (0.79)	.64
Shape Parameter P	0.75 (0.15)	.16	0.72 (0.12)	.06
N	47		58	
Log Pseudo-Likelihood	−56.52		−76.01	

number of cases, I also include results with that variable dropped from the analysis (column 2). The substantive effects are much the same, though some variables that are not significant in the former model are so in the latter.[5]

While many of the effects fail to pass tests of statistical significance (probably because of the relatively small N), almost all of them are in the expected direction. The risk of another war is higher the higher the infant

[5] The differences appear to be the result of dropping cases for which data are missing, rather than correlation between the neighbor support variable and other variables in the model. The results are similar to column 1 if cases for which data are missing are deleted from the analysis in column 2.

mortality in the country. Democracy reduces the risk of another war. Ethnic wars are more susceptible to renewal, but, surprisingly, secessionist wars are less likely to resume than are wars fought for other goals.[6] The higher the deaths and displacement from the war, the more likely it is to resume. These last three effects are statistically significant, or close to it, in column 2, where missing data do not affect results. Wars ending with a clear victory for one side are significantly less likely to resume, while treaties also seem to reduce the risk of another war (relative to mere truces), though this latter effect is not significant. Wars in which there was significant contraband financing available to rebels are significantly more likely to resume. Peace also appears to fall apart more quickly after complicated wars pitting more than two factions against each other, though this result may be an artifact of chance in the data, as it is not significant.

The low levels of statistical significance mean that many of these findings should be taken with a grain of salt. I include them in the predictions because others have found them to have substantial effects, and because my purpose here is not to prove or disprove theories about what drives the prospects for peace, but rather to come up with as informative an indicator as possible about the degree of difficulty in the post–Cold War cases.

[6] Note that this means that the *same* conflict is less likely to recur, not that a country facing one secessionist challenge will be less likely to face another (the opposite is probably true but is not tested here).

REFERENCES

BOOKS AND ARTICLES

Achen, Christopher H. 2005. Let's Put Garbage-Can Regressions and Garbage-Can Probits Where They Belong. *Conflict Management and Peace Science* 22 (4): 327–39.

Adebajo, Adekeye. 2002. *Building Peace in West Africa: Liberia, Sierra Leone, and Guinea-Bissau*. Boulder: Lynne Rienner.

Adebajo, Adekeye, and David Keen. 2007. Sierra Leone. In *United Nations Interventionism, 1991–2004*, edited by M. Berdal and S. Economides. Cambridge: Cambridge University Press.

Alden, Chris. 2001. *Mozambique and the Construction of the New African State: From Negotiations to Nation Building*. New York: Palgrave.

Andersson, Andreas. 2000. Democracies and UN Peacekeeping Operations, 1990–1996. *International Peacekeeping* 7 (2): 1–22.

Ballentine, Karen, and Jake Sherman, eds. 2003. *The Political Economy of Armed Conflict: Beyond Greed and Grievance*. Boulder: Lynne Rienner.

Bangura, Yusuf. 2002. Strategic Policy Failure and State Fragmentation: Security, Peacekeeping, and Democratization in Sierra Leone. In *The Causes of War and the Consequences of Peacekeeping in Africa*, edited by R. R. Laremont. Portsmouth, NH: Heinemann.

Barnes, Sam. 1998. Peacekeeping in Mozambique. In *Peacekeeping in Africa*, edited by O. Furley and R. May. Aldershot: Ashgate.

BBC News. 2007. S Leone War Crimes Suspect Dies. February 22, 2007. Available from http://news.bbc.co.uk/2/hi/africa/6387673.stm (consulted May 25, 2007).

Beardsley, Kyle. 2004. UN Intervention: Selection, Endogeneity, and Authority. Paper presented at Annual Meeting of the International Studies Association, Montreal.

Behera, Ajay Darshan. 1996. Insurgency in the Bangladesh Hills: Chakmas' Search for Autonomy. *Strategic Analysis* 19 (7): 985–1005.

Bennett, D. Scott, and Allan C. Stam. 2003. EUGene: Expected Utility Generation and Data Management Program. Version 3.0.

Bennis, Phyllis. 1996. *Calling the Shots: How Washington Dominates Today's U.N.* New York: Olive Branch Press.

Bercovitch, Jacob, and Robert Jackson. 1997. *International Conflict: A Chronological Encyclopedia of Conflicts and Their Management, 1945–1995*. Washington, DC: Congressional Quarterly.

Berdal, Mats. 1999. UN Peacekeeping and the Use of Force: No Escape from Hard Decisions. In *Security in a Post–Cold War World*, edited by R. G. Patman. New York: Macmillan and St. Martin's Press.

Blinkenberg, Lars. 1972. *India-Pakistan: The History of Unsolved Conflicts*. Copenhagen, Denmark: Munksgaard Dansk Udenrigspolitisk Institut.

Box-Steffensmeier, Janet M., and Bradford S. Jones. 1997. Time Is of the Essence: Event History Models in Political Science. *American Journal of Political Science* 41 (4): 1414–61.

Box-Steffensmeier, Janet M., Dan Reiter, and Christopher Zorn. 2003. Nonproportional Hazards and Event History Analysis in International Relations. *Journal of Conflict Resolution* 47 (1): 33–53.

Boyce, James K. 2002. *Investing in Peace: Aid and Conditionality after Civil Wars.* Adelphi Paper 351. Oxford: Oxford University Press for the International Institute for Strategic Studies, London.

Bright, Dennis. 2000. Implementing the Lomé Peace Agreement. *Paying the Price: The Sierra Leone Peace Process.* London: Conciliation Resources. *Accord 9.*

Bueno de Mesquita, Bruce, Alastair Smith, Randolph M. Siverson, and James D. Morrow. 2003. *The Logic of Political Survival.* Cambridge: MIT Press.

Byman, Daniel L. 2002. *Keeping the Peace: Lasting Solutions to Ethnic Conflicts.* Baltimore: Johns Hopkins University Press.

Carter, Timothy A. 2007. United Nations Intervention Decisions: A Strategic Examination. Unpublished paper, Wayne State University.

Charters, David A., ed. 1994. *Peacekeeping and the Challenge of Civil Conflict Resolution.* New Brunswick: University of New Brunswick, Centre for Conflict Studies.

Chester, Lucy. 2002. The 1947 Partition: Drawing the Indo-Pakistani Boundary. *American Diplomacy* 7 (1).

Chesterman, Simon. 2004. *You, the People: The United Nations, Transitional Administration, and State-Building.* Oxford: Oxford University Press.

Chopra, Jarat. 1998. *The Politics of Peace-Maintenance.* Boulder: Lynne Rienner.

Chowdhury, Bushra Hasina. 2002. *Building Lasting Peace: Issues of Implementation of the Chittagong Hill Tracts Accord.* Urbana: Program in Arms Control, Disarmament, and International Security, University of Illinois at Urbana-Champaign.

Clapham, Christopher. 1998. Being Peacekept. In *Peacekeeping in Africa*, edited by O. Furley and R. May. Aldershot: Ashgate.

———. 2000. Peacekeeping and the Peacekept: Developing Mandates for Potential Intervenors. In *Peacekeeping and Peace Enforcement in Africa*, edited by R. I. Rotberg and others. Washington, DC: Brookings Institution Press.

Cockayne, James, and David M. Malone. 2005. The Ralph Bunche Centennial: Peace Operations Then and Now. *Global Governance* 11 (3): 331–50.

Cohen, Herman J. 1995. African Capabilities for Managing Conflict: The Role of the United States. In *African Conflict Resolution: The U.S. Role in Peacemaking*, edited by D. R. Smock and C. A. Crocker. Washington, DC: United States Institute of Peace.

Collier, Paul, V. L. Elliot, Håvard Hegre, Anke Hoeffler, Marta Reynal-Querol, and Nicholas Sambanis. 2003. *Breaking the Conflict Trap: Civil War and Development Policy.* Washington, DC: World Bank and Oxford University Press.

Collier, Paul, and Anke Hoeffler. 2004. Greed and Grievance in Civil War. *Oxford Economic Papers* 56 (4): 563–95.

Conciliation Resources. 1997. Nigerian Intervention in Sierra Leone. Available from www.c-r.org/pubs/occ_papers/briefing2.htm (consulted May 7, 2003).

Cousens, Elizabeth M., and Charles K. Cater. 2001. *Toward Peace in Bosnia: Implementing the Dayton Accords*. Boulder: Lynne Rienner.

Cousens, Richard P. 1998. Providing Military Security in Peace-Maintenance. In *The Politics of Peace-Maintenance*, edited by J. Chopra. Boulder: Lynne Rienner.

de Jonge Oudraat, Chantal. 1996. The United Nations and Internal Conflict. In *The International Dimensions of Internal Conflict*, edited by M. E. Brown. Cambridge: MIT Press.

DeRouen, Karl, and Michael Barutciski. 2005. Refugees and Civil War Dynamics. Paper presented at Annual Meeting of the International Studies Association, Honolulu.

DeRouen, Karl, and David Sobek. 2004. The Dynamics of Civil War Duration and Outcome. *Journal of Peace Research* 41 (3): 303–20.

Diehl, Paul F. 1993. *International Peacekeeping*. Baltimore: Johns Hopkins University Press.

Diehl, Paul F., Jennifer Reifschneider, and Paul R. Hensel. 1996. United Nations Intervention and Recurring Conflict. *International Organization* 50 (4): 683–700.

Dobbins, James, Seth G. Jones, Keith Crane, Andrew Rathmell, Brett Steele, Richard Teltschik, and Anga Timilsina. 2005. *The UN's Role in Nation-Building*. Santa Monica: RAND Corporation.

Downs, George, and Stephen John Stedman. 2002. Evaluation Issues in Peace Implementation. In *Ending Civil Wars: The Implementation of Peace Agreements*, edited by S. J. Stedman, D. Rothchild, and E. M. Cousens. Boulder: Lynne Rienner.

Doyle, Michael W. 1995. *UN Peacekeeping in Cambodia: UNTAC's Civil Mandate*. Boulder: Lynne Rienner.

———. 2001. War Making and Peace Making: The United Nations' Post–Cold War Record. In *Turbulent Peace: The Challenges of Managing International Conflict*, edited by C. A. Crocker, F. O. Hampson, and P. Aall. Washington, DC: United States Institute of Peace.

Doyle, Michael W., and Nicholas Sambanis. 2000. International Peacebuilding: A Theoretical and Quantitative Analysis. *American Political Science Review* 94 (4): 779–801.

———. 2006. *Making War and Building Peace: United Nations Peace Operations*. Princeton: Princeton University Press.

Dubey, Amitabh. 2002. Domestic Institutions and the Duration of Civil War Settlements. Paper presented at Annual Meeting of the International Studies Association, New Orleans.

Durch, William J, ed. 1993. *The Evolution of UN Peacekeeping*. New York: St. Martin's Press.

———. 1996a. Keeping the Peace: Politics and Lessons of the 1990s. In *UN Peacekeeping, American Policy, and the Uncivil Wars of the 1990s*, edited by W. J. Durch. New York: St. Martin's Press.

———, ed. 1996b. *UN Peacekeeping, American Policy, and the Uncivil Wars of the 1990s*. New York: St. Martin's Press.

Durch, William J., Victoria K. Holt, Caroline R. Earle, and Moira K. Shanahan. 2003. *The Brahimi Report and the Future of UN Peace Operations*. Washington, DC: Henry L. Stimson Center.

Eckstein, Harry. 1975. Case Study and Theory in Political Science. In *Handbook of Political Science: Strategies of Inquiry*, edited by F. I. Greenstein and N. W. Polsby. Reading, MA: Addison-Wesley.

Elbadawi, Ibrahim, and Nicholas Sambanis. 2000. External Interventions and the Duration of Civil Wars: World Bank Policy Research Working Paper 2433.

Enzensberger, Hans Magnus. 1994. *Civil Wars: From L.A. to Bosnia*. New York: New Press.

Farrell, Joseph, and Matthew Rabin. 1996. Cheap Talk. *Journal of Economic Perspectives* 10 (3): 103–18.

Fearon, James D. 1992. Threats to Use Force: Costly Signals and Bargaining in International Crises. Ph.D. dissertation, Political Science, University of California, Berkeley.

———. 1995. Rationalist Explanations for War. *International Organization* 49 (3): 379–414.

———. 1997. Signaling Foreign Policy Interests. *Journal of Conflict Resolution* 41 (1): 68–90.

———. 2004. Why Do Some Civil Wars Last So Much Longer Than Others? *Journal of Peace Research* 41 (3): 275–302.

Fearon, James D., and David D. Laitin. 1999. Weak States, Rough Terrain, and Large-Scale Ethnic Violence since 1945. Paper presented at Annual Meeting of the American Political Science Association, Atlanta.

———. 2003. Ethnicity, Insurgency, and Civil War. *American Political Science Review* 97 (1): 75–90.

Fetherston, A. B. 1994. *Towards a Theory of United Nations Peacekeeping*. New York: St. Martin's Press.

Findlay, Trevor. 2002. *The Use of Force in UN Peace Operations*. Oxford: SIPRI and Oxford University Press.

Finnemore, Martha. 2003. *The Purpose of Intervention: Changing Beliefs about the Use of Force*. Ithaca, NY: Cornell University Press.

Fortna, Virginia Page. 1995. Success and Failure in Southern Africa: Peacekeeping in Namibia and Angola. In *Beyond Traditional Peacekeeping*, edited by D. C. F. Daniel and B. C. Hayes. London: Macmillan.

———. 2003. Scraps of Paper? Agreements and the Durability of Peace. *International Organization* 57 (2): 337–72

———. 2004a. Does Peacekeeping Keep Peace? International Intervention and the Duration of Peace after Civil War. *International Studies Quarterly* 48 (2): 269–92.

———. 2004b. Interstate Peacekeeping: Causal Mechanisms and Empirical Effects. *World Politics* 56 (4): 481–519.

———. 2004c. *Peace Time: Cease-Fire Agreements and the Durability of Peace*. Princeton: Princeton University Press.

———. 2005. Where Have All the Victories Gone? War Outcomes in Historical Perspective. Paper presented at Annual Meeting of the International Studies Association, Honolulu.

———. 2008. Peacekeeping and Democratization. In *From War to Democracy: Dilemmas of Peacebuilding*, edited by A. Jarstad and T. Sisk. Cambridge: Cambridge University Press.

Fortna, Virginia Page, and Lisa L. Martin. Forthcoming. Peacekeepers as Signals: The Demand for International Peacekeeping in Civil Wars. In *Power Interdependence and Non-state Actors in World Politics: Research Frontiers*, edited by Helen Milner. Princeton: Princeton University Press.

Furley, Oliver, and Roy May. 1998. Introduction. In *Peacekeeping in Africa*, edited by O. Furley and R. May. Aldershot: Ashgate.

Gartzke, Erik, and Dong-Joon Jo. 2002. The Affinity of Nations Index, 1946–1996. Version 3.0.

Gberie, Lansana. 2000. First Stages on the Road to Peace: The Abidjan Process (1995–96). In *Paying the Price: The Sierra Leone Peace Process*, edited by D. Lord. London: Conciliation Resources. *Accord 9*.

Geddes, Barbara. 1990. How the Cases You Choose Affect the Answers You Get: Selection Bias in Comparative Politics. *Political Analysis* 2 (1):131–50.

George, Alexander L., and Andrew Bennett. 2004. *Case Studies and Theory Development in the Social Sciences*. Cambridge: MIT Press.

George, Alexander, and Richard Smoke. 1974. *Deterrence in American Foreign Policy*. New York: Columbia University Press.

Gerring, John. 2004. What Is a Case Study and What Is It Good For? *American Political Science Review* 98 (2): 341–54.

Ghosh, Partha S. 1989. *Cooperation and Conflict in South Asia*. New Delhi: Manohar.

Gibbs, David. 1997. Is Peacekeeping a New Form of Imperialism? *International Peacekeeping* 4(1):122–28.

Gilligan, Michael J., and Ernest J. Sergenti. 2007. Does Peacekeeping Keep Peace? Using Matching to Improve Causal Inference. Unpublished paper, New York University and Harvard University.

Gilligan, Michael J., and Stephen John Stedman. 2003. Where do the Peacekeepers Go? *International Studies Review* 5 (4): 37–54.

Goemans, H. E. 2000. *War and Punishment: The Causes of War Termination and the First World War*. Princeton: Princeton University Press.

Greif, Avner. 1998. Self-Enforcing Political Systems and Economic Growth: Late Medieval Genoa. In *Analytic Narratives*, edited by R. H. Bates, A. Greif, M. Levi, J.-L. Rosenthal, and B.R. Weingast. Princeton: Princeton University Press.

Hampson, Fen Osler. 1996a. *Nurturing Peace: Why Peace Settlements Succeed or Fail*. Washington, DC: United States Institute of Peace Press.

———. 1996b. The Pursuit of Human Rights: The United Nations in El Salvador. In *UN Peacekeeping, American Policy, and the Uncivil Wars of the 1990s*, edited by W. J. Durch. New York: St. Martin's Press.

Harbom, Lotta, ed. 2004. *States in Armed Conflict 2003*. Department of Peace and Conflict Research. Research Report 70. Uppsala: Uppsala University.

Hartzell, Caroline, Mathew Hoddie, and Donald Rothchild. 2001. Stabilizing the Peace after Civil War. *International Organization* 55 (1): 183–208.

Heldt, Birger. 2004. UN-Led or Non-UN-Led Peacekeeping Operations? *IRI Review* 9:113–38.

Herbst, Jeffrey. 2000. African Peacekeepers and State Failure. In *Peacekeeping and Peace Enforcement in Africa*, by R. I. Rotberg and others. Washington, DC: Brookings Institution Press.

Hillen, John. 2000. *Blue Helmets: The Strategy of UN Military Operations.* 2nd ed. Washington, DC: Brassey's.

Hirsch, John L. 2001a. *Sierra Leone: Diamonds and the Struggle for Democracy.* Boulder: Lynne Rienner.

———. 2001b. War in Sierra Leone. *Survival* 43 (3): 145–62.

Hoile, David. 1994. *Mozambique: Resistance and Freedom.* London: Mozambique Institute.

Holiday, David, and William Stanley. 1993. Building the Peace: Preliminary Lessons from El Salvador. *Journal of International Affairs* 46 (2): 415–38.

Howard, Lise Morjé. 2008. *UN Peacekeeping in Civil Wars.* Cambridge: Cambridge University Press.

Human Rights Watch. 2004. Failure to Protect: Anti-Minority Violence in Kosovo, March 2004. 16 (6) D.

Hume, Cameron. 1994. *Ending Mozambique's War: The Role of Mediation and Good Offices.* Washington, DC: United States Institute of Peace.

Humphreys, Macartan, and Jeremy Weinstein. 2007. Demobilization and Reintegration. *Journal of Conflict Resolution* 51(4):531–67.

Huth, Paul. 1988. *Extended Deterrence and the Prevention of War.* New Haven: Yale University Press.

Ibrahim, Syed Muhammad. 1991. Insurgency and Counterinsurgency: The Bangladesh Experience in Regional Perspective—the Chittagong Hill Tracts. *Military Papers* 4. Dhaka: AHQ Military Training Directorate.

International Crisis Group (ICG). 2001. *Sierra Leone: Time for a New Military and Political Strategy.* Africa Report 28. Freetown: International Crisis Group.

———. 2002. *Sierra Leone after Elections: Politics as Usual?* Africa Report 49. Freetown: International Crisis Group.

———. 2003. *Sierra Leone: The State of Security and Governance.* Africa Report 67. Freetown: International Crisis Group.

Jakobsen, Peter Viggo. 1996. National Interest, Humanitarianism, or CNN: What Triggers UN Peace Enforcement after the Cold War? *Journal of Peace Research* 33 (2): 205–15.

———. 2000. The Emerging Consensus on Grey Area Peace Operations Doctrine: Will It Last and Enhance Operational Effectiveness? *International Peacekeeping* 7 (3): 36–56.

James, Alan. 1969. *The Politics of Peace-keeping.* New York: Praeger.

———. 1990. *Peacekeeping in International Politics.* New York: St. Martin's Press.

———. 1994. Internal Peacekeeping. In *Peacekeeping and the Challenge of Civil Conflict Resolution*, edited by D. A. Charters. New Brunswick: University of New Brunswick, Centre for Conflict Studies.

Jervis, Robert. 1978. Cooperation under the Security Dilemma. *World Politics* 30 (2): 167–86.

Jett, Dennis C. 1999. *Why Peacekeeping Fails.* New York: St. Martin's Press.

Jones, Bruce D. 2001. *Peacemaking in Rwanda: The Dynamics of Failure.* Boulder: Lynne Rienner.

Kalyvas, Stathis N. 2006. *The Logic of Violence in Civil War.* New York: Cambridge University Press.

Kaplan, Robert D. 1996. *The Ends of the Earth: A Journey at the Dawn of the 21st Century*. New York: Random House.

Kaufmann, Chaim. 1996. Possible and Impossible Solutions to Ethnic Civil Wars. *International Security* 20 (4): 136–75.

Kecskemeti, Paul. 1964. *Strategic Surrender: The Politics of Victory and Defeat*. New York: Atheneum.

Keen, David. 2005. *Conflict & Collusion in Sierra Leone*. New York: Palgrave.

Krasno, Jean, Bradd C. Hayes, and Donald C. F. Daniel, eds. 2003. *Leveraging for Success in United Nations Peace Operations*. Westport, CT: Praeger.

Kumar, Anand. 2003. *Discord in the Chittagong Hill Tracts*. Institute of Peace and Conflict Studies 955, New Delhi.

Kumar, Radha. 1997. The Troubled History of Partition. *Foreign Affairs* 76 (1): 22–34.

Last, David M. 1997. *Theory, Doctrine, and Practice of Conflict De-Escalation in Peacekeeping Operations*. Clementsport, Nova Scotia: Canadian Peacekeeping Press of the Lester B. Pearson Canadian International Peacekeeping Training Centre.

———. 2000. Organizing for Effective Peacebuilding. *International Peacekeeping* 7 (1): 80–96.

Licklider, Roy. 1995. The Consequences of Negotiated Settlements in Civil Wars, 1945–1993. *American Political Science Review* 89 (3): 681–90.

Lin, Ann Chih. 1998. Bridging Positivist and Interpretivist Approaches to Qualitative Methods. *Policy Studies Journal* 26 (1): 162–80.

Lindley, Dan. 2007. *Promoting Peace with Information: Transparency as a Tool of Security Regimes*. Princeton: Princeton University Press.

Lord, David, ed. 2000. *Paying the Price: The Sierra Leone Peace Process*. London: Conciliation Resources. *Accord 9*.

Luttwak, Edward N. 1999. Give War a Chance. *Foreign Affairs* 78 (4): 36–44.

Mackinlay, John. 1995. Military Responses to Complex Emergencies. In *The United Nations and Civil Wars*, edited by T. G. Weiss. Boulder: Lynne Rienner.

Malan, Mark, Phenyo Rakate, and Angela McIntyre. 2002. *Peacekeeping in Sierra Leone: UNAMSIL Hits the Home Straight*. ISS Monograph Series, vol. 68. Pretoria: Institute for Security Studies.

Malone, David M., and Karin Wermester. 2000. Boom and Bust? The Changing Nature of UN Peacekeeping. *International Peacekeeping* 7 (4): 37–54.

Manning, Carrie L. 2002. *The Politics of Peace in Mozambique: Post-Conflict Democratization, 1992–2000*. Westport, CT: Praeger.

Marshall, Monty G., and Keith Jaggers. 2002. Polity IV Project: Political Regime Characteristics and Transitions, 1800–2002. College Park, MD: Center for International Development and Conflict Management (CIDCM), University of Maryland.

Marten, Kimberly Zisk. 2004. *Enforcing the Peace: Learning from the Imperial Past*. New York: Columbia University Press.

Maxwell, Michael. 1998. Peace for the Chittagong Hill Tracts? *Fourth World Bulletin*, 64–69.

McCartney, Clem, Martina Fischer, and Oliver Wils, eds. n.d. *Security Sector Reform: Potentials and Challenges for Conflict Transformation*, Berghof Handbook for

Conflict Transformation. Berlin: Berghof Research Center for Constructive Conflict Management.

Mendelson, Sarah E. 2005. *Barracks and Brothels: Peacekeepers and Human Trafficking in the Balkans.* Washington, DC: Center for Strategic and International Studies.

Minorities at Risk. 2004a. Assessment for Chittagong Hill Tribes in Bangladesh. December 31, 2003. Available from http://www.cidcm.umd.edu/mar/assessment.asp?groupId=77101 (consulted September 2, 2007).

———. 2004b. Chronology for Chittagong Hill Tribes in Bangladesh. Available from http://www.cidcm.umd.edu/mar/chronology.asp?groupId=77101 (consulted October 4, 2007).

Mohsin, Amena. 1997. *The Politics of Nationalism: The Case of the Chittagong Hill Tracts.* Dhaka, Bangladesh: University Press Limited.

———. 2003. *The Chittagong Hill Tracts, Bangladesh: On the Difficult Road to Peace.* Boulder: Lynne Rienner.

Morgan, Patrick. 1977. *Deterrence: A Conceptual Analysis.* Beverly Hills: Sage.

Morrow, James D. 1999. The Strategic Setting of Choices: Signaling, Commitment, and Negotiation in International Politics. In *Strategic Choice and International Relations,* edited by D.A. Lake and R. Powell. Princeton: Princeton University Press.

Mullenbach, Mark J. 2005. Deciding to Keep Peace: An Analysis of International Influences on the Establishment of Third-Party Peacekeeping Missions. *International Studies Quarterly* 49 (3): 529–55.

Otunnu, Olara A., and Michael W. Doyle, eds. 1998. *Peacemaking and Peacekeeping for the New Century.* Lanham, MD: Rowman and Littlefield.

Paris, Roland. 2004. *At War's End: Building Peace after Civil Conflict.* New York: Cambridge University Press.

Peace Campaign Group. 2002. A Report on the Demonstration against the Government of Bangladesh at Paris Consortium, 2002. Peace Campaign Group, New Delhi.

Perlez, Jane. 2005. Indonesia Orders Foreign Troops Providing Aid to Leave by March 26. *New York Times,* January 13, A12.

Pugh, Michael, ed. 1997. *The UN, Peace and Force.* Portland, OR: Frank Cass.

Pugh, Michael, and Neil Cooper. 2004. *War Economies in a Regional Context: Challenges of Transformation.* Boulder: Lynne Rienner.

Ramsbotham, Oliver. 2000. Reflections on UN Post-settlement Peacebuilding. *International Peacekeeping* 7 (1): 169–89.

Rashid, Ismail. 2000. The Lomé Peace Negotiations. In *Paying the Price: The Sierra Leone Peace Process,* edited by D. Lord. London: Conciliation Resources. *Accord 9.*

Reed, Pamela L. 1996. The Politics of Reconciliation: The United Nations Operation in Mozambique. In *UN Peacekeeping, American Policy, and the Uncivil Wars of the 1990s,* edited by W. J. Durch. New York: St. Martin's.

Regan, Patrick M. 2000. *Civil Wars and Foreign Powers: Outside Intervention in Intrastate Conflict.* Ann Arbor: University of Michigan Press.

———. 2002. Third Party Intervention and the Duration of Intrastate Conflict. *Journal of Conflict Resolution* 46 (1): 55–73.

Reno, William 2003. Sierra Leone: Warfare in a Post-State Society. In *State Failure and State Weakness in a Time of Terror,* edited by R. I. Rotberg. Washington, DC: Brookings Institution Press.

Rikhye, Indar Jit. 1984. *The Theory & Practice of Peacekeeping.* London: C. Hurst.

Ron, James. 2005. Paradigm in Distress? Primary Commodities and Civil War. In *Journal of Conflict Resolution*, special issue, 49 (4): 443–50.

Ross, Michael L. 2004. What Do We Know about Natural Resources and Civil War? *Journal of Peace Research* 41 (3): 337–56.

Rotberg, Robert I. 2000. Peacekeeping and the Effective Prevention of War. In *Peacekeeping and Peace Enforcement in Africa*, by R. I. Rotberg and others. Washington, DC: Brookings Institution Press.

Ryan, Stephen. 2000. United Nations Peacekeeping: A Matter of Principles? *International Peacekeeping* 7 (1): 27–47.

SAHRDC. 1999. See South Asia Human Rights Documentation Centre 1999.

Salomans, Dirk. 2003. Probing the Successful Application of Leverage in Support of Mozambique's Quest for Peace. In *Leveraging for Success in United Nations Peace Operations*, edited by J. Krasno, B. C. Hayes, and D. C. F. Daniel. Westport, CT: Praeger.

Sambanis, Nicholas. 2000. Partition as a Solution to Ethnic War: An Empirical Critique of the Theoretical Literature. *World Politics* 52 (4): 437–83.

———. 2004. What Is Civil War? Conceptual and Empirical Complexities of an Operational Definition. *Journal of Conflict Resolution* 48 (6): 814–58.

Sambanis, Nicholas, and Jonah Schulhofer-Wohl. 2007. Evaluating Multilateral Interventions in Civil Wars: A Comparison of UN and Non-UN Peace Operations. In *Multilateralism and Security Institutions in an Era of Globalization*, edited by D. Bourantonis, K. Ifantis, and P. Tsakonas. London: Routledge.

Sambanis, Nicholas, and Annalisa Zinn. 2003. The Escalation of Self-Determination Movements: From Protest to Violence. Paper presented at Annual Meeting of the American Political Science Association, Philadelphia.

Schelling, Thomas C. 1966. *Arms and Influence*. New Haven: Yale University Press.

Schmidt, Holger. Forthcoming. Do Brokers Always Have to Be Honest? Impartiality and the Effectiveness of Third-Party Guarantees for Negotiated Civil War Settlements. Ph.D. dissertation, Department of Political Science, Columbia University.

Shelley, Mizanur Rahman, Abdur Rob Khan, and Mohammad Humayun Kabir. N.d. Tribal Insurgency in the Chittagong Hill Tracts of Bangladesh: A Case of Non-violent Conflict Resolution. In *Conflict Prevention Survey: Bangladesh*. Dhaka.

SIPRI. 1992–98. See Stockholm International Peace Research Institute 1992–98.

Smith, Michael G. 2003. *Peacekeeping in East Timor: The Path to Independence*. Boulder: Lynne Rienner.

Snyder, Jack, and Robert Jervis. 1999. Civil War and the Security Dilemma. In *Civil War, Insecurity, and Intervention*, edited by B. F. Walter and J. Snyder. New York: Columbia University Press.

Söderberg Kovacs, Mimmi. 2007. From Rebellion to Politics: The Transformation of Rebel Groups to Political Parties in Civil War Peace Processes. Ph.D dissertation, Department of Peace and Conflict Research, Uppsala University.

South Asia Human Rights Documentation Centre (SAHRDC). 1999. *Elusive Peace in the Chittagong Hill Tracts*. Asia-Pacific Human Rights Network. Available from www.hrdc.net/sahrdc/hrfeatures/HRF11.htm (consulted June 8, 2004).

Stanton, Jessica. Forthcoming. In Search of Legitimacy: Compliance with International Laws of War during Civil War. Ph.D dissertation, Department of Political Science, Columbia University.

Stedman, Stephen John. 1997. Spoiler Problems in Peace Processes. *International Security* 22 (2): 5–53.

Stockholm International Peace Research Institute (SIPRI). 1992–98. *SIPRI Yearbook: World Armaments and Disarmament*. Stockholm: Almquist & Wiksell.

Synge, Richard. 1997. *Mozambique: UN Peacekeeping in Action, 1992–94*. Washington, DC: United States Institute of Peace.

Tharoor, Shashi. 1995–96. Should UN Peacekeeping Go 'Back to Basics'? *Survival* 37 (4): 52–64.

Toft, Monica Duffy. 2003. Peace through Victory? Paper presented at Annual Meeting of the American Political Science Association, Philadelphia.

United Nations. 1995. *The United Nations and Mozambique, 1992–1995*. New York: United Nations.

———. 1996a. *The Blue Helmets: A Review of United Nations Peace-keeping*. 3rd ed. New York: United Nations.

———. 1996b. *Multidisciplinary Peacekeeping: Lessons from Recent Experience*. New York: Lessons Learned Unit, Department of Peacekeeping Operations.

Uppsala Conflict Data Program (UCDP). N.d. Department of Peace and Conflict Research, Uppsala University. Available from http://www.pcr.uu.se/research/UCDP/.

Venâncio, Moisés, and Stephen Chan. 1998. War and Gropings toward Peace. In *War and Peace in Mozambique*, edited by M. Venâncio and S. Chan. New York: St. Martin's Press.

Vines, Alex. 1996. *RENAMO: From Terrorism to Democracy in Mozambique?* Revised ed. London: James Currey.

Vreeland, James Raymond. 2002. Selection and Survival. Unpublished paper, Yale University.

———. 2003. *The IMF and Economic Development*. New York: Cambridge University Press.

Walter, Barbara F. 1997. The Critical Barrier to Civil War Settlement. *International Organization* 51 (3): 335–64.

———. 1999. Introduction. In *Civil Wars, Insecurity, and Intervention*, edited by B. F. Walter and J. Snyder. New York: Columbia University Press.

———. 2002. *Committing to Peace: The Successful Settlement of Civil Wars*. Princeton: Princeton University Press.

———. 2004a. Does Conflict Beget Conflict? Explaining Recurring Civil War. *Journal of Peace Research* 41 (3).

———. 2004b. What We Know about Renewed Civil War. Unpublished paper, University of California, San Diego.

Walter, Barbara F., and Jack Snyder, eds. 1999. *Civil Wars, Insecurity, and Intervention*. New York: Columbia University Press.

Weinstein, Jeremy M. 2002. Mozambique: A Fading UN Success Story. *Journal of Democracy* 13 (1): 141–56.

———. 2005. Autonomous Recovery and International Intervention in Comparative Perspective. Unpublished paper. Center for Global Development, Washington, DC.

———. 2007. *Inside Rebellion: The Politics of Insurgent Violence*. New York: Cambridge University Press.

Werner, Suzanne. 1999. The Precarious Nature of Peace: Resolving the Issues, Enforcing the Settlement and Renegotiating the Terms. *American Journal of Political Science* 43 (3): 912–34.

Wesley, Michael. 1997. *Casualties of the New World Order: The Causes of Failure of UN Missions to Civil Wars.* New York: St. Martin's Press.

Woodward, Susan. 2004. Why Do We Fail at State Building? Presentation at Columbia University, March 30, New York.

World Development Indicators (WDI). World Bank. Available from http://devdata .worldbank.org/dataonline/.

Zacarias, Agostinho. 1996. *The United Nations and International Peacekeeping.* London: Tauris Academic Studies.

Zongwe, Mitonga. 2001. Preliminary Assessment of the Disarmament and Demobilisation in Sierra Leone. Unpublished manuscript.

———. 2002. Summary Report on Lessons Learned from Disarmament and Demobilization in Sierra Leone. Paper presented at the Workshop on Lessons Learned from Disarmament and Demobilization in Sierra Leone, July 25–26, Paris.

UNITED NATIONS DOCUMENTS

UN General Assembly and Security Council. A/55/305-S/2000/809. *Report of the Panel on United Nations Peace Operations* [Brahimi Report]. August 21, 2000.

UN Security Council. S/1997/80. Report of the Secretary-General on Sierra Leone. January 26, 1997.

———. S/1998/486. Fifth Report of the Secretary-General on the Situation in Sierra Leone. June 9, 1998.

———. S/1998/750. First Progress Report of the Secretary-General on the United Nations Observer Mission in Sierra Leone. August 12, 1998.

———. S/1999/750. Sixth Report of the Secretary-General on the United Nations Observer Mission in Sierra Leone. June 4, 1999.

———. S/Res/1299. Security Council Resolution 1299. May 19, 2000.

———. S/2000/455. Fourth Report of the Secretary-General on the United Nations Mission in Sierra Leone. May 19, 2000.

———. S/2000/832. Sixth Report of the Secretary-General on the United Nations Mission in Sierra Leone. August 24, 2000.

———. S/2001/228. Ninth Report of the Secretary-General on the United Nations Mission in Sierra Leone. March 14, 2001.

———. S/Res/1346. Security Council Resolution 1346. March 30, 2001.

———. S/2001/394. *No Exit without Strategy: Security Council Decision-Making and the Closure or Transition of United Nations Peacekeeping Operations.* Report of the Secretary-General. April 20, 2001.

———. S/2002/1417. Sixteenth Report of the Secretary-General on the United Nations Mission in Sierra Leone. December 24, 2002.

———. S/2003/321. Seventeenth Report of the Secretary-General on the United Nations Mission in Sierra Leone. March 17, 2003.

———. S/2004/536. Twenty-Second Report of the Secretary-General on the United Nations Mission in Sierra Leone. July 6, 2004.

UN Security Council. S/2005/273. Twenty-Fifth Report of the Secretary-General on the United Nations Mission in Sierra Leone. April 26, 2005.

———. S/2005/777. Twenty-Seventh Report of the Secretary-General on the United Nations Mission in Sierra Leone. December 12, 2005.

INTERVIEWS

Note that this list is slightly longer than the actual number of interviews conducted because in a few cases interviewees indicated that part, but not all, of their interview was for attribution. Some interviews are thus listed as "anonymous" in one citation, and by name in another. I have omitted dates and some place-names from the anonymous interview entries to prevent identification.

Bangladesh

Ahmed, Aftab. Professor of political science, University of Dhaka. Dhaka, January 6, 2002.

Ahmed, Imtiaz. Professor of international relations, University of Dhaka. Dhaka, January 15, 2002.

Ahmed, Sharif Uddin. Director, Archives and Libraries, Cultural Affairs Ministry. Dhaka, January 13, 2002.

Alam, Nurul. Member, CHT Regional Council. Rangamati, January 9, 2002.

Anonymous. Awami League member, negotiator of 1997 accord. January 2002.

Anonymous. Bangladeshi academic. Dhaka, January 2002.

Anonymous. Embassy official, Royal Danish Embassy. Dhaka, January 2002.

Anonymous. Embassy official, US Embassy. Dhaka, January 2002.

Anonymous. United Peoples Democratic Front leader. Dhaka, January 2002

Anonymous. United Peoples Democratic Front leader. Dhaka, January 2002

Chakma, Barun. Staff member, CHT Regional Council. Rangamati, January 9, 2002

Chakma, Kalparanjan. Former minister of Chittagong Hill Tracts, member of the National Committee on the CHT. Dhaka, January 14, 2002.

Chakma, Pradanendu Bikash. Professor of management, University of Dhaka. At his home, Dhaka, January 14, 2002.

Dewan, Gautam. Former member, Rangamati Local District Council. Peda Ting Ting, Lake Kaptai, January 9, 2002.

Dewan, Rupayan. Chitttagong Hill Tracts Regional Council member and secretary of international relations, PCJSS. Regional Council, Rangamati, January 8, 2002.

Huq, A.K.M. Zahoorul. Correspondent, Bangladesh Sangbad Sangstha (National News Agency). Regional Council, Rangamati, January 9, 2002.

Hussain, Syed Anwar. Professor of history, University of Dhaka. Dhaka, January 3, 2002.

Ibrahim, Maj. Gen. (Ret.) Syed M. Executive director, Centre for Strategic and Peace Studies, former commander of Rangamati District. Dhaka, January 14, 2002.

Islam, M. Nazrul. Professor of political science, University of Dhaka. Dhaka, January 3, 2002.

Islam, Mufakharal. Professor of history, University of Dhaka. Dhaka, January 6, 2002.

Islam, Shafriqul. Joint secretary, Ministry of Chittagong Hill Tracts Affairs. Dhaka, January 3, 2002.

Kaiser, Ataur Rahman Khan. Awami League member and member of the National Committee on the CHT. Rotary Club, Chittagong, January 10, 2002.

Khan, Abdur Rob. Research director, Bangladesh Institute of International and Strategic Studies. Dhaka, January 3, 2002.

Larma, Jyotirindra Bodhipriya (Shantu). Chairman, Chittagong Hill Tracts Regional Council and leader of PCJSS. Regional Council, Rangamati, January 8, 2002.

Mohsin, Amena. Professor of international relations, University of Dhaka. At her home, Dhaka, January 2 and January 15, 2002.

Rahman, Kazi Ghulam. Negotiatior of 1997 accord. Telephone interview, Dhaka, January 12, 2002.

Rashiduzzaman, Mohammed. Professor of political science, Rowan University. By telephone December 12, and in person in Dhaka, January 3, 2002.

Roy, Raja Devashish. Chakma king. At his residence, Rangamati, January 8, 2002.

Sen, Sukanta. Director, Integrated Action Research and Development. Dhaka, January 2, 2002.

Shelley, Mizanur Rahman. Chairman, Centre for Development Research Bangladesh. Dhaka, January 1 and January 14, 2002.

Tawhid, Major. Bangladesh Military Intelligence. Parjatan Hotel, Rangamati, January 7 and 8, 2002.

Tripura, Mrinal Kanti. Coordinator, Hill Tracts NGO Forum, PCJSS staff member, and aide to Devashish Roy. Rangamati, January 7–10, 2002.

GROUP INTERVIEWS

Bengali settler villagers. Lake Kaptai, January 9, 2002.
Tripura villagers. Lake Kaptai, January 9, 2002.

Sierra Leone

Adetuberu, George. Political Affairs, UNAMSIL. UNAMSIL Headquarters (Mammy Yoko Hotel), Freetown, November 26, 2002.

Alam, Lt. Col. BANMED-2. UNAMSIL, Magburaka, November 22, 2002.

Ali, Maj. Gen. Syed Athar. Deputy force commander, and chief military observer, UNAMSIL. UNAMSIL HQ, Freetown, November 25, 2002.

Anyidoho, Charles. UNAMSIL Civil Affairs. Koidu, November 28, 2002.

Anonymous UNAMSIL military official. Freetown, November 2002.

Bangura, Zainab. Civil society activist, former director, Campaign for Good Governance. At her home, Freetown, November 29, 2002.

Dankwa, Joseph. Civilian police (CIVPOL) commissioner, UNAMSIL. UNAMSIL HQ, Freetown, November 25, 2002.

Diallo, Ismael. Head of Civil Affairs, UNAMSIL. UNAMSIL HQ, Freetown, November 25, 2002.

Douglas, Col. Stewart. Chief of staff, MILOBS, UNAMSIL. UNAMSIL HQ, Freetown, November 25, 2002.

Ellery, Brig. Gen. James. Chief of staff (Force), UNAMSIL. UNAMSIL HQ, Freetown, November 25 and 27, 2002.

Hagoss, Gebremedhin. Chief, Policy Planning Section, UNAMSIL. UNAMSIL HQ, Freetown, November 28, 2002.

Hasan, Col. Commander of Pakistani UNAMSIL contingent in Kono District. Koidu, November 28, 2002.

Hirsch, John. Former US ambassador to Sierra Leone. International Peace Academy, New York, May 28, 2002.

Ijawazan, Brig. Gen. Sector-5 force commander, UNAMSIL. Koidu, November 28, 2002.

Kabir, Major. BANBATT-6. Camp Charlie, Mile 91, November 22, 2002.

Kai-Kai, Dr. Francis. Executive secretary, National Commission for Demobilization, Disarmament, and Reintegration (NCDDR). Freetown, November 23, 2002.

Kamara. Commissioner, National Commission for Demobilization, Disarmament, and Reintegration (NCDDR), Magburaka, November 22, 2002.

Khiolfa II, Paramount Chief Bai Jossoh. Magburaka, November 22, 2002. (Through an interpreter).

Lecoq, Hervé. Special assistant to the deputy special representative to the secretary-general, UNAMSIL. UNAMSIL HQ, Freetown, November 25, 2002.

Malloy, Desmond. Reintegration coordinator, DDR, UNAMSIL. UNAMSIL HQ, Freetown, November 26, 2002.

Massaquoi, Gibril. Former RUF spokesman. UNAMSIL HQ, Freetown, November 26, 2002.

Maturi, Lt. Col. commander, Sector 2, UNAMSIL. Sector 2 HQ, Freetown, November 26, 2002.

Norman, Chief Hinga. Minister of Internal Affairs and Civil Defense Forces (CDF), national coordinator (formerly deputy minister of defense). Office of the Ministry of Internal Affairs, Freetown, November 29, 2002.

Opande, Lt. Gen. Daniel. Force commander, UNAMSIL. UNAMSIL HQ, Freetown, November 25, 2002.

Razaq, Abdul. Ex-RUF leader and negotiator, now executive director, Global Youth Foundation against Drug Abuse. Freetown, November 27, 2002.

Sadry, Behrooz. Acting special representative to the secretary-general, UNAMSIL. UNAMSIL HQ, Freetown, November 25, 2002.

Sarwardy, Lt. Col. Chy. Hasan. General staff officer, Sector-4, UNAMSIL. Magburaka, November 22, 2002.

Sesay, Gen. Issa. Head of the RUF-P. UNAMSIL Sector 2 HQ, Freetown, November 26, 2002. (Met, refused interview.)

Sessay, Moksin. Ex(?)-RUF leader (original contact between UN and RUF after May 2000 crisis). Mile 91, November 22, 2002.

Shawkat, Col. Force commander, BANBATT-6, UNAMSIL. Magburaka, November 22, 2002.

Zenenga, Raisedon. United Nations Department of Peacekeeping Operations. UN Headquarters, New York, June 4, 2002.

GROUP INTERVIEWS

Child combatants. NCDDR Magburaka, November 22, 2002.

Religious leaders (approximately 60 imams and priests). Mile 91, November 22, 2002.

Ex-combatants (approximately 40 ex-RUF, ex-CDF, and ex-SLA). Mile 91, November 22, 2002.

Global Youth Foundation against Drug Abuse: Mariama Faysal, Christian Adekele, Fatmah Sherifa, and Sahr Joseph Brina. Freetown, November 27, 2002.

Kono Ex-Combatant Development Organization (approximately 15 members). Koidu, Kono District, November 28, 2002.

Kono Youth League (approximately 10 members). Koidu, Kono District, November 28, 2002.

Mozambique

Almirante, João. Member of Parliament (Renamo), delegate to peace negotiations. Hotel Cardoso, Maputo, December 11, 2002. (Abdul Manafi translating.)

Anonymous. Frelimo leader. Maputo, December 2002.

Anonymous. Former UN official. Maputo. December 2002.

Anonymous. International NGO worker. Maputo, December 2002.

Anonymous. USAID official. Maputo, December 2002.

de Castro, José (aka Francisco Xavier Marcelino). Member of Parliament (Renamo), delegate to peace talks. At his home, Maputo, December 7, 2002. (Abdul Manafi translating.)

Forquilha, Albino. National coordinator, Christian Council of Mozambique, Department of Peace Justice and Reconciliation, Transforming Arms into Ploughshares (TAE). TAE offices, Maputo, December 11, 2002.

Guebuza, Armando Emilio. Chief negotiator of peace accords for Frelimo (became president of Mozambique in 2004). Frelimo Headquarters, Maputo, December 11, 2002.

Hunguana, Teodato. Member of Parliament (Frelimo), representative at peace negotiations, and on commission implementing the accords. Parliament building, Maputo, December 6, 2002.

Macaringue, Brig. Gen. Paulino. Director of Defence Policy, Department of Defence, Frelimo member. (Involved in reintegration and training of new army). Hotel Cardoso, Maputo, December 9, 2002.

McDonald, Mike. GTZ (German NGO involved with reintegration process). Maputo, December 6, 2002.

Ngonhamo, Lt. Gen. Mateus. Deputy chief of staff of defense, Renamo member. Defense Headquarters, Maputo, December 9, 2002. (Abdul Manafi translating).

Simpson, Mark. Carter Center representative in Mozambique, and former political aide to SRSG in UNAVEM III, Angola. Hotel Cardoso, Maputo, December 4, 2002.

Weimer, Bernard. Swiss Agency for Development and Cooperation (SDC). At his home, Maputo, December 9, 2002.

Zacarias, Augustinho. UN Department of Peacekeeping Operations. United Nations, New York, October 21, 2002.

INDEX